Insurgency & Terrorism

From Revolution to Apocalypse

Attention Authors

Manas Publications is fighting a war to tell the world that India can win the battle not only by bullet but also by pen. We are converting fighters into writers since our country is full of intellectuals but their knowledge is only confined to them. No sincere effort has been made by any publisher to give the right direction to their knowledge and the talent of intellectual is still hidden. An author always gives the raw material in the shape of manuscript and it is the sense of publisher to make it a finished product. We are motivating the intellectuals' mind and publishing their manuscripts for more than two decades and would like to publish your manuscript too. If you or your colleagues have any manuscript or are working on, please don't hesitate to contact us with detailed synopsis and contents for its publication. We take utmost care in production and give a wide publicity to the book and its author. We can also suggest you the title for writing related to your subject since we are the publishers who believe more in quality than in quantity.

Insurgency
&
Terrorism

From Revolution to Apocalypse

Bard E. O'Neill

*(Published in collaboration with Potomac Books, Inc.
formerly Brassey's Inc.)*

Manas Publications
New Delhi - 110 002 (India)

MANAS PUBLICATIONS

(We Convert Fighters into Writers)
(Publishers for IAS, IPS, IFS, IRS, Defence, Press, Judges etc)

4402/5-A, Ansari Road (Opp HDFC Bank)
Darya Ganj, New Delhi-110 002 (India)
Off.: 23260783, 23265523, Fax: 011-23272766
E-mail: manaspublications@gmail.com
manaspublications@yahoo.com

2013 (FP-2006)

ISBN: 81-7049-284-X

Rs. 595/-

Designed at
Manas Publications

Printed in India at
RKOffsets, Delhi and published by Mrs Suman Lata for
Manas Publications, 4402/5-A,
Ansari Road (Opp HDFC Bank),
Darya Ganj, New Delhi-110 002 (INDIA)

CONTENTS

PREFACE

Forty years ago I developed what became a life-long interest in the subject of insurgency. I was interested in both particular cases and, most especially, how to analyze them. As I pored over the literature, it became evident that there were two kinds of writings on the subject: descriptive and theoretical. Seldom did the two come together, and the theoretical materials often focused on only part of the problem. The more I read, the more I became convinced that there was a need for a comprehensive framework for analysis that integrated and added to the collective understanding and insights about insurgency.

My observations led me to devise a framework for analysis in 1970. Since then, it has appeared in several iterations, each of which has sought to build upon and improve the previous one. After countless case studies—written and oral—and numerous visits to countries facing insurgencies, I decided the time had come to pull together what I had learned and develop a book that would be useful to various individuals and groups interested in the subject, be they participants, observers, scholars, students, or government analysts.

I have kept two subsidiary aims in mind: to keep the book succinct and to avoid being overly theoretical. This is by no means to dismiss the value of more theoretical undertakings, such as Ted Robert Gurr's *Why Men Rebel.* To the contrary, as the reader will soon discover, I have incorporated a number of ideas from these important works. My purposes, however, are different from theirs. Whereas the theoretical works are intended primarily for academics, I am writing for a more general audience that includes, most importantly, military and civilian members of the national security policy community. Hence, while obviously concerned about explicit and structured analysis, I have tried to tilt away from social science jargon, not because it lacks utility but because it tends to turn off more general readers.

The study of insurgency is fraught with perils because of the zealotry and partisanship that surround the subject. There is no poverty of commentary on issues having to do with supporting or opposing particular insurgencies or broader phenomena such as revolution and counterrevolution. Suffice it to say that I am not interested in taking positions. I am concerned with straightforward, dispassionate analysis of the status of insurgencies that "tells it like it is."

A number of colleagues gave their time to read and critique all or portions of the manuscript. Among those who made constructive suggestions were Dr. William Heaton; Margaret Dean and Ruth Van Heuven, Department of State; Alice Maroni, Congressional Research Service; and Col. Michael Diffley and Col. Terrence "Rock" Salt, U.S. Army. Two friends who were especially important in this undertaking were Dr. Donald J. Alberts and Dr. John Schulz. Dr. Alberts's impressive knowledge of insurgency and his analytical insights were invaluable at many points along the way. Dr. Shultz's painstaking review of the manuscript and numerous editorial suggestions were indispensable.

I would also like to acknowledge Dorle Hellmuth for the terrific job she did finalizing the format of the manuscript. The last steps were accomplished in a smooth and adroit manner thanks to her intelligence, efficiency, and cheerfulness.

I remain indebted to a truly great soldier-scholar, Maj. Gen. Perry M. Smith, USAF Retired, for encouraging and supporting me in the initial undertaking when he was commandant of the National War College.

I would also like to thank the National Defense University Foundation for its continuous and generous support of faculty and student research.

Finally, I would like to express my gratitude to Congressman Ike Skelton for the inspiration and motivation he has provided to the faculty and students of the National War College with his untiring commitment to the qualitative enhancement of professional military education.

Responsibility for this effort is, of course, solely my own. The views expressed herein do not necessarily represent those of either the Department of Defense or the U.S. government.

1

INSURGENCY IN THE CONTEMPORARY WORLD

To say that the beginning of the twenty-first century has been tumultuous would be an understatement. If the attacks by Al Qaida and its affiliates and the insurgencies in Iraq and Afghanistan are harbingers of things to come, we are in for continued rough times. This should come as no surprise. In the years prior to September 11, we were faced with an unstable, dangerous, and frequently violent international political environment. In fact, since World War II there was an average of eight wars going on somewhere in the world at any given time. Casualties have been estimated in the unnumbered millions.

The violence is striking in that so much of it occurs in the context of internal wars or insurgencies. Pick up a copy of either the *New York Times* or the *Washington Post* on any day, and you are likely to find several articles on insurgencies. These so-called small wars, which can be found on virtually all continents, are often very costly and frequently involve vital or major interests of regional and global powers. The conflicts in Iraq and Afghanistan are striking examples. Because of their continuing and predicted future importance, insurgencies deserve serious and systematic analysis, and in this book, I set forth a way to do precisely that.

Insurgency, of course, is hardly a new phenomenon, as Roman armies could have reported from Gaul, Judea, or elsewhere. Indeed, insurgency has probably been the most prevalent type of armed conflict since the creation of organized political communities. It would be difficult, perhaps impossible, to find many volumes on political history that do not mention rebellions, revolutions, uprisings, and the like.

Our contemporary era is no different; since World War II, terrorism and guerrilla warfare have been predominant types of political violence. Between 1969 and 1985, for instance, the number of major international terrorist incidents alone jumped from just under two hundred to over eight hundred per year, sparking international headlines and leaving people everywhere bewildered, polarized in their opinions, and often afraid. Most of those incidents were the handiwork of insurgent groups seeking to achieve a variety of objectives. Consequently, to understand most terrorism, we must first understand insurgency. We begin the quest for understanding with some preliminary comments on international and domestic factors that have accounted for the prevalence of insurgency since the early 1950s.

THE INTERNATIONAL SYSTEM

The structure of power in the international system that emerged after World War II was asymmetrical and bipolar, divided between Western and Eastern blocs, led by the United States and the Soviet Union, respectively. The United States enjoyed a clear advantage because of its enormous economic capacity and nuclear-weapons superiority until the 1960s. The Soviet Union, meanwhile, acquired recognition as a superpower by virtue of the perceived threat posed by its larger land forces and the tight control it appeared to have over Communist parties around the world, particularly in Eastern Europe. This bifurcation of capabilities and the ideological hostility between the two sides gave rise to a global struggle for power and influence that persisted until the breakup of the former Soviet Union, despite structural changes in the international system that had gradually become evident by the 1970s.

Europe was the most immediate arena of the struggle for power in the postwar era. Nations such as France, Italy, and Greece, suffering from postwar political instability and severe economic dislocation, were believed vulnerable to Communist political inroads. While the conflicts in France and Italy centered on the fear that well-organized Communist parties might come to power through domestic political processes, a civil war in Greece prompted concern that violence might also play a part in Soviet designs. As things turned out, Moscow's commitment to the Greek Communists was less than originally perceived and proved to be short-lived. As for the rest of Europe, the aid provided by the Marshall Plan, together with astute political and economic leadership in the European countries, led to a dramatic recovery and gradual stabilization.

As the threat in Europe receded, attention shifted to the newly emerging countries that were products of the rapidly disintegrating European colonial empires. Although some of these countries achieved independence peacefully, others such as Vietnam and Algeria underwent a lengthy period of violent conflict. In cases where the anticolonial insurrections were led by Marxist parties (e.g., in Vietnam and Malaya), the prevailing perception of the bipolar international structure of power led to fears that victories by the insurgents were tantamount to losses for the West, due in part to the belief that international struggle for power was considered a zero-sum game. Within this context, policies of the West in general, and the United States in particular, were widely seen as oriented toward, or actively supporting, the status quo, while the Soviet Union and its allies were perceived to have the revolutionary mission of upsetting the existing order and structure of power.

Both ideological predispositions, dating back to Vladimir Lenin's critique of imperialism, and the fragility of the new, less-developed countries, which came to be known collectively as the Third World, led Soviet and, shortly thereafter, Chinese leaders to conclude that the Achilles' heel of the West was the Third World. Accordingly, Moscow and Beijing extended moral, political, and material support to both "progressive" governments and Marxist insurgents in underdeveloped countries. The underlying assumption behind support to various insurgents was that deplorable economic, social, and political conditions in many of the new nations were the products of imperialist or neoimperialist exploitation by Western countries, and this made insurgent leaders natural allies of the Communist bloc. Neither Moscow nor Beijing foresaw that in later years their clients would jealously guard their newly won independence and be as defiant toward them as they were toward the West. But while they may have miscalculated the eventual relationships they would have with their clients, the Soviet Union and the People's Republic of China (PRC) correctly assessed the opportunities inherent in the unstable domestic situations of many Third World countries.

THE DOMESTIC CONTEXT

In general, two fundamental challenges confronted most Third World nations following independence: lack of national integration and economic underdevelopment. The lack of national integration was rooted in societal divisions along one or more lines—racial, ethnic, linguistic, or religious—and in the absence of a political tradition that included legitimate centralizing values and structures that transcended parochial loyalties. Accordingly, it was not surprising to find intergroup antagonism and distrust eventually giving rise to insurrections directed at governments dominated by personalities from rival groups in such places as Burma, Malaya, India, Pakistan, Ethiopia, Nigeria, Iraq, and the Sudan, to note but a few. Moreover, even in countries where group rivalries did not lead to major outbreaks of violence, these rivalries were often just one of several impediments to economic development.

The obstacles to economic development went beyond the lack of national cohesion to include such things as a dearth of the requisite human, capital, and natural resources; psychological and cultural resistance to change; corruption; nonexistent, poorly trained, or cumbersome, inefficient bureaucracies; lack of an adequate communications and transportation infrastructure; and the disadvantageous competitive position of less-developed countries vis-à-vis the major powers in the international economic system. Further exacerbating this situation was the frequent misuse of foreign assistance on showplace projects, conflicts with regional rivals that devoured already scarce resources, and frustrations engendered by political leaders who failed to make good on promises that they would improve their peoples' standard of living. Such failures normally had one or more causes. In many cases, leaders were incompetent, saw their own power base as threatened by needed changes, or simply were overwhelmed by the magnitude of their problems and their lack of resources.

The factors that gave rise to insurgencies varied from case to case. Particularly violent situations arose where societal divisions were cumulative and were combined with economic and political disparities. In the Sudan, for instance, the bloody conflict between black insurgents in the south and the Arab government in the north was an outgrowth of racial, ethnic, linguistic, and religious differences, as well as political and economic discrimination against the southern populace. While there were some specific differences, essentially similar situations arose in Iraq, where Kurds revolted against the Arab government in Baghdad; in Ethiopia, where Eritreans initiated a long, bitter, and ultimately successful struggle against Amhara-based regimes in Addis Ababa; and in Sri Lanka, where Tamil Hindus attacked the Sinhalese Buddhist ruling establishment.

In addition to insurgencies rooted in intergroup antagonisms, others had as their main cause socioeconomic disparities between classes. Whether it was the Philippines in the early 1950s, Cuba in the late 1950s, Laos and Vietnam in the late 1950s and 1960s, or El Salvador, Guatemala, Nicaragua, and Peru in later years, the story was a familiar one: small ruling establishments supported by vested interests (e.g., landowners, the military, or religious leaders) controlled the lion's share of economic wealth and political power. In a few cases, such as the Philippines, modest reforms were inaugurated and played a role in undercutting the insurgencies, but in most of these situations, staunch resistance to reform and change, accompanied by repression, fueled and prolonged hostilities. Where colonial powers and colonists constituted the ruling elite, as in Algeria, Rhodesia, Angola, and

Mozambique, a nationalist dimension merged with socioeconomic disparities and resulted in prolonged sanguinary conflicts.

The insurrections based on socioeconomic disparities and concomitant demands for political change opened the door to local Communist Party involvement. The parties articulated an ideology that identified the source of deprivation (class exploitation and imperialism or neoimperialism) and promised a new political and economic order that would address popular needs and usher in a new era based on a fair distribution of socioeconomic resources. Equally important, the Communist parties provided sophisticated organizational formats and a flexible approach that brought together Communists and non-Communists in what they called national liberation or democratic fronts. Finally, they enjoyed various kinds of support from the Soviet Union and the PRC.

THE DOMESTIC-INTERNATIONAL INTERPLAY

While all insurgencies were potentially disruptive as far as international order was concerned, those based on class conflicts and led by Communist parties appeared to pose a significant threat to the overall balance of power between East and West. As the major Communist powers gradually extended various types of assistance to insurgent movements, the Western powers, most notably the United States, increased their aid to beleaguered governments. By the early 1960s, public pledges of assistance to wars of liberation by both Chinese and Soviet leaders led President John F. Kennedy and his national security advisers to conclude that special counterinsurgency forces and doctrinal principles would be necessary to stabilize friendly governments threatened by Communist insurgents. They stressed the combination of political, military, social, psychological, and economic measures.

Although the United States preferred to keep its troops out of insurgencies, deteriorating situations in Laos and Vietnam prompted U.S. leaders to send advisers and, later, regular military forces to Southeast Asia. Closer to home, the United States began extensive training and advisory efforts to shore up Latin American regimes increasingly threatened by Marxist insurgents in the wake of the Cuban revolution. The direct and indirect involvement of Washington, Moscow, and Beijing in Third World insurgencies led many to conclude that the East-West struggle was being waged through proxies in the less-developed nations.

The involvement of the major powers in various internal conflicts and their ability to produce and rapidly transport weapons and other assets around the world resulted in a general trend toward the internationalization of insurgencies. Despite the eventual American setback in Southeast Asia and alterations in the international structure of power that had become evident by the time Richard M. Nixon became president in 1968, this trend continued.

In the late 1960s, the Nixon administration presented a more sophisticated conceptual framework than its predecessors in its analyses of international politics. This framework, articulated principally by Henry A. Kissinger, special assistant for national security affairs, depicted a new pentagonal structure of power comprising the United States, the Soviet Union, the PRC, Japan, and Europe. Although Washington and Moscow maintained military preeminence, the other actors asserted considerable influence because of their economic or demographic resources. While the U.S. administration acknowledged the emergence of smaller regional powers like Brazil and Iran, the key arena for international politics consisted of relationships among the major powers. President Nixon and his advisers saw America's role and power in that arena threatened by the debilitating effects of the Vietnam War on the U.S. economy and social cohesion.

The administration therefore sought to disengage from Southeast Asia in order to concentrate on "more important" areas like Western Europe. As is well known, the disengagement process was not an easy one, given the persistence of North Vietnam, the failure of South Vietnam to defend itself, and Washington's commitment to achieve "peace with honor." The phrase "peace with honor" did not refer to prestige per se; it meant leaving Vietnam with America's credibility intact.

As things turned out, the Vietnam War actually intensified for a period of time, leading to increased public and congressional protests in the United States. Though peace accords were negotiated and the American troop withdrawal began, Hanoi eventually renewed large-scale fighting, and South Vietnam fell. The negative experience in Vietnam reinforced the administration's view that American involvement in Third World insurgencies should be more selective and limited to aid and military assistance. Furthermore, Congress, reflecting public opinion, tried to forestall future debacles like Vietnam by passing the War Powers Act and specific pieces of legislation like the Clark amendment, which ended U.S. support for insurgents in Angola. The Department of Defense, meanwhile, concentrated its attention on nuclear and conventional warfare and de-emphasized the role and capability of its special forces. The administration was not entirely comfortable with these developments. It still perceived potential threats by Marxist insurgent groups or governments in Third World countries but was unable to turn the situation around. Furthermore, the Defense Department continued to downplay the role and capability of Special Forces during the first three years of the Carter administration.

The American desire to avoid future Vietnams did not mean an end to international involvement in insurgencies. To begin with, Moscow, Beijing, and Cuba continued to aid insurgents in places like Eritrea, Thailand, Oman, El Salvador, and Nicaragua. At times, Soviet and Chinese support was as much, if not more, a product of a growing Soviet-Chinese rivalry than it was a product of continued antipathy toward the West. Whatever the motivations of the Communist states, their involvement frequently generated a negative reaction by powers that felt threatened by their activity. In a number of cases, countries other than the United States became involved in counterinsurgency on the local government side. In Oman, for instance, Jordan, Iran, Saudi Arabia, and Great Britain supported the sultan against the Popular Front for the Liberation of Oman, which was backed by the Soviet Union and, for a time, the PRC.

Another development that fostered continued international involvement in internal conflicts was the appearance of new regional actors motivated by power politics, ideological considerations, or a combination of both. To achieve their aims against regional rivals, various governments backed insurgent groups across their borders and sometimes beyond. For example, the Shah of Iran gave aid to Kurdish rebels in Iraq to gain leverage against Baghdad in negotiations over land and border disputes; Algeria assisted (some would say "created") the Front for the Liberation of Rio d'Oro and Saguia el-Hamra (Polisario) rebels in the western Sahara, who were fighting against Morocco, Algeria's rival for hegemony in North Africa; and the Republic of South Africa backed insurgents with the National Union for the Total Independence of Angola (UNITA) as part of an overall security policy aim of weakening neighboring states that threatened both South Africa's position in Namibia and its apartheid policies at home.

The actions of some governments were significantly inspired by ideology. Libyan leader Muammar al-Qaddafi propagated what he called his "third universal theory," a blend of populist, Islamic, pan-Arab, and socialist tenets that he believed should be adopted everywhere. Identifying the principal obstacles to the spread of his ideas as the imperialist powers, Israel, and reactionary Arab regimes in the Middle East, Qaddafi sought to undermine them by sponsoring and aiding insurgents of various stripes who shared his opposition to these enemies. In the late 1970s, the Iranian revolution brought to power an Islamic government that also sought to spread its doctrines and ideas through the support of insurgents in various Middle Eastern countries (e.g., Bahrain, Kuwait, Saudi Arabia, and Lebanon).

An important point worth noting is that even though the United States partially retreated from involvement in insurgencies during the 1970s, the international dimension of insurgencies remained important because of the continued involvement of the Communist powers and the actions of regional states. In the 1980s this trend was reinforced by renewed American involvement in situations involving insurgent groups.

RENEWED AMERICAN INVOLVEMENT

During the Nixon years, the administration's move away from entanglement in foreign insurrections was reflected in the Nixon Doctrine, which allowed for advice and assistance to friendly governments threatened by insurgents but precluded military involvement. As noted earlier, this policy was the result of both the public aversion to "new Vietnams" and the administration's strategic assumption that the East-West conflict should be addressed primarily in terms of major-power politics, with less attention paid to peripheral, Third World areas.

The Nixon Doctrine notwithstanding, flexible response remained the conceptual cornerstone of U.S. defense policy. Although this strategy meant that theoretically the United States should be able to respond differentially and proportionately to threats on the nuclear, conventional, and insurgent levels of conflict, the attention and resources devoted to the insurgent level of conflict diminished considerably in the Nixon, Ford, and Carter years. But, as is so often the case, at the very time this trend was dominant, new events in the international arena were slowly giving rise to a countertrend that eventually refocused American attention on insurgent conflicts. Among these events were transnational terrorism, the oil embargo and production cutbacks of 1973, the Iranian revolution, and the 1979 Soviet invasion of Afghanistan.

The upsurge of transnational terrorism came in the wake of Jordan's rout of the Palestinian guerrillas in 1970 and 1971. Motivated by a variety of aims, the Black September Organization and other Palestinian groups carried out a series of bombings, assassinations, kidnappings, skyjackings, and the like outside the Middle East. Their acts, together with similar ones by a growing number of ideologically disparate insurgent groups, compelled the United States to adopt political and military countermeasures to protect its citizens.

The renewed attention to insurgent conflicts created by terrorism was reinforced by the oil embargo of 1973 and subsequent price increases, which made the West acutely aware of its vulnerability to disruptions in the supply and price of vital raw materials. Of the many dangers to the supply of raw materials that defense planners envisaged, one of the most troublesome was the threat posed to governments of oil-producing states by insurgents hostile to Western interests. As analysts looked at the problem, questions reminiscent of the Kennedy years began to resurface: Which regimes are vulnerable? Is their existence vital to American interests? What are the social, economic, and political sources of instability? What American policies could prevent or mitigate political upheaval? Under what circumstances should the United States intervene? How should it intervene?

Whatever fears the West had about the potential of insurgent movements to threaten its interests were realized by the overthrow of the seemingly durable shah of Iran and the establishment of an Islamic regime antipathetic to both the United States and neighboring Arab oil producers in the critical Persian Gulf. Before long, Teheran became a center for various insurgent groups opposed to governments in the area that were either major oil producers (Saudi Arabia) or contiguous to the major producers (Oman).

The renewed concern about insurgent warfare increased further with the Soviet invasion of Afghanistan in December 1979. In this case, however, attention was focused on how effectively insurgency might be used against the Soviets by rebels who were already actively opposing the Marxist regime that had seized power in April 1978.

When the Reagan administration came to office in the wake of these events, differences emerged and sharpened between advisers who wished to avoid involvement in insurgencies and those who felt it might not be possible. The latter attitude was due, in large part, to the convergence of two factors: the general threat perceptions of the president and the growing insurrection in El Salvador. As far as President Reagan and most of his advisers were concerned, the Soviet threat was paramount because a long-term nuclear- and conventional-arms buildup by the Soviet Union had shifted the superpower military balance in its favor and enabled it to expand its influence geographically through the deployment of its own personnel, or surrogates, to places like Angola, Afghanistan, Ethiopia, Libya, Syria, South Yemen, and Vietnam. The Reagan administration further believed that unless the Soviets were checked, they would continue this process of expansion, using in some cases the instigation of, or support for, insurgencies in countries that had pro-Western governments.

Even though the Soviet threat was uppermost in the minds of the Reagan defense establishment, there was increased concern that serious threats to American interests could be posed by radical insurgents independent of Moscow. But, even in these cases, there was still apprehension that the Soviet Union would benefit from a diminution of Western power, which could result from insurgent victories. In light of its assumptions about the Soviet Union's improved capability to project military power and proclivity toward exploiting Western vulnerabilities, it was not surprising that the Reagan administration exhibited fears about revolutionary insurgencies in Guatemala and, especially, El Salvador. From the administration's point of view, both situations were part of a Soviet design to spread Marxism in the Western Hemisphere, and they had to be contained. Consequently, the United States gave strong moral and political support to the threatened governments, increased military and economic assistance, established a counterinsurgency training program for the Salvadoran military, and dispatched advisers to the area. Pressure, albeit uneven, was exerted on El Salvador to implement human rights reforms and land redistribution. Although American combat units were not directly engaged, it became clear that events had overtaken the post-Vietnam aversion to involvement in insurgencies.

Despite its very busy domestic agenda and immersion in relations with the Soviet Union and the Middle East, the Reagan administration's involvement with insurgencies during its second term did not change perceptibly. Attention and various forms of assistance were directed not just to governments like those of El Salvador and the Philippines, which were threatened by Marxist insurgents, but also to rebels who were fighting Marxist regimes in Angola, Nicaragua, and Afghanistan. Moreover, the regional conflicts became an important part of the diplomatic discussions between the superpowers, while the Department of Defense, as part of its overall buildup, once again devoted increased resources to various kinds of forces designed for special operations.

Insurgencies were not the only concern of the national security policy community, however. By the time of the George H. W. Bush administration it was evident that drug dealers and international terrorists acting on behalf of governments posed new threats. Their actions and those of insurgents hostile to the West were viewed as manifestations of "low-intensity conflicts" that could threaten the security interests of the United States and its friends. This led various U.S. government agencies dealing with national security policy to search for doctrinal principles and organizational formats for waging low-intensity conflicts.

The search for a general, cohesive doctrine and organization for dealing with low-intensity conflict was not successful, largely because drug dealing, international terrorism, and insurgency differ substantially with respect to purpose, modus operandi, and vulnerability to various countermeasures. Moreover, efforts to sort this out were quickly eclipsed by the attention devoted to managing the after effects of the dramatic collapse of the Soviet Union and its Eastern European empire. Further compounding matters was the Iraqi invasion of Kuwait in the summer of 1990 and the subsequent war.

While successful liberation of Kuwait seemed to guarantee the election of President Bush, economic problems asserted themselves and were effectively exploited by his opponent, William Jefferson Clinton, in what turned out to be a successful quest for the presidency. Consistent with his campaign motto, "It's the economy stupid," Clinton focused on economic issues early in his administration. But this would soon change as internal violence in Somalia and then Bosnia compelled the administration to devote more attention to foreign affairs, a trend reinforced by ethnic cleansing in Kosovo, which led to American-led military intervention, and by transnational terrorist attacks by a new and increasingly deadly nemesis, Osama bin Ladin. The latter was responsible for attacks on the American embassies in Tanzania and Kenya in August 1998 and the USS *Cole* in October 2000. The embassy attacks led to ineffectual cruise missile strikes in Afghanistan and the Sudan.

The growing menace of terrorism led the Clinton administration to characterize it as the most important threat to national security. This carried over into the administration of George W. Bush. As things turned out, however, neither the Clinton nor the Bush administration dealt effectively with the bin Ladin threat, despite adequate warnings about his hostility and intentions to harm the United States. The result was the attack of September 11.

The shock engendered by Al Qaida's blow regenerated interest in insurgency, a subject that with a few exceptions (most notably in the American special operations forces and the education and training component of the CIA) had faded in importance inside the U.S. government and the larger national security community during the last decade of the twentieth century. Two factors galvanized the new interest in insurgency. The first was the realization that Al Qaida conceptualized its struggle with the West as an effort ultimately to change the international order by creating a global caliphate (Islamic state). To do so, it vowed to conduct a worldwide insurrection in countless places, including Afghanistan, where, along with the deposed Taliban, it commenced guerrilla and terrorist attacks against the new government. The second factor was the aftermath of the conventional war in Iraq in 2003, which gave rise to chronic insurgency waged by a multiplicity of groups. The grave challenge posed by the Al Qaida and Iraqi insurgents brought the study of insurgency back to center stage where it stands today as analysts, practitioners, and commentators seek to discover its dynamics, principles, and lessons by looking at past experiences and analogies and their implications for the present and future.

PURPOSE

This brief summary of the role of insurgencies since World War II is not intended as a moral or political critique of past roles played by internal and external participants in these conflicts. Its purpose is to underscore the persistent importance of insurgency as a type of conflict in the international system. As was the case in 1990, when the first edition of this book appeared, there is little doubt that insurgency will continue to be prominent because there are no signs that the problems of national cohesion, economic development, and political legitimacy that gave rise to earlier conflicts will be solved any time soon. Indeed, in many places they may be exacerbated by the inequities of the globalization process. In the meantime, there is every reason to expect that rivalries between major and regional powers will persist and that subversion of adversaries will be viewed in many countries as an attractive and rational alternative to the costs of major interstate wars.

As a consequence of the persistence of many current insurgencies and the emergence of unforeseen ones, participants, journalists, students, government analysts, and scholars in many parts of the world will be spending considerable time trying to better understand and evaluate them. The main purpose of this book is to provide a general and holistic framework for analysis that will be helpful in these endeavors. The framework is designed to bring together factors that can have a crucial bearing on the progress and outcome of insurgent conflicts. These factors, which are set forth in succeeding chapters, focus attention on key questions that should be asked about all insurgencies, regardless of time and place.

The components of the framework are not the product of a random selection process. They were abstracted from an exhaustive review of the literature that included theoretical and historical writings by scholars, participants, journalists, and other observers. Once these components were identified, the literature was again reviewed to collate, compare, and synthesize various insights regarding them. The framework for analysis was then applied to a wide range of cases to test for consistency and validity. Although there is a continuous effort throughout the study to identify, define, and suggest relationships among the factors, there is no pretense that the framework is a formal theory or model. The framework does, however, provide a systematic, straightforward format for comprehensively analyzing or comparing insurgencies.

There is no assumption that all concepts, definitions, propositions, hypotheses, and examples in the framework are flawless. Experiences with both this framework and other conceptual devices in the social sciences suggest that all conceptual schemata should be open to refinements, deletions, additions, and qualifications. Accordingly, case studies are crucial because of what we learn about particular situations under consideration and because of ideas and findings that will improve the framework. The framework used in this book is the product of an evolutionary process, involving many changes suggested by the case studies and by academic colleagues and countless students. While its value has hopefully been improved, the evolutionary process will continue, for there is much still to be learned.

There is no effort to pass judgment on whether such things as particular insurgencies, governments, strategies, forms of warfare, types of organization, and external support are inherently good or bad, moral or immoral. The object is to develop concepts that can be used to pose essential questions.

The concepts used in the framework will be defined, discussed, and illustrated extensively. Definitions are, of course, somewhat arbitrary and, with respect to insurgency, can be quite contentious. Terms like *insurgency, guerrilla warfare, terrorism,* and *revolutionary* have not only been defined in various ways but have often been used interchangeably. To avoid the confusion and obfuscation that are inevitable when definitions are unclear, a conscious effort has been made to set forth what the various terms mean and then to use them explicitly and consistently. Analysis, communications, and mutual understanding are all served by adhering to common concepts, however imperfect, until such time as they are redefined.

The discussion of the concepts is based on a wide variety of written works, including my own. The examples and illustrations are drawn from both these sources and extensive case studies completed by either graduate students at civilian universities or highly select groups of mid-career government officials, including members of all the armed services, various intelligence agencies, and the Department of State, to name but a few. Cases, such as the insurgencies in Eritrea, the western Sahara, El Salvador, Northern Ireland, Guatemala, Angola, Afghanistan, Nicaragua, Italy, Sri Lanka, Peru, Spain, Italy, and the Philippines, have been analyzed at various times in the last twenty years by more than thirty different groups, all of which used continually updated information and sought new insights. Many of the strong points of consensus that emerged from these analyses are reflected in the commentary and illustrations in the pages ahead.

The presentation of the framework begins in chapter 2 with a definition of insurgency and a discussion of various goals insurgents pursue, types of insurgencies, and forms of warfare. Chapter 3 deals with different strategic approaches insurgents may adopt and suggests the relative importance they ascribe to the environment, popular support, organization and unity, external support, and government response. Chapters 4 through 8 discuss each of those factors separately and a number of relationships among them are drawn.

2

THE NATURE OF INSURGENCY

Insurgency may be defined as a struggle between a nonruling group and the ruling authorities in which the nonruling group consciously uses *political resources* (e.g., organizational expertise, propaganda, and demonstrations) and *violence* to destroy, reformulate, or sustain the basis of legitimacy of one or more aspects of politics.[1] *Legitimacy* and *illegitimacy* are terms used to determine whether existing aspects of politics are considered moral or immoral—right or wrong—by the population or selected elements thereof. Simply defined, *politics* is the process of making and executing binding decisions for a society. Generally, the major aspects of politics may be identified as the political community, the political system, the authorities, and policies. Insurgents may consider any or all of these illegitimate, and it makes a great deal of difference precisely which one is at stake.[2]

ASPECTS OF POLITICS

Political Community

The political community consists of those who interact on a regular basis in the process of making and executing binding decisions. These interactions may consist of active participation in the policy process or simply passive acceptance of the decisions. Although political communities have varied in size throughout history, with some even being empires, in the contemporary international system, the political community is, for the most part, equivalent to the nation-state. Most citizens in the West take the political community for granted, although their respective countries may contain a multiplicity of ethnic, religious, and racial groups. Even where group animosities and conflicts over political and material resources are evident (e.g., the Flemings and Walloons in Belgium), people have been accustomed to being part of geographically distinct states that enjoy historical continuity and international recognition. There are, of course, exceptions, such as the members of the Basque Homeland and Liberty (ETA) in Spain and of the Irish Republican Army (IRA) in the United Kingdom, both of which violently reject the idea that they should be in the political communities of which they are nominally a part.

While violent rejection of the political community is the exception rather than the rule in most Western nations, Japan, and a number of other countries, the Third World has experienced substantial conflict related to the legitimacy of political communities. For the most part, this is because the boundaries of many states in the developing world were established by former imperial powers with little regard to the distribution of ethnic groups. Thus, in Africa, the Middle East, and Asia, it is not uncommon to find major ethnic and religious groups either living in two or more contiguous states (e.g., the Pashtuns in Afghanistan and Pakistan; the Kurds in Iraq, Iran, Turkey, the Soviet Union, and Syria; and the Baluchis in Afghanistan, Pakistan, and Iran) or being incorporated into political entities in which they are subjected to rule by rival groups (e.g., the subordination of the Islamic Moros to Christian rule in the Philippines and the Eritreans to Amhara rule in Ethiopia). In all these examples, as well as in a number of other situations, violent conflict over the legitimacy of the political community has occurred at some time or another in the past few decades.

Political System

Where a consensus on the legitimacy of the political community exists, there may be other grounds for internal warfare. A case in point is violent discord over the political system—that is, the salient values, rules, and structures that make up the basic framework guiding and limiting the making and executing of binding decisions.[3] *Values* are general ideas as to what is desirable, such as equality, justice, liberty, and individualism, whereas *rules* encourage desired patterns of behavior (e.g., prohibition of private property is a rule that supports the value of equality). Over the years, political scientists, anthropologists, and sociologists have used many different terms and concepts (e.g., high and low authoritarian, pluralistic, polyarchic, traditional, autocratic, oligarchical, monarchical, and totalitarian) to describe and contrast political systems. From several that could be adopted, this framework uses four models developed by Charles F. Andrain. Although they are ideal types from which actual systems may diverge in specific ways, they nonetheless capture the basic differences among systems.

The first political system, *traditional autocracy*, is one in which elitism, ascription (birthright), and highly personalized relationships are key values. Top decision makers are drawn from a small group—a family, clan, or lineage—that is considered to have the exclusive right to rule. The personal traits of the top leader are extolled, and his right to rule is further legitimized by sacred (religious) values that often portray him as divinely anointed. Government is marked by limited institutional development. Such groups as the clergy, the economic elite, and the military provide support for the regime and, in return, gain security and various socioeconomic privileges. And, while local leaders are left to control affairs at the lowest levels, they play little or no role in national-level policy making. The general public, meanwhile, is expected to be apathetic and loyal.

While in the past they paid little attention to economic modernization and bureaucratic development, in today's world, traditional leaders are compelled to attend more to these matters because of the rising expectations of their populations. When this occurs, as it did in Saudi Arabia and Iran, traditional autocracies may be forced to transform themselves into a second type of system, *modernizing autocracies*, which, like traditional systems, are characterized by elite rule. While political systems in transition from traditional to modernizing autocracies may continue to stress birthright and religious values as a basis for rule, building state power is the highest value of the modernizing autocracy. As this value is pursued, rule becomes more bureaucratic and impersonal, and the structure of power evolves into a hierarchical one, with a president, military officer, or similar personage at the top. The leader functions as a patron who dispenses favors to military, police, bureaucrats, and landowners in return for their support. Unlike the traditional system, a more complex administrative apparatus manages affairs. While the state may control or even own more economic enterprises, a good deal of regulated private activity is permitted. Changes tend to be directed from the top, and participation by the masses in the political process is minimal or carefully circumscribed. Contemporary Iran functions in this manner. Although elections for parliament (*majlis al-shura*, or consultative council) and municipal offices are held and ascription is not a requisite to rule, the Velayat-e Faqih (supreme jurisconsult) and interlocking key families hold the real power, and challenge to theocratic rule is not tolerated.

The third and most authoritarian political system is the *totalitarian* one. Its goal is to control completely all aspects of the political, economic, and social life of its citizens. Accomplishing this goal is, of course, far from easy, especially in developing countries with weak technological or bureaucratic infrastructures. Whatever the case, the values of consensus and equality are primary in totalitarian regimes. And while populist rhetoric is commonplace and mass participation is encouraged in the process of reconstructing society, participation is controlled and orchestrated by a leadership elite, usually organized in a vanguard party that claims to represent the popular will. Top leaders use a complex bureaucracy, the media, the educational system, and a host of societal groups (e.g., peasants', workers', writers', and women's organizations) to carry out and control ambitious socioeconomic programs. With few exceptions, economic activity is in the hands of the public sector. Marxist-controlled systems have been the most notable example.

The fourth type of political system, the *pluralistic* (i.e., democratic), differs substantially from the authoritarian types. The principal values are individual freedom, liberty, and compromise. Numerous political structures exist within, and outside of, government. Those outside, such as political parties, the media, and interest groups, act autonomously. In the past, this was referred to as structural, or subsystem, autonomy; in more recent times, the term *civil society* has been used. While precise institutional arrangements vary among pluralist systems, in all cases limits are placed on the powers of the top leaders by written or unwritten constitutions that provide mechanisms for their periodic approval or removal.

No doubt the most notable contemporary examples of insurgencies motivated by a rejection of a given political system have been those led by Marxists, who view traditional and modernizing autocracies, as well as pluralist systems, to be exploitative of workers and peasants because the values, norms, and structures of such systems serve the interests of feudal or capitalist classes. The Popular Front for the Liberation of Oman, for example, accepted the political community but utterly rejected the traditional autocracy led by the sultan. Through political efforts and through violence, it sought during the late 1960s and 1970s to replace the values of elitism, birthright, and religion (in this case, Islam), as well as the patrimonial structures of the sultanate, with a system in which a single mass party that extols the values of equality, secularism, and populism would make binding decisions.[4] Traditional systems are not the only ones targeted by insurgents. In the recent past, Muslim insurgents opposed modernizing autocratic systems in Syria and Iraq; anarchist and Marxist insurgents confronted pluralist systems in West Germany, Belgium, France, and Japan; and, quasitotalitarian systems in Angola, Cambodia, and Vietnam came under attack. The common goal of the insurgents in all these and similar cases was to radically transform the political system.

Authorities

Another aspect of politics that may lead to insurrection involves the authorities. While some groups may not quarrel with the political community or the system, they may consider specific individuals illegitimate because their behavior is inconsistent with existing values and norms or because they are viewed as corrupt, ineffective, or oppressive. This situation is normally exemplified by coups in which insurgents seize top decision-making offices without changing the system of their predecessors. The well-known Latin American cases of the 1950s and the 1970 overthrow of Sultan Said bin Taimur of Oman by his son Qabus provide illustrations.[5]

Policies

Finally, nonruling groups may resort to violence to change existing social, economic, or political policies that they believe discriminate against particular groups (e.g., ethnic, religious, racial, or economic) in the population. A recent example is the Sudanese insurgency in the 1960s, where blacks in the south demanded a change in policies related to economic power and resources; another is the periodic attempts by moderate Shiite and Druze elements in Lebanon to redress the perceived unequal distribution of political and economic assets that favored the Christian community. While insurgents clearly focus on policies, in some cases they may also seek to displace authority figures they consider uncompromising.

It is important to bear in mind that insurgency is essentially a political-legitimacy crisis of some kind. The task of the analyst, therefore, is to identify exactly what is at stake. To do so, it is necessary to ascertain the long-term goal of the insurgents and the relationship of that goal to the above-described aspects of politics (the political community, political system, authorities, and policies).

TYPES OF INSURGENCIES

When we look at the ultimate goals of insurgent movements and the aspects of politics they focus on, some very important distinctions emerge. If we fail to see the fundamental differences with respect to goals, we make a major mistake because, as will be clear later, differentiating among goals has not only academic value but also some vital practical implications for those involved in insurgent conflicts. So, the first question an analyst must answer is, what type of insurgency are we dealing with? In answering that question, we will find it helpful to be aware of the several types, their differences, and their goals.

Our research suggests nine types of insurgents: anarchists, egalitarians, traditionalists, pluralists, apocalyptic-utopians, secessionists, reformists, preservationists, and commercialists. The first five are all revolutionary because they seek to change an existing political system completely.

Anarchist

Anarchist groups espouse the farthest-reaching goal. Highly diffuse and individualistic, their members believe that since all authority patterns are unnecessary and illegitimate, political systems should be destroyed but not replaced. Examples include the Black Cells and Black Help in Germany in the 1970s, the Revolutionary Initiative Group in Italy, the Black Star in Austria, 17 November in Greece, the International Anarchist Organization in Spain, and the New Revolutionary Alternative in Chechnya. Not included are Al Qaida, Marxist organizations, or others that pursue a breakdown of law, order, and authority as an intermediate strategic aim pursuant to their ultimate objective of replacing a political system with one of their own liking. None of the contemporary anarchist groups has been particularly significant, which cannot be said of our second category, the egalitarians.[6]

Egalitarian

Egalitarian insurgent movements seek to impose a new system based on the ultimate value of distributional equality and centrally controlled structures designed to mobilize the people and radically transform the social structure within an existing political community. This type of insurgency was a familiar part of the post–World War II international political landscape and was epitomized by violent Marxist groups such as the Malayan Communist Party, the Huks in the Philippines, the Vietcong in South Vietnam, the Thai National Liberation Front, the Japanese Red Army, the Fedayeen-i-Khalq in Iran, the Popular Front for the Liberation of Oman, and principal groups in the Farabundo Marti National Liberation Front in El Salvador. Baathist groups in the Middle East that seized power in Iraq and Syria provide examples of non-Communist egalitarian insurgents.[7]

Despite their populist rhetoric, egalitarian insurgents who came to power normally established political systems that were authoritarian, repressive, and elitist. Nevertheless, it is wishful thinking to assume that egalitarianism, especially its Marxist variant, has somehow evaporated with the collapse of Soviet communism and China's decision to pursue what some call "Market-Leninism." Since the underlying social, economic, and political deprivations that gave rise to violent behavior in the previous century have either remained unchanged or worsened in many places, the appeal of egalitarians will remain attractive for some dispossessed and disenfranchised people. This is not meant to suggest that the cold war is about to be reborn but simply to point out that violence stemming from egalitarian motives will cause significant problems in specific situations. Present examples include the remnants of Sendero Luminoso (Shining Path) in Peru, the New People's Army in the Philippines, the Revolutionary Armed Forces of Colombia (FARC), and the surprisingly effective Front for the Liberation of Nepal.

Traditionalist

Without question, traditionalist insurgents who articulate primordial and sacred values rooted in ancestral ties and religion have posed the greatest threat in the early twenty-first century. Unlike the egalitarians, traditionalists would opt for a less inclusive and less intrusive system with two features. As adumbrated above, the first is an emphasis on values and norms that legitimatize a small, centralized ruling elite (either a single family or a restricted network of interconnected select families). For the most part, the values are—to a lesser or greater degree—familiar sacred or religious ones. The second feature is passive rather than active involvement in politics on the part of the majority of the population. Traditionalists seek to establish political structures characterized by limited or guided participation and low autonomy, with political power in the hands of an autocratic leader supported by economic, military, and clerical elites. While the majority of the population may enjoy some autonomy at the local level, widespread participation in politics, especially by organized opposition groups, is discouraged, if not proscribed.

Many, if not most, traditionalists seek to restore a political system from the recent or distant past. Examples of such groups include the Nationalists in Spain from 1936 to 1939, who fought to destroy the republic and restore the church, monarchy, and army to former positions of prestige; the Contras in Nicaragua during the 1980s, who sought to reconstitute the old oligarchic triumvirate of landowners, military, and clergy; and insurgents in Yemen during the 1960s who aimed to restore the tribally based rule of the Zaydi (Shia faction) imamate by carrying out an insurrection against a newly established "republican" government inspired and backed by Egypt's secular and socialist government.

Within the category of traditionalist insurgents, one also finds more zealous groups seeking to reestablish an ancient political system that they idealize as a golden age. We refer to this subtype as *reactionary-traditionalist.* It includes a plethora of present day Islamic militants, or *jihadis* ("holy warriors"), such as the Shia-based Party of God (Hezbollah) in Lebanon and the Islamic Call (Al-Dawa al-Islamiyya) in Iraq, as well as Sunni-based organizations like the Armed Islamic Group in Algeria, Hamas ("zeal," the acronym for Harakat al-Muqawama al-Islamiyya, or Islamic Resistance Movement) in Palestine, the Islamic Group (Jama'a al-Islamiyya) in Egypt and, of course, Al Qaida ("the Base"). Whatever their sectarian composition, groups like these believe that political rule should be based on the Koran and Sunnah-Hadith (traditions and sayings of Muhammad) as codified in the sharia (Islamic law). While exact details of the structures and functions of the new system are not spelled out, most jihadis wish to emulate what they consider the purest form of Islamic rule as practiced by Mohammad and his first three successors (caliphs), Abu Bakr, Umar, and Uthman. Frequently, they are referred to as *salafis* (from *al-salaf al-salih*, or "pious forbearers").

Jihadis further believe that rulers who do not apply sharia must be overthrown and that only Muslims should exercise political and military responsibilities. In the words of Al Qaida theoretician Faris Al Shuwayl al-Zaharani, "The rulers of the countries of Islam in this age are all apostate, unbelieving tyrants who have departed in every way from Islam. Muslims who proclaim God's unity have no other choice than iron and fire, jihad in the way of God, to restore the caliphate according to the Prophet's teachings." As for Christians and Jews, in the final analysis, they must either obey authority or be eliminated. Moreover, since some Sunni militants like Abu Mussab al-Zarqawi condemn Shia Muslims as polytheists and mankind's worst evil (in his words, as "the lurking snake, the crafty and malicious scorpion, the spying enemy, and the penetrating venom"), they also must be converted or expunged.[8]

Until the turn of the century, most militant Islamic organizations focused on replacing the political systems of the states where they were located. In the later 1990s, this would begin to change as Al Qaida and its affiliates indicated their desire to establish a worldwide Islamic political system, or caliphate, in which everyone would accept, or be compelled to accept, Islamic rule; they thereby posed a truly revolutionary threat within the context of the international system.

Strikingly similar to the dogmatism and intolerance of the militant Islamic worldview is the outlook of Jewish and Christian militants. In Israel, the General Security Service (Shin Bet) refers to such militants as the Jewish Underground. Its notable (albeit small) groups include the Kach movement of the late Rabbi Meir Kahane and its successor, Kahana Chai ("Kahane Lives"), Herev David ("Sword of David"), EYAL (Irgun Yehudi Lohem, or "Jewish Fighting Organization"), Zu Artzenu ("This Is Our Land"), and Bereshit ("Genesis"). Many, if not most, members of these groups deride pluralist democracy as a passing phenomenon that will eventually be replaced by a recrudescent kingdom based on Jewish religious law (halacha). Unlike the militant salafis, they have no global aspirations.[9] Despite its limited size and geographic ambitions, the Jewish Underground has the potential to have a disproportionate impact. One can only imagine the enormity of the repercussions that would follow if it fulfilled the worst fears of the Shin Bet and attacked the sacred Islamic holy places (Dome of the Rock and Al-Aqsa Mosque) in Jerusalem.

Some militant Christian groups manifest the same kind of thinking. While clearly less capable than Islamic insurgents and even the Jewish Underground in Israel and the Occupied Territories, they are every bit as ideological, rigid, and committed to their ultimate goal. In the United States, these "Soldiers for Christ," as Mark Juergensmeyer has called them, subscribe to dominion theology, which calls for the dominion of God over all things. The more extreme among them believe in reconstruction theology's aim of creating a biblical-based Christian theocracy, which is destined to rule the world. As with Islamic and Jewish fundamentalists, their ranks include both opponents and proponents of violence. Even more radical is the Christian Identity Movement, which has spawned a plethora of groups like the Aryan Nation, Posse Comitatus, and the Order. Unconcerned about a past golden age, they believe in the supremacy of the white race and merging the state with their version of Christian law.[10]

Whatever their religious affiliation, reactionary traditionalists believe they are repositories of truth; their rhetoric is self-righteous, and they feel contempt (usually hatred) for those who do not share their views. Enemies are demonized and dehumanized, being referred to as monkeys, dogs, pigs, mud people, and the like. Like more pragmatic traditionalists, they believe economic and technological progress can take place in a traditional political-religious setting. Gulbudin Hekmatyar, leader of the Party of Islam (Hezb-i-Islami) in Afghanistan, for example, argues that there has never been a conflict in Islam between science and religion. This is important to keep in mind since it belies the common but erroneous assumption that all traditionalists oppose economic and technological change.

Apocalyptic-Utopian

A fringe insurgent grouping that merits brief attention includes religious cults with political aims, some of which transcend the confines of the nation-state. Essentially, they envisage establishing a world order—in some cases, involving divine intervention—as the result of an apocalypse precipitated by their acts of terrorism. As Robert Jay Lifton has persuasively argued, Aum Shinrikyo ("Supreme Truth") in Japan is a case in point.[11] Theologian Hiromi Shimada notes that in Aum Shinrikyo's eschatology (belief systems about the end of the world), which blends "junk stories" from Buddhism, yoga, European theosophy, ancient Shintoism, and Christianity, a depraved and wrong world should be ruined in order to achieve spiritual salvation.[12] The Mahdaviyat ("Last Imam") group in Iran exhibits somewhat similar thinking. It believes the mahdi ("savior") will not appear until the world is filled with cruelty and injustice. This being so, it is necessary to facilitate and expedite the spread of cruelty and injustice by destroying and removing institutions and people that foster justice![13]

Pluralist

The last of the insurgent groups seeking a revolutionary transformation of the political system, the pluralists, is neither authoritarian nor apocalyptic. Pluralist insurgents aim to establish a system that emphasizes the values of individual freedom, liberty, and compromise and in which political structures are differentiated and autonomous. The history of Western civilization is marked by a number of pluralist insurgencies. Among the so-called liberals with bombs were the People's Will and Social Revolutionaries in Russia in the 1890s and early twentieth century and elements of the African National Congress (Spear of the Nation) during the struggle against apartheid in the Republic of South Africa in the 1970s and 1980s.[14]

Today, the National Council of Resistance of Iran (NCRI), the umbrella organization that includes the Mujahidin-e Khalq (MKO), claims that it aims ultimately to supplant the traditionalist theocracy of Iran with a pluralist system. Doubters argue that past violence, Iranian authoritarian political culture, and centralized control within the NCRI militate against such an outcome. Supporters say that past violence was the work of organizational dissidents and has been repeatedly censured, that the NCRI's political thinking transcends Iran's old thinking, and that the multiplicity of groups within the NCRI is evidence of emerging pluralism. History will judge which assessment is correct. In the meantime, the MKO acts in the name of pluralist democracy.

Secessionist

The ultimate aim of secessionist (separatist) insurgents is even farther-reaching than the revolutionary goals espoused by the five types of groups we have just discussed. Secessionists renounce and seek to withdraw from the political community (nation-state) of which they are formally a part. Perhaps the best-known historical example is the secession of the Southern states and their formation of the Confederate States of America during the American Civil War (1861–1865).

Secessionists have been among the most notable insurgents since World War II. Today they are found in all corners of the globe. T. David

Mason has hypothesized that where relatively deprived ethnic groups live in distinct areas and have their own class-stratification systems (what he calls unranked systems), the ultimate goal of insurgent activity is usually secession, whereas in systems where groups are intermixed geographically (ranked systems), insurrectionary aims tend to be revolutionary.[15]

Some secessionists seek either to form their own nation-state or to join another. The first category includes World War II, anticolonialist, national-liberation movements such as the Vietminh in Indochina, the National Liberation Front in Algeria, and the Mau Mau in Kenya, all of which fought to separate from imperial political control. Also included are numerous recent and current secessionists. In Africa, examples include Eritrean and Afar liberation organizations in Ethiopia, the Front for the Liberation of Rio d'Oro and Saguia el-Hamra in the western Sahara (controlled by Morocco), and the South-West African People's Organization in Namibia (controlled until 1990 by the Republic of South Africa). Asian secessionists include radical Sikhs of the Khalistan Liberation Front in India, the Liberation Tigers of Tamil Eelam in Sri Lanka, the Pattani United Liberation Organization in southern Thailand, and the Baluchistan National Liberation Front in the Pakistan-Iran-Afghanistan triborder region. In the Middle East, Kurdish insurgents in Iraq and tribal rebels in Oman's Dhofar Province have, at times, articulated secessionist aims. Key Chechen groups in Russia, the Front for the Liberation of Corsica, the Brittany Liberation Front in France, Tirol and the Sardinian Armed Movement in Italy, Basque Homeland and Liberty in Spain, and the Quebec Liberation Front in Canada are examples in Europe and North America.[16]

Groups seeking to separate from one nation-state and merge into or with another are also not hard to find. Albanians in the Kosovo Liberation Army, the National Liberation Front for Presevo in Yugoslavia, and the National Liberation Army in Macedonia envisage a Greater Albania made up of Kosovo, Albania, Macedonia, and perhaps Montenegro. Nationalists of the Irish Republican Army–Provisional Wing (herein referred to as simply the IRA) and smaller factions (the Real IRA, the Continuity Army Council, and the Irish National Liberation Army) seek to withdraw from the United Kingdom and join the Republic of Ireland. Likewise, Islamic factions in Kashmir wish to escape Indian political control in favor of joining Pakistan.

Secessionist insurgents vary with respect to the type of political system they would establish in their new state. Whereas many are pragmatic or vague, others set forth ideological goals that explicitly address this issue. For example, militant Uighur Muslims of the Party of Allah seeking to liberate China's Xinjiang-Uighur Autonomous Region, like their Kashmiri counterparts, want an Islamic political system. Similarly, the Eritrean

People's Liberation Front articulated ideas that were supposed to define the political system. In this case, the aim was a secular Marxist people's republic. Where members of a secessionist movement have profoundly different visions about the political system they seek to establish, it is not uncommon to have factional strife marked by conspiratorial maneuvering and violence.

Whatever the type of political system secessionists favor, the primary goal that inspires their efforts is secession. Regardless of their size and whether their focus is regional, ethnic, racial, religious, ideological, or some combination thereof, secessionists consider themselves nationalists. Accordingly, bona fide wars of national liberation, such as China's anti-Japanese struggle and the Vietnamese and Algerian wars with France, fall within the secessionist category because the *primary* aim was independence, not the establishment of an authoritarian political system of one sort or another.[17]

Reformist

The seventh type of insurgency, the reformist, is nonrevolutionary. Reformists target policies that determine distribution of the economic, psychological, and political benefits that society has to offer. Here we confront groups of various political persuasions that see themselves as reformists and whose aims vary according to their specificity. Those who have carried out acts of violence to effect policy changes related to abortion, animal rights, and the environment are among the most specific. In England, for example, there is a very active array of small groups that threaten and carry out acts of violence on behalf of their "animal brothers and sisters." Acting under such names as Animal Rights Militia, the Animal Liberation Front, Band of Mercy, and so on, they seek to terminate laboratory testing by publishing death lists and targeting, among others, researchers and their family members. That they are taken seriously is evident from a separate data bank maintained by Scotland Yard called the Animal Rights National Index.[18]

More familiar and ambitious are reformists who see themselves as acting on behalf of aggrieved social classes or primary social groups perceived to be victims of relative deprivation and discrimination with respect to material benefits, political rights, and status. Typical of such groups is the National Liberation Army in Macedonia, which argues that Macedonia should remain a unified, multiethnic state in which Albanians will have equal status with respect to linguistic and political issues. While most of such groups have been associated with the left, some are extremely right-wing, such the neo-Nazi White Wolves in the United Kingdom. While they do not reject the overall political system, they do wish to turn political and social policies back by reestablishing white dominance through exclusionary laws and policies.[19] In this manner, they straddle the borderline between reactionary traditionalists and reformists.

On a much larger scale, the notion of using violence to effect reforms was clearly the dominant motive behind the first round of terrorist and guerrilla attacks by rebel groups in the southern Sudan in the 1960s. Although some insurgents entertained secessionist ambitions, the movement ended up seeking—but failing to obtain, as things turned out—a more equitable distribution of political and economic power for the black Christian and animist population at the expense of the ruling Arab Muslims. In 2004, two Muslim groups demanding political and economic rights in Sudan's western province of Darfur—the Sudan Liberation Army (SLA) and the Justice and Equality Movement—carried out a similar insurrection. As SLA official Adam Shogar put it, "we are not fighting for self-determination or an independent state of Darfur. . . . [W]e want justice and equality in Sudan, a democratic system in Sudan. . . . [W]e want our role in ruling Sudan, not to be ruled by others." Elsewhere in the world, reformist insurgents have included the Zapatistas in Mexico, who champion Indian rights; militant Kurds seeking more autonomy and a better economic deal in Iran; and at least a segment of Albanian insurgents in Macedonia.[20]

Preservationist

Preservationists differ from insurgents in all other categories in that they carry out illegal acts of violence against nonruling groups and authorities that are trying to effect change.[21] They are essentially oriented toward maintaining the status quo because of the relative political, economic, and social privileges they derive from it. Groups like this are infamous in American political history. During the eighteenth and nineteenth centuries, for example, loosely organized outfits in the West, like the Wyoming Stock Grower's Association, defended the political and economic dominance of ranchers and cattle companies by directing acts of violence at anyone who threatened their interests, such as homesteaders and sheepherders.[22] Meanwhile, in the South, the Ku Klux Klan (KKK) terrorized blacks in order to maintain the white-controlled social, political, and economic order at the local level. Although the Western groups gradually faded away, the KKK would reorganize by the early 1920s and reappear as a nationwide phenomenon that enjoyed its largest political successes not in the South but in Colorado and Indiana.[23] In recent times, preservationists have included organizations like the Afrikaner Resistance Movement in South Africa, which sought to sustain the apartheid system, and the Ulster Volunteer Force and the Ulster Defense Association, both of which used violence to retain the political community, political system, and policies that they believe the IRA, Catholic moderates, the Irish Republic, and "British capitulationists" threaten. Among the more notorious preservationists have been right-wing "death squads" in Latin American countries, which are neither sanctioned by, nor have official ties with, the ruling political authorities. This category also includes borderline cases like the United Self-Defense Forces in Colombia, which has links with some elements of the military but retains its ability to operate independently.[24] Not included are violent groups directed by the authorities, such as the Saddam Fedayeen during Saddam Hussein's rule in Iraq, the Al Quds faction of the Revolutionary Guards in Iran, and the Janjaweed militia in the just-noted Darfur situation, since they are considered agents of the state rather than insurgents.

Commercialist

The last type of insurgent group is one that Steven Metz has aptly called commercial insurgents.[25] Many have a narrow tribal or clan basis and are led by self-styled chiefs, warlords, and the like. Their main aim appears to be nothing more than the acquisition of material resources through seizure and control of political power. Essentially, they consider political legitimacy to be relatively unimportant. Coercive power is what counts. Arthur Helton of the Open Society Institute has characterized their indifference to ideas as follows:

> Ideas are much smaller now. The circumstances are far more driven by self-interest or the perception of self-interest. Ordinary people are the targets and the fodder of rogue militias. Nine times more civilians than combatants die. Battles are fought over no apparent principles, only greed and power.[26]

Given this noticeable absence of a serious rationale for what they seek, such groups are essentially self-aggrandizing nihilists, although predators would also be an appropriate term. A particularly noxious example is the Revolutionary United Front (RUF) in Sierra Leone, which during the late 1990s evinced a penchant for exacting general compliance by systematically burning civilians alive, disemboweling them, or hacking off their arms and legs to render them helpless, unemployable, and compliant. Commenting on the motives of the RUF, presidential spokesperson Septimus Kaikai noted, "There are no issues for these people. They do not have a political agenda. They do not have a social agenda. They do not have a religious agenda. What they're simply doing is simply personal; it's personal aggrandizement, selfishness on their part, just to amass wealth."[27]

IDENTIFYING INSURGENT TYPES: SIX PROBLEMS

Identifying types of insurgent movements is not always easy. One or more of five complications render some cases problematic, the first being a change in goals.

Changing Goals

Some insurgent movements experience goal transformation because leaders emerge with new goals in mind or because existing leaders calculate that they stand a better chance of accomplishing less ambitious aims. The evolution of the insurgency in Oman's Dhofar Province during the 1960s from a secessionist to an egalitarian one as the result of a Marxist takeover is a straightforward case in point; more chaotic has been the transformation of the Sudanese insurrection carried out by blacks in the southern area of that country for more than forty years. The warfare in the Sudan began during the 1960s with a secessionist aim, was temporarily interrupted by a 1972 political accord based on a reformist solution, and was reignited by groups seeking either secession or a change in the political system. Within this context, the major group, the Sudanese People's Liberation Front (SPLM), led by John Garang, demanded an egalitarian Marxist system; then, when the Communist bloc disintegrated, he called for a pluralist polity. In 1998, the SPLM joined forces with northern opponents of the governing elite who wanted to reform the existing political system. Meanwhile, in the midst of this confusion over ultimate ends, the SPLM seemed ready at times once more to accept a reformist outcome (i.e., a federal state).[28]

Conflicting Goals

A second complicating factor presents itself in situations where distinct groups or factions of an insurgent movement have different, sometimes mutually exclusive, goals. The Afghan insurrection against the Soviets contained several traditionalist groups competing with one another and with a smattering of smaller egalitarian and putative pluralist groups. An even sharper division could be seen in clashes between traditionalists and egalitarians in the Palestinian ranks in the late 1960s and 1970s, which outside supporters seeking influence with the resistance and adversaries looking for ways to discredit it both exploited. This divisive trend continued in the

1990s as those who violently opposed the peace process were themselves divided into secular and Islamic camps, which prevented them from cooperating politically or militarily.[29] This suggests that a careful analysis of contradictions among the ultimate goals of terrorists has great practical significance; indeed, as we shall see later, it may present an opportunity for driving a wedge into insurgent ranks.

Misleading Rhetoric

The third difficulty confronting a researcher is the frequent masking of ultimate goals by democratic rhetoric. When this occurs, it is particularly important to examine carefully the public and internal documents of the insurgents and the way the movement is governed before rendering a judgment about its primary or essential aspirations. The democratic pronouncements of movements that are politically pluralistic, like the Jewish Agency in Palestine during the 1940s, are far more convincing than those of centrally controlled and authoritarian organizations, such as Marxist and religiously inspired ones that claim a monopoly on the truth. In the Jewish case, democratic values were actualized by the multiparty structure of the Jewish Agency, which became the basis for a democratic system once statehood was achieved. In sharp contrast, the Popular Front for the Liberation of Oman imposed harsh, centralized rule in liberated zones during the 1960s, despite its democratic verbiage. This clearly suggests that any assessment of insurgent goals should include careful attention to how insurgents actually conduct their own political affairs.

Ambiguous Goals

Another complication that may arise when researchers try to identify insurgent goals is ambiguity. This occurs when two or more aims may be evident, neither of which clearly predominates. Pinning down the precise aims of the Red Brigades in Italy and the Shining Path in Peru, for instance, has proven difficult. The temptation to classify the Red Brigades as egalitarians because of their Marxist-Leninist rhetoric has been mitigated by their clear emphasis on destroying the existing political system and the paucity of comments on what will replace it. Likewise, the Shining Path's goal in Peru is not as clear as its Maoist ideological pronouncements might suggest, because Indian mysticism and symbols are extolled in what seems to be an attempt to synthesize traditional communalism with egalitarianism.

Confusion of Ultimate and Intermediate Goals

A fifth problem stems from the occasional tendency to confuse the intermediate and ultimate strategic aims of terrorists. Many insurgents who want a new political system believe a necessary condition for success is a prior breakdown of authority and control patterns in a society. When this happens, the activity and rhetoric of an insurgent organization tends to focus on fomenting disorder. Since this tactic has the earmarks of anarchism, it may easily obscure the ultimate purposes of the group. The behavior of some apocalyptic utopians that believe political chaos and violent eruptions must precede the establishment of the ultimate utopia comes to mind. In situations like this, observers tend to focus on the destructive aims and lose sight of the desired outcome.

IDENTIFYING GOALS

It should not be inferred from the preceding discussion that all insurgent movements are difficult to classify. To the contrary, the ultimate goals of many are straightforward, consistent with behavior, and easy to identify. Whatever the difficulty, ascertaining the goals of insurgent organizations is a crucial first step in any analysis; aside from its academic merits, it has a number of significant practical implications, which should become evident at various points later in this study. For now, a few general comments may help clarify this point.

To begin with, different goals place different demands on insurgents with respect to resources. Since secessionist, and most especially anarchistic, traditionalist, pluralist, egalitarian, and apocalyptic-utopian aims are by their nature not amenable to compromise, they normally result in strong resistance from authorities. This, in turn, means that in nearly all cases, the insurgents must mobilize greater support and be prepared for a sustained commitment if they are to have any hope of success. Some egalitarian movements, like the Thai National Liberation Front in the 1980s, which are based on geographically isolated minority groups, are at a tremendous disadvantage initially because of their limited ability to mobilize support from the majority group, which sustains the political system and authorities. In contrast, reformist and preservationist groups may find that limited insurgent activity can convince the authorities to make concessions because their aims do not require the political system to collapse or the authorities to abdicate. In response to reformist insurgents, the authorities may decide to cut their losses by agreeing to a more equitable distribution of political and economic benefits (e.g., the accord between the government and the southern rebels that ended the Sudanese insurrection in the 1960s). As far as preservationist challenges are concerned, the authorities may simply steer away from basic changes in the system in order to mitigate violence (e.g., as the British did in Northern Ireland).

Clarifying insurgent goals is crucial for outside powers that are thinking about becoming involved on one side or the other. Indeed, an argument can be made that the United States' fears, commitments, and tendency to intervene in local conflicts in the 1960s resulted in part from an inclination to equate all insurgencies with the revolutionary aspirations of egalitarian movements. It is thus worth pointing out that calculations about intervention that gloss over ultimate insurgent aims can lead to ill-informed and costly entanglements and the creation of enemies where none existed before. This is a particular danger within the current framework of the American Global War on Terrorism since the ultimate goals of many groups that rely on terrorism, either in whole or in part, may not threaten U.S. vital interests. This is arguably the case with respect to the Front for the Liberation of Nepal, the FARC in Colombia, and the New People's Army in the Philippines. Some would even include Hamas and the Palestinian Islamic Jihad.

THE MEANS: POLITICS AND FORMS OF WARFARE

Political Means

Insurgent movements use political resources and instruments of violence against the ruling authorities to accomplish their goals. Political activity includes such things as the dissemination of information (propaganda) through meetings, pamphlets, media broadcasts, the Internet, and the like; arranging protest demonstrations; recruiting cadres (insurgent officials); training and infiltrating agents into the official establishment; persuading outside powers to extend various kinds of assistance; raising and managing finances; creating supportive groups (e.g., workers', farmers', women's, writers', and youth associations); providing services to the people; and devising and implementing strategies and plans. The importance of activities like these has led many analysts to characterize insurgency as primarily a political phenomenon and to attribute the success of individuals such as Mao Tse-tung and Ho Chi Minh more to their political acumen than their prowess as military leaders.

Success in marshaling and utilizing resources depends on effective organization. On a general level, there are two types: *selective,* where small, elite groups threaten or carry out violent acts, and *mobilizational,* where insurgent elites attempt to involve large segments of the population actively on behalf of their cause.[30] While a mobilizational organization is the most familiar to students of insurgency because of the well-known Chinese, Vietnamese, Cambodian, Algerian, and Portuguese colonial conflicts, there are numerous examples of selective insurgencies, such as the Red Brigades in Italy, the Red Army in Japan, the Muslim Brotherhood in Syria, and Al Qaida. Because some selective groups gradually evolve into mobilizational movements, the two are best viewed as the ends of a continuum, with many cases falling between them.

The organizational effort necessary for coordinating both violent and nonviolent activity is not as demanding for a selective organization because there is far less concern with linking the insurgency to the masses. But, in the long term, this neglect of the population often renders such groups impotent and, as a result, becomes one of the contentious issues dividing leaders of insurgent movements. We will elaborate on this theme when we look at insurgent strategies, popular support, and organization.

The other aspect of insurgency, the use of violence, sets it apart from political protest movements like Gandhi's in India, Khomeini's in Iran, Solidarity in Poland, and the civil rights movement in the United States. One need not dispute the prominence of the political dimension of insurgencies in order to call attention to the important role that violent acts play, whether they are small-scale or take place in the context of large-scale warfare. It is not a matter of *either* politics *or* violence; rather, it is a matter of *both*—and the relative parts they play in different situations.

Forms of Warfare

The violent aspect of insurgency is manifested in different forms of warfare. A *form of warfare* may be viewed as one variety of organized violence emphasizing particular armed forces, weapons, tactics, and targets. Three forms of warfare have been associated with insurgent conflicts: terrorism, guerrilla war, and conventional warfare.[31]

Terrorism is herein defined as the threat or use of physical coercion, primarily against noncombatants, especially civilians, to create fear in order to achieve various political objectives. Achieving such objectives requires behavioral change on the part of specific audiences.[32] The target *audience* whose behavioral modification is sought will vary from case to case and may involve individuals, selected groups, the general public, governments, or some combination thereof. While, in some cases, victims and target audiences may coincide, normally they are different. A well-known example over the past decade is the killing and maiming of passengers (victims) during several bus bombings in Israel by secular and Islamic Palestinian militants seeking to undermine peace negotiations by inflaming Israeli public opinion and goading the government to overreact (behavioral change of two audiences). One of the more bizarre cases along these lines was an attack against passengers arriving on an Air France flight carried out on behalf of the Popular Front for the Liberation of Palestine by the Japanese Red Army at Lod airport in Israel on May 30, 1972. When the firing and explosions terminated, sixteen Puerto Rican religious pilgrims lay among the dead victims. Needless to say, it would be a stretch of the imagination to conclude that the pilgrims had been the targeted audience. Of more recent vintage were the bombings of the train stations in Madrid in 2004 by Al Qaida elements, which were designed to influence the Spanish electorate to vote for a new government that would withdraw troops from Iraq.

Civilian casualties that are unintended consequences of military operations (so-called collateral damage) are not included in this definition. Also excluded are spontaneous and sometimes intensifying episodes of violence between ethnic and religious groups that are often triggered by rumors and false information and fueled by mutual hatred, distrust, and desires for revenge. Examples abound and in recent times have included violence between Hindus and Christians and between Muslims and Hindus in India, as well as between Christians and Muslims in East Timor and the Spice Islands of Indonesia.

The active units of terrorist organizations are normally smaller than those of guerrillas, being composed of individuals organized covertly into cells. Their actions are familiar, consisting of assassinations, bombings, grenade tossing, arson, torture, mutilation, hijacking, and kidnapping. While the targets of such violence may at times be arbitrary, often they are carefully chosen in order to maximize political impact.[33] Although such terrorism has generally occurred within the borders of states where insurgents have challenged the legitimacy of the political system, authorities, or policies, there has been an increasing tendency since the mid-1970s to conduct attacks against targets outside the country. In fact, for a group like Al Qaida, the world at large is a battlefield. Such attacks by nonstate actors are herein referred to as *transnational terrorism* to distinguish them from similar behavior on the part of individuals or groups controlled by sovereign states (*international terrorism*).[34]

Insurgent terrorism is purposeful rather than mindless violence because terrorists seek to achieve specific long-term, intermediate, and short-term goals. The long-term goal is, of course, to change the political community, political system, authorities, or policies. The intermediate goal of terrorism is not so much the desire to deplete the government's physical resources as it is to erode its psychological support by instilling fear into officials and their domestic and international supporters. In the short term, terrorists often pursue one or more objectives, such as extracting particular concessions (e.g., payment of ransom or the release of prisoners), gaining publicity, undermining or seeking to join a negotiating process, demoralizing the population through the creation of widespread disorder, provoking repression by the government, enforcing obedience and cooperation from those inside and outside the movement, enhancing the political stature of specific factions within an insurgent movement, and fulfilling the need to avenge losses inflicted upon the movement. The last is especially vexing since the insurgents sometimes eschew credit for acts of revenge and, thus, mislead their opponents into concluding they were uninvolved.[35]

Given the multitudinous proximate aims that terrorist acts may serve, care must be exercised when generalizing about them. This is especially important since similar actions may have quite different objectives. The hostage and barricade incidents in the Israeli towns of Qiryat Shemona and Maalot in the spring of 1974 illustrate this point well. While the release of Palestinian prisoners was demanded in each case, other, more important aims were revealed by insurgent statements. At Qiryat Shemona, the Popular Front for the Liberation of Palestine–General Command, an extreme, hard-line group, intended to sabotage the peace process by increasing tensions, whereas at Maalot, the Democratic Popular Front for the Liberation of Palestine sought to ensure its participation in any negotiations that might occur.

In contrast to terrorism, *guerrilla warfare* is more complex and requires more resources. In essence, guerrilla warfare is highly mobile hit-and-run attacks by lightly to moderately armed groups that seek to harass the enemy and gradually erode his will and capability. Guerrillas place a premium on flexibility, speed, and deception. The following comments by Mao provide an excellent summary of the basic features of guerrilla warfare:

> What is basic guerrilla strategy? Guerrilla strategy must be based primarily on alertness, mobility, and attack. It must be adjusted to the enemy situation, the terrain, the existing lines of communication, the relative strengths, the weather, and the situation of the people.
>
> In guerrilla warfare, select the tactic of seeming to come from the east and attacking from the west; avoid the solid, attack the hollow; attack; withdraw; deliver a lightning blow, seek a lightning decision. When guerrillas engage a stronger enemy, they withdraw when he advances; harass him when he stops; strike him when he is weary; pursue him when he withdraws. In guerrilla strategy, the enemy's rear, flanks, and other vulnerable spots are his vital points, and there he must be harassed, attacked, dispersed, exhausted, and annihilated.[36]

While victories are always important, they consist of relatively modest engagements followed by withdrawal and dispersal rather than large positional battles designed to seize and hold the territory. Robert N. Watt has provided one reason for this, noting that a key principle of one of the great practitioners of guerrilla warfare, the Apache Indians in the American Southwest, was maximum damage inflicted for minimal loss sustained. Like most guerrillas, the Apaches simply could not afford significant casualties, given their small size relative to their adversaries'.[37]

Guerrilla warfare differs from terrorism because its primary targets are the government's armed forces, police, or support units and, in some cases, key economic targets, rather than unarmed civilians.[38] As a consequence, guerrilla units are larger than terrorist cells and tend to require a more elaborate logistical structure as well as base camps. While their locus of activity has normally been associated with rural areas, urban areas are not immune; witness the original IRA campaign under Michael Collins against the British in the early twentieth century, which concentrated on British soldiers, police, and their intelligence apparatus.[39]

Like terrorism, guerrilla warfare is usually a weapon of the weak; it is decisive only where the government fails to commit adequate resources to the conflict. Although Mao's ideological frame of reference led him to associate successful guerrilla warfare with left-wing revolutions and to dismiss its use by traditionalists as a contradiction of the "law of historical development," its successful use by traditionalists in Afghanistan suggests that such a limited perspective is myopic, to say the least.

Whether or not guerrilla warfare alone can be successful is another matter. In many cases, it has been necessary to combine guerrilla warfare with other forms of violence or to make a transition into *conventional warfare*, defined as the direct confrontation of large units in the field, to achieve success. The transition to conventional warfare depends on the strategy of the insurgents and their judgments about the vulnerability of the government's armed forces to conventional attacks.

Three points should be kept in mind when identifying the forms of warfare used by insurgents. First, insurgents may use more than one form of warfare, with the combination of terrorism and guerrilla warfare being the most common. An example would be indiscriminate bombings in civilian areas (terrorism) and guerrilla attacks in the countryside by the mujahedin during the insurgencies against the Russians in both Afghanistan and Chechnya. Where this occurs, the analyst will want to ascertain which form of warfare is most prominent.

The second point is that although many actions of insurgents are often categorized very easily, others may not be since they fall into gray areas. As noted, terrorism is primarily directed at noncombatants, while guerrilla warfare is aimed at the government's military and police forces. With this in mind, it is easy to designate attacks such as indiscriminate bombing by the IRA of civilians in department stores, pubs, and the like as terrorism. But the bombings of military barracks and vehicles and sniper attacks on police and military officers by the IRA and by other groups, such as ETA in Spain, are more akin to guerrilla warfare. Indeed, these same acts in rural settings have always been subsumed within the category of guerrilla warfare.[40] In the IRA and ETA cases, of course, the setting is urban and the size of the armed units is smaller. In addressing the differences between guerrilla warfare in rural and urban settings, Che Guevara pointed out that guerrilla operations in cities are less independent than those in rural areas, and units are very small (four or five men) because in urban areas the government's vigilance is greater and the possibilities of betrayal and reprisals increase enormously.[41]

The third thing to remember when dealing with forms of warfare is that *terrorism* is a highly politicized and emotive term. Nobody wants to admit that his or her group, or the group he or she supports, engages in terrorism. As a result, groups that carry out terrorist actions call themselves freedom fighters. The dichotomy between terrorist and freedom fighter is a false one because the term *freedom fighter* has to do with ends (e.g., the secessionist goal of freeing one's people from control by another or the egalitarian aim of freeing workers and peasants from the oppression of an exploitative political system), while *terrorism* connotes the means of achieving this goal. Hence, one can be a freedom fighter who uses terrorism to achieve his purposes. The analyst, of course, must depict things as they are. For the neutral or outside analyst, this is easier than for an analyst who supports insurgents. But for the partisan analyst, it may be more important because prolonged and indiscriminate terrorism can (as we shall see later) undercut support for insurgents, and ignoring or refusing to admit to their use of terrorism means that insurgents never address the problems or come to terms with the counterproductive aspects of terrorism as an instrument for furthering their cause. In short, the partisan analyst may fail to identify correctly and promptly the problems that the use of prolonged terrorism will eventually cause the movement. The bottom line is that all analysts need to be scrupulously objective. If insurgent actions meet the criteria of terrorism as defined above, then they are using terrorism as a form of warfare.

SUMMARY

When seeking to understand an insurgency, the first consideration is the nature of the insurgency. It is essential to ascertain first what type or types of insurgents one is dealing with by carefully examining their ultimate goals and the means they use to achieve them. It is especially important to distinguish among forms of warfare because they not only differ in terms of their purposes, targets, activities, and scale of organization but also with regard to the problems they pose for, and the requirements they place on, both sides.

Once we have identified the type of insurgency and forms of warfare it uses, the next step is to address various strategic approaches that insurgents adopt to maximize the effectiveness of political techniques and forms of warfare in their quest for victory. Strategies vary in terms of the relative importance they ascribe to six general variables: environment, popular support, organization, unity, external support, and the government response. The next chapter therefore addresses the crucial question of insurgent strategies.

NOTES

1. The definition of *insurgency* here is similar to that for civil war in J. K. Zawodny, "Civil War," in *International Encyclopedia of the Social Sciences* (New York: Macmillan 1968), 7:499, as cited in Sam C. Sarkesian, "Revolutionary Guerrilla Warfare: An Introduction," in *Revolutionary Guerrilla Warfare*, ed. Sam C. Sarkesian (Chicago: Precedent Publishing, 1975), 4. The use of violence by opponents of the government distinguishes insurgencies from sociopolitical protest movements, such as those led by Gandhi in India, Khomeini in Iran, and Solidarity in Poland. Those interested in systematically analyzing such movements will find Jerrold Green's use of the concept "countermobilization" in the Iran case very helpful; see his "Countermobilization as a Revolutionary Form," *Comparative Politics* (January 1984). The centrality of legitimacy in insurgencies is noted by Harry Eckstein, "On the Etiology of Internal Wars," *History and Theory* 4, no. 2 (1965): 133, and Max G. Manwaring and John T. Fishel, "Insurgency and Counter-Insurgency: Toward a New Analytical Approach," *Small Wars and Insurgencies* (winter 1992): 285–86.
2. On the question of legitimacy and parts of the political system, see Charles F. Andrain, *Political Life and Social Change*, 2nd ed. (Belmont, Calif.: Duxbury Press, 1974), 150–59, and David Easton, *A Systems Analysis of Political Life* (New York: John Wiley and Sons, 1965), 171–219.
3. In previous iterations of the framework, the term *regime* referred to salient values, rules, and structures. However, since the term *regime* has sinister connotations, I have chosen to replace it with *political system*. Although *political system* is often associated with all aspects of politics, the more restricted definition used herein should be less distracting to the general readership for whom this book is intended.
4. Andrain, *Political Life and Social Change*, 7, 191–262.
5. Military coups fall within the broad scope of the definition. Even though those who engineer coups may occupy supportive roles in the political system, they are not, strictly speaking, part of the "ruling authorities." Indeed, one of the reasons for coups is to seize control of the highest offices or create new ones.

6. Marco Imarisio, "Parcel Bombs: Shadow of Former Terrorists," *Corriere della Sera* (Milan), August 25, 1998, in *FBIS-Terrorism Internet Edition* (hereafter *INE*), August 25, 1998; Alexsandr Strogin, "Chechens Want to Spoil Easter," *Kommersant* (Moscow), April 10,1999, in *FBIS-Terrorism (INE)*, April 13, 1999; *Oesterreich Eins Radio Network*, May 21, 1999, in *FBIS-Terrorism (INE)*, May 21, 1999. Although anarchists and Marxists have different long-term goals, they occasionally cooperate in the short term. See the comments of Italian interior minister Beppe Pisanu in *La Repubblica*, June 8, 2004, in *FBIS-Terrorism (INE)*, June 8, 2004.
7. The term *revolution* as used in this book refers primarily to political revolution. Whether or not one will be followed by a social revolution that drastically changes the class stratification system will depend upon subsequent actions by the new revolutionary elite and the response to those actions. The importance of value changes and the relationship between values and structures is the principal focus of Chalmers Johnson's *Revolutionary Change* (Boston: Little, Brown, 1965), a seminal work on the application of systems theory to revolution. For a comparison and evaluation of the explanatory power of Johnson's work vis-à-vis several other approaches, see Waltraud Q. Morales, *Social Revolution: Theory and Historical Explanation* (Denver, Colo.: Denver University, 1973).
8. Ian O. Lesser, Bruce Hoffman, John Arquilla, David Ronfeldt, Michele Zanini, and Brian Jenkins, *Countering the New Terrorism* (Santa Monica, Calif.: RAND Corporation, 1999), 9. An example of such thinking is, of course, Osama bin Ladin. See Anonymous, *Imperial Hubris* (Washington D.C.; Brassey's, 2004), 127–61. For the text of the Abu Mussab al-Zarqawi letter that excoriates the Shiites, see www.globalsecurity.org/wmd/library/new/iraq/2004/02/040212-al-zarqawi.htm, 1–4 (accessed August 18, 2004). The Zahrani quote is from *Al Hijaz* (London), August 15, 2004, in *FBIS–Near East South Asia* (hereafter NESA) *(INE)*, August 15, 2004.
9. For a discussion of the utopian (golden age) conceptualization of Islamic groups, see Gilles Kepel, *Muslim Extremism in Egypt* (Berkeley: University of California Press, 1984), 226–40. A comparative assessment of Islamic and Jewish militants' utopian visions and political preferences may be found in Ilana Kass and Bard O'Neill, *The Deadly Embrace* (Lanham, Md.: National Institute for Public Policy and University Press of America, 1997). Also see Ehud Sprinzak, *The Ascendance of Israel's Radical Right* (Oxford: Oxford University Press, 1991), 231–50. There is a long history of tolerance for despotic rulers who uphold Islam. In a recent reaffirmation, Abu Hamza stated, "I do not support rebellion against the ruler who rules according to Islamic shariah. Even if al-Hajjaj Bin-Yusuf al-Thaqafi [early Islamic ruler famous for his harsh rule] is ruling us, I do not believe we should rebel against him. I will do like what the companions of the Prophet did. God will judge him for killing people so that he can remain in power." Quoted in "Interview with Abu-Hamza al-Masri," *Al-Majallah* (London), March 21–27, 1999, in *FBIS-Terrorism (INE)*, March 29, 1999. On Sunni-Shiite violence in Pakistan see the Associated Press report in *The New York Times*, January 5, 1999. A very useful run down on militant Islamic groups is Monte Palmer and Princess Palmer, *At the Heart of Terror: Muslim Extremism and America's War on Terror* (Lanham, Md.: Rowman & Littlefield, 2004).
10. Mark Juergensmeyer, *Terror in the Mind of God* (Berkeley: University of California Press, 2001), 24–36.

11. Robert Jay Lifton, *Destroying the World to Save It* (New York: Henry Holt and Co., 2000), 62–88, 201–13.
12. Hiromi Shimada, "Analyzing Aum in Depth—Spell of the Promised Land," *Ronza* (Tokyo), March 29, 1999, in *FBIS-Terrorism (INE)*, March 29, 1999.
13. On the Mahdaviyat, see "A Look at the Appearance of a Deviant Group," *Abrar* (Tehran), April 25, 1999, in *FBIS-NESA (INE)*, May 19, 1999.
14. Walter Laqueur, *The New Terrorism* (New York: Oxford University Press 1999), 17. The uncomfortable fact that the African National Congress was responsible for acts of terrorism was well known to observers of the antiapartheid struggle and was confirmed in 1998 by the Truth and Reconciliation Commission.
15. T. David Mason, "Structures of Ethnic Conflict: Revolution versus Secession in Rwanda and Sri Lanka," *Terrorism and Political Violence* (winter 2003): 83–113.
16. Readers interested in secessionist groups will find *Conflict* 8, nos. 2/3 (1988), very informative because it contains several good articles. These include Wade Wheelock, "The Sikhs: Religious Militancy, Government Oppression or Politics as Usual," 97–109; Vittorfranco Pisano, "Terrorist Ethnic Separatism in France and Italy," 83–95; Robert C. Oberst, "Sri Lanka's Tamil Tigers," 185–202; and Paul Henze, "Ethnic Strains and Regional Conflict in Ethiopia," 111–40.
17. The difference between secessionists and other types of insurgents is exemplified in the following comments by Yasir Ahmad, a member of the Afar Sultanate Liberation Front in Ethiopia, a Muslim organization that seeks to separate from Christian-controlled Ethiopia:

    We are not a revolution that broke out to change the existing regime or corrupt rule. We have existed as a distinct nation, with its people, land, leadership, and culture, for centuries. We are a nation which was exposed to a crusader invasion, followed by a Communist invasion with the support of a superpower. We are resisting this invasion with the faith we derive from our Islamic belief.

    We fought the Abyssinian empires until they became exhausted. We imposed a peaceful-coexistence agreement on them under which we allowed them safe passage through our territory to the sea in return for money. They exploited our goodwill, and through the help of the crusader states they included our territory in the map of the empire.

    See "Afar Liberation Leader Interviewed on Struggle," *Al Qabas (Kuwait)*, June 10, 1988, in FBIS-Africa (INE), June 14, 1988.
18. For an interesting account of animal rights terrorists, see Warren Hoge's piece on the animal-rights movement's death list in the *New York Times*, January 10, 1999.
19. On the White Wolves see London Press Association, in *FBIS-Terrorism (INE)*, April 30, 1999.
20. Shogar is quoted in the *New York Times*, September 11, 2004. The Darfur situation is nicely summarized in *New York Times*, August 16, 2004. While the Kurds in Iraq at one time had a secessionist goal, their demands during the mid-1970s were essentially reformist (to wit, increased revenues from oil, more social services, and a substantial degree of political autonomy within the framework of Iraq). The current Kurdish insurrection in Iran also has reformist aims, despite claims by the government that they are secessionist.
21. Quite often the term *counterrevolutionary* is used to refer to preservationist insurgents. See, for instance, Don R. Bowen, "Counterrevolutionary War: Missouri,

1861–1865," *Conflict* 8, no. 1 (1988): 69–70. Some scholars have analyzed preservationist insurgents within the context of *vigilantism*, that is, acts or threats of coercion that are conducted by individuals and groups seeking to defend the existing order against subversion and that transgress the accepted normative restraints on coercion in a polity. See H. Jon Rosenbaum and Peter C. Sederberg, "Vigilantism: An Analysis of Establishment Violence," in *Vigilante Politics*, ed. H. Jon Rosenbaum and Peter C. Sederberg (Philadelphia: University of Pennsylvania Press, 1976), 4–5. The concept of vigilantism is broader than the category of preservationist insurgency in that it encompasses coercion that receives support from the ruling authorities, but we are interested only in autonomous groups. Otherwise put, we concentrate on insurgent vigilantism. For an incisive commentary on the Protestant preservationist insurgents (regime-control vigilantes), see Richard Ned Lebow, "Vigilantism in Northern Ireland," in Rosenbaum and Sederberg, *Vigilante Politics*, 248–50. Also see Julian Braum, "Northern Ireland's Fighting Protestants," *Christian Science Monitor*, March 31, 1988.

22. C. J. M. Drake, "The Phenomenon of Conservative Terrorism," *Terrorism and Political Violence* (autumn 1996): 32.
23. See William Loren Katz, *The Invisible Empire: The Ku Klux Klan Impact on History* (Seattle: Open Hand Publishing, 1986); Nancy Maclean, *Behind the Mask of Chivalry: The Making of the Second Ku Klux Klan* (New York: Oxford University Press, 1994); Wyn Craig Wade, *The Fiery Cross: The Ku Klux Klan in America* (New York: Simon Schuster, 1987); Shawn Lay, ed., *The Invisible Empire in the West: Toward a New Historical Appraisal of the Ku Klux Klan of the 1920s* (Urbana: University of Illinois Press, 1992); Kenneth T. Jackson, *The Ku Klux Klan in the City: 1915–1930* (New York: Oxford University Press, 1967); and Robert Alan Goldberg, *Hooded Empire: The Ku Klux Klan in Colorado* (Urbana: University of Illinois Press, 1981).
24. While revelations about particular incidents are less than objective and represent the point of view of one side or another in a conflict, there is little dispute about the overall viciousness of certain Latin American governments. The Guatemalan Commission for Historical Clarification put forth a searing nine-volume indictment of the state's complicity and involvement in terrorism, including genocide during the rule of Rios Montt in the 1980s. See *New York Times*, February 27, 1999. Human rights groups have attributed 70 percent of the human rights violations in Colombia to the right-wing paramilitaries. See Steven Dudley's article in the *Washington Post*, June 22, 2000. The Castano group has admitted to dozens of civilian massacres. See the Associated Press report in the *New York Times*, April 11, 1999.
25. Steven Metz, *The Future of Insurgency* (Carlisle Barracks, PA: Strategic Studies Institute, December 10, 1993), 13–15. Also see Steven Metz, *Counterinsurgency: Strategy and the Phoenix of American Capability* (Carlisle Barracks, PA: Strategic Studies Institute, February 28, 1995), 28–29, and Robert Kaplan, "The Coming Anarchy," *Atlantic Monthly* (February 1994): 44–54.
26. Quoted by Barbara Crossette, *New York Times*, January 24, 1999. While Crossette's point about nonideological groups is well made, I would qualify her statement that the new world order is without ideologies since, as noted in the text, both Marxism and Islam currently provide ample ideational rationale for a range of groups.
27. On the National Liberation Front of Macedonia see Timothy Garton Ash, "Is There a Good Terrorist?" *The New York Review of Books* (November 19, 2001): 6. Quoted by

Norimitsu Onishi, *New York Times*, January 31, 1999. The vague leftist utterances of the RUF hardly constitute a systematic series of ideas. Hence, it is not surprising that observers pay little attention to them. Indeed, the common perception is one of pillage, murder, and materialist motives. See *Washington Post*, January 1, 1998; *Washington Post*, January 7, 1999; *New York Times*, July 30, 1998; and *New York Times*, January 26, 1999.

28. Francis Mading Deng, "War of Visions for the Nation," *Middle East Journal* (autumn 1990): 596–98.
29. Kass and O'Neill, *The Deadly Embrace*, 269–73.
30. On this distinction, see Ted Robert Gurr, *Why Men Rebel* (Princeton, N.J.: Princeton University Press, 1970), 10–11. I have substituted the terms *selective* and *mobilizational* for *conspiratorial* and *internal* war to avoid confusion, since I use the latter terms for different purposes later in the book.
31. Samuel P. Huntington, "Guerrilla Warfare in Theory and Policy," in *Modern Guerrilla Warfare*, ed. Franklin Mark Osanka (New York: The Free Press of Glencoe, 1962), xvi; Arthur Campbell, *Guerrillas* (New York: The John Day Co., 1968), 3.
32. Needless to say, countless books, articles and the like define *terrorism*. Although much attention has been given it, a precise definition agreeable to all or most scholars has remained elusive. For a representative sampling of recent attempts to grapple with the definitional problem, see Paul Wilkinson, *Political Terrorism* (New York: Wiley and Sons, 1974), 9–31; David Fromkin, "The Strategy of Terrorism," *Foreign Affairs* (July 1975): 692–93; H. Edward Price, Jr., "The Strategy and Tactics of Revolutionary Terrorism," *Comparative Studies in Society and History* (January 1977): 52–53; Jay Mallin, "Terrorism as a Military Weapon," *Air University Review* (January–February 1977): 60; Central Intelligence Agency, Research Study, *International and Transnational Terrorism: Diagnosis and Prognosis,* 8–9; Jordan J. Paust, "A Definitional Focus," in *Terrorism: Interdisciplinary Perspectives*, ed. Yonah Alexander and Seymour Maxwell Finger (New York: John Jay Press, 1977), 19–25; and Martha Greenshaw Hutchinson, "The Concept of Revolutionary Terrorism," *Journal of Conflict Resolution* (September 1972): 383–85. An especially good source is Boaz Ganor, "Terror as a Strategy of Psychological Warfare," *Herzliyya International Policy Institute for Counterterrorism*, in *FBIS-Near East (INE)*, July 15, 2002.
33. The attributes of political terrorism are analyzed cogently by Wilkinson in *Political Terrorism*, 14–18.
34. See U.S. Central Intelligence Agency, Research Study, *International and Transnational Terrorism: Diagnosis and Prognosis* (Washington, D.C.: CIA, April 1976), 8–9. The University of Oklahoma Study Group on Terrorism subsumes both international and transnational terrorism within a broader category that it calls "non-territorial terrorism." See Charles Wise and Stephen Sloan, "Countering Terrorism: The U.S. and Israeli Approach," *Middle East Review* (spring 1977): 55. Needless to say, actions by governments may also be considered terrorist acts.
35. On terrorist aims, see Brian Jenkins, "International Terrorism: A Balance Sheet," *Survival* (July/August 1975): 158–60; Bard E. O'Neill, "Towards a Typology of Political Terrorism: The Palestinian Movement," *Journal of International Affairs* (spring/summer 1978); 35–37, 42; and Brian Crozier, *A Theory of Conflict* (New York: Charles Scribner's Sons, 1974), 127–28. Chechen women known as black widows exemplify carrying out terrorist attacks to achieve revenge. See *New York Times*, September 10, 2004.

36. Mao Tse-tung, *On Guerrilla Warfare,* trans. Samuel B. Griffith (New York: Fredrick A. Praeger, 1962), 46. On the attributes of guerrilla warfare, see Julian Paget, *Counter-Insurgency Campaigning* (New York: Walker & Co., 1967), 15.
37. Robert N. Watt, "Raiders of a Lost Art? Apache War and Society," *Small Wars and Insurgencies* (autumn 2002): 4–5.
38. My definition of *guerrilla warfare* is similar to the one Robert B. Asprey uses in his *War in the Shadows,* 2 vols. (Garden City, N.Y.: Doubleday, 1975). Whereas Asprey identifies the target of the small-scale attacks as "orthodox military forces" (p. 1:xi), I have expanded the definition to include police and key economic targets. Further insights concerning guerrilla warfare may be found in Edward E. Rice, *Wars of the Third Kind* (Berkeley: University of California Press, 1988), 61–66, and *Guerrilla Warfare,* ed. John Pimlott (New York: Bison Books, 1985), 34, 44–45.
39. Tim Pat Coogan, *The Man Who Made Ireland: The Life and Death of Michael Collins* (Niwot, Colo.: Roberts Rinehart Publishers, 1996), see particularly pp. 55–234 for the period of the Anglo-Irish war; Tim Pat Coogan, *The IRA: A History* (Niwot, Colo.: Roberts Rinehart Publishers, 1993), 7–22; and, Michael Hopkinson, *Green against Green: The Irish Civil War* (New York: St. Martin's Press, 1998), 6–14.
40. *New York Times,* August 23, 1988. My own research on the ETA, which included conversations with both Spanish and American officials in Madrid in the spring of 1988, uncovered a strong consensus that ETA targets were primarily military and Guardia Civile personnel.
41. Che Guevara, *Guerrilla Warfare* (New York: Vintage Books, 1961), 29–31.

3

INSURGENT STRATEGIES

Chapter 2 discusses goals and forms of warfare insurgents may adopt. How their ends and means are related brings us to the crucial matter of strategy. For our purposes, *strategy* is defined as the systematic, integrated, and orchestrated use of various means (diplomatic, informational, economic, and military instruments of power) to achieve goals. What kinds of goals are chosen, which means are emphasized, and how systematic the plans are will differ considerably from case to case.

Strategies also vary in terms of conceptual sophistication, ranging from the clearly and carefully articulated to the inchoate. Moreover, like the grand strategies of states, insurgents implement their strategies in less-than-ideal fashion either because of the interplay of conflicting political interests, limited material resources, and unanticipated events or because insurgents sometimes adopt strategies that others have used successfully but that are inappropriate for the different environment in which they are operating. One reason for the latter phenomenon is that the previously successful insurgent leaders were able to convince others that their strategy had universal applicability.

STRATEGIC APPROACHES

To make it easier to understand and evaluate insurgent strategies, I concentrate on four broad strategic approaches that have provided guidance, if not inspiration, for many recent and contemporary insurgent leaders. We also sketch out a fifth strategy that is still evolving. Where appropriate, we examine the importance of popular and external support, organization, cohesion, the environment, and the government's role (the strategic factors that comprise the criteria for evaluating insurgencies that we will discuss in later chapters). We also look at significant shifts in emphasis and new ideas within the contexts of the four approaches.

Conspiratorial Strategy

Perhaps the oldest and least complicated insurgent strategy is the conspiratorial one, which seeks to remove the ruling authorities through a limited but swift use of force. Conspiracies are basically coups led by either military officers, who are not part of the ruling elite, or civilians. In many cases, the removal of the authorities is considered necessary to achieve the real goal, which is to change policies or a political system that insurgents consider illegitimate. In other situations, the aim may be to replace the authorities either because they are threatening to undertake major policy initiatives that will upset the existing distribution of social, economic, and political privileges (and are thus opposed by preservationist insurgents) or because the leaders are perceived to be corrupt and inefficient (and are thus opposed by reformist insurgents).

Whatever the ultimate goal, the crucial instrument for seizing power is a small, secretive, disciplined, and tightly organized group, an example being the Islamic Liberation Organization in Egypt during the 1980s. The decisive arena for insurgent activity is the major urban centers, especially the capital city, where political and economic power is concentrated. Military conspiracies, such as those in Latin America in the 1960s, pay little or no attention to the organized involvement of the public. To the extent that the views of the masses are taken into consideration, calculations center on assuring public acceptance of the outcome. Like popular support and organization, external support is not a major consideration. While environmental factors, such as economic regression and maldistribution, political disorder, and corruption, may be the underlying causes of the insurrection, defection of military officers is the crucial variable. Although military insurrections have occurred throughout history and are hardly uncommon now, the fact remains that in many cases where governments confront social, economic, and political problems, they still manage to retain the loyalty of the military. When this happens, civilian-led conspiracies may be hatched. The continued loyalty of the military to the governing authorities is a formidable obstacle for civilian insurgents, who must then engage in more extensive political activity and preparations for using violence. In some cases, part of their effort involves attempts to infiltrate and subvert the military, particularly rank-and-file officers and enlisted personnel.

Of course, the most striking example of this situation is the 1917 Bolshevik insurrection in Russia, which popularized the conspiratorial strategy, particularly among Marxist revolutionaries. Vladimir Lenin, the key Bolshevik strategist and tactician, was convinced that the ultimate seizure of power depended on a highly organized political party that would obtain support from certain discontented social groups, such as the rank-and-file military and the workers, especially in the capital city (which in the Russian case was Petrograd). A critical part of Lenin's conspiratorial strategy was the assumption that the government was undergoing a general crisis, was alienated from significant sectors of the population (workers, soldiers, and peasants), and would capitulate when confronted with low-level violence, subversion of the military and police, and the final seizure of the media, government offices, and other state-controlled institutions. In the words of John Shy and Thomas W. Collier, in this scheme, battles were "conceived as brief, climactic encounters fought for control of the nerve centers of a modern society."[1]

Although segments of the population beyond the party were organized into soviets (committees) to play a role in the Bolshevik scheme, Lenin's strategy was essentially elitist. As Lenin bluntly put it, "We are apprehensive of an excessive growth of the Party, because careerists and charlatans, who deserve only to be shot, inevitably do all they can to insinuate themselves into the ranks of the ruling party."[2] He had no intention of mobilizing the general population within the framework of an extensive shadow government. And although there was always a readiness to exploit mass grievances where they existed, there was no systematic effort to solicit them. In fact, one of the reasons for creating the vanguard party was Lenin's lack of confidence in the ability of the workers to understand either their own predicament or the requirements for a successful revolutionary insurgency; this was something that only the intellectual elites of the party could do.

Although Lenin denigrated the idea of enduring alliances with non-Bolshevik dissidents, he argued strenuously that under certain circumstances, it was necessary to pursue "united-front tactics" by cooperating temporarily with groups he despised, such as "reactionary trade unions" and the Social Democratic and Socialist Revolutionary parties. At all times, however, a limited group of dedicated activists, whose activities could be more easily controlled and coordinated, was to constitute the vital leadership echelon.[3] Lenin placed a premium on ideological, strategic, and tactical unity; deviations were unacceptable. While a key aim of the leadership elites and cadres was to exploit mass discontent, only segments of the population, mainly in the urban centers, became the targets of infiltration, proselytism, manipulation, and, ultimately, control. Although scattered terrorist acts took place, violence was basically confined to the direct seizure of key government facilities. Neither systematic terrorism nor guerrilla warfare was important. In theory, there was little need for external support because deteriorating social and economic conditions and the government's political and military ineptitude made it vulnerable to a quick, decisive, and forceful move by the insurgents. Although foreign financial inputs and sanctuaries across the borders were not unwelcome, their importance was downplayed or denied altogether.

Because of Lenin's success in Russia and its profound historical impact, there was a belief that other revolutionary insurgents could effectively follow his conspiratorial strategy. This overlooked, of course, the fact that the czarist regime had been toppled (March 1917) because of its own blunders and a spontaneous uprising of the citizenry of Petrograd, events that had little or nothing to do with Lenin or his strategy. In fact, Lenin, who was in exile, initially refused to believe reports that the Romanov dynasty had fallen and accepted them only after he read about the events in the Zurich newspapers. From that moment onward, Lenin concentrated his efforts on overthrowing the provisional government.

When the provisional government proved incapable of establishing its authority and failed to extricate Russia from its disastrous and unpopular involvement in World War I, Lenin and his cohorts, particularly Leon Trotsky, who joined forces with Lenin and became chairman of the Military Revolutionary Committee, eventually carried out a coup on November 7 (October 25 o.s.), 1917. It is worth recalling that the coup took place after several months of hesitation and indecisiveness by Lenin and came in response to a weak crackdown by the Kerensky government. Robert H. McNeal has thoughtfully summarized the import of these events:

> The October Revolution conformed to Lenin's conception of proletarian revolution. Unlike the March Revolution (or the mass upheavals of May and July), it was not a spontaneous upsurge of the proletariat but a *coup d'état* in which the "vanguard of the proletariat" had organized and directed elements of the lower classes. The party of Lenin's design had shown little ability to topple the tsarist government under normal conditions, and it is highly unlikely that it could have done better in a parliamentary democratic system. But in the crucible of revolution the party had proven its strength.[4]

It does not detract from Lenin's historical stature to point out that the success of his strategy depended as much on events beyond his control as it did on his considerable conceptual, organizational, and political acumen. Yet, when it came to replicating his strategy in other countries, especially in Europe, where the Bolsheviks had great hopes, the main problem was the absence of the particular combination of political, economic, and social factors that in Russia had created a vacuum with respect to political legitimacy and authority. In spite of the psychological aftershocks of World War I and the traumas of the Great Depression, the political systems of the West retained their legitimacy, and governments continued to exercise control over critical institutions, such as the military and the police. Even in China, where the decay of the traditional system, the diffusion of power to warlords, widespread corruption, and socioeconomic problems had led some Marxists to believe they could seize power in the late 1920s, the various ruling authorities proved resilient. As a consequence, the Chinese Communists were compelled to devise a markedly different strategy for insurgency, one that emphasized prolonged armed struggle based on mobilizing mass support.

Strategy of Protracted Popular War

The strategy of protracted popular war articulated by Mao Tse-tung is undoubtedly the most conceptually elaborate and, perhaps, the most widely copied insurgent strategy. It was a response to conditions in China, which differed substantially from those faced by Lenin and his cohorts in Russia. In contrast to the Bolsheviks, who confronted a feeble provisional government, the Chinese Communists had to overcome adversaries who enjoyed obvious superiority during the 1930s and 1940s—first the Japanese and then the Kuomintang (Chinese Nationalist Party), led by Chiang Kai-shek. Under such circumstances, it became apparent that although a strong, well-organized party along Leninist lines would be necessary for success, a quick victory based on support from the urban proletariat was not feasible. In spite of contrary views held by fellow Chinese Communist leaders and Soviet advisers, Mao came to the conclusion that the revolutionary struggle would be a long one and that the peasantry, not the urban proletariat, was the most important revolutionary class. As things turned out, the Chinese Communist insurgents did engage in a long conflict, during which they mobilized substantial popular support by means of extensive organizational efforts. Militarily, the struggle consisted mainly of hit-and-run guerrilla attacks in the countryside, which eventually gave way to mobile conventional warfare.[5]

Although Mao eventually succeeded, his road to power was not an easy one. During the 1930s, he experienced not only battlefield setbacks but also opposition from comrades who resisted his strategy and influence within the party. Nevertheless, the tenacity of Mao and his followers enabled them to survive the celebrated Long March (a costly and arduous retreat to Shensi in the north), to establish control over the party, and to carry out operations against the Japanese invaders.

The Japanese occupation was fortuitous for Mao because it provided a nationalist appeal around which to rally support and also because it diverted the attention of the Kuomintang away from Chinese Communist insurgents. Moreover, as the war dragged on, Mao's stature as a heroic nationalist was enhanced, while the dislocation and costs of the fighting further weakened Chiang Kai-shek's position. Indeed, there is reason to question whether Mao's strategy would have been successful against the Kuomintang if the Japanese had not invaded China. The fact remains that Mao did win, and his strategy became increasingly attractive to insurgents around the world because it offered them a cohesive, systematic blueprint for their own struggles against colonial occupiers or oppressive indigenous regimes. The Chinese, of course, welcomed the emulation of their strategy and were vigorously encouraging it by the time the Cultural Revolution began in the 1960s.

The Maoist version of the protracted-popular-war strategy, which was used in both the anti-Japanese and anti-Kuomintang wars, consists of three sequential but overlapping phases, each of which differs with respect to the correlation of forces. First is the *strategic defensive,* a time when the enemy is on the offensive, and the insurgents must concentrate on survival, political organization, and low-level violence. As the insurgents gradually gain support and achieve military successes, they enter the second and longest phase, the *strategic stalemate,* which is characterized mainly by guerrilla warfare. Further escalation and victories, which lead to demoralization, lethargy, and defections on the government side, usher in the *strategic offensive,* during which the insurgents move from guerrilla warfare to mobile conventional attacks on a large scale, and the political and psychological effects of the insurgent victories lead to a collapse of the government.[6]

The three stages in Mao's scheme have specific objectives, involve different combinations of political and military actions, and depend on the outcomes of the preceding stages. The strategic defensive phase emphasizes political mobilization. In Mao's words,

> This move is crucial; it is indeed of primary importance, while our inferiority in weapons and other things is only secondary. The mobilization of the common people throughout the country will create a vast sea in which to drown the enemy, create the conditions that will make up for our inferiority in arms and other things, and create the prerequisites for overcoming every difficulty in the war. To win victory, we must persevere in the War of Resistance, in the united front and in the protracted war. But all these are inseparable from the mobilization of the common people. To wish for victory and yet neglect political mobilization is like wishing to "go south by driving the chariot north," and the result would inevitably be to forfeit victory.[7]

Pursuant to political mobilization, cellular networks are created, political organizers engage in propaganda activities to win popular support, and terrorists carry out selective acts of intimidation against recalcitrant individuals. At this point, fronts composed of various social groups (e.g., religious, occupational, youth, and women's) may be organized, along with pressure groups and parties, to gain popular support. Simultaneously, insurgents usually try to infiltrate enemy institutions; foment strikes, demonstrations, and riots; and perhaps carry out sabotage missions.

As part of their political effort, the insurgents stress appeals based on both ideology and material grievances and try to provide social services and engage in mutual self-help projects (e.g., harvesting crops or building schoolhouses) to demonstrate their sincerity and to gain acceptance and support. A key objective at this time is the recruitment of local leaders, who, once in the organization, play a key role in detaching the people from the government. To institutionalize support, insurgents begin to construct shadow-government structures (parallel hierarchies) that will provide de facto control of the population. If the government fails to react, it will lose by default; if it responds successfully, the insurgents may suffer a decisive fate similar to that of the Tudeh Party insurgents in Iran during the shah's reign.[8]

Selective terrorism during this period serves many purposes, including the attempt to gain both popular and external support. This can be very significant where the insurgent organization is too rudimentary to support guerrilla warfare. In situations where the regime's strength is the key reason for the use of terror, the insurgent movement is worse off than where its own organizational deficiencies are the problem. The movement is worse off because the government may be ameliorating the conditions that provide motivation and support for the insurgency, or it may be using force effectively to eliminate the insurgents. If the movement's own organizational failings are the problem, the insurgents may rectify them and move toward guerrilla warfare.

Guerrilla warfare is the most important activity in the strategic stalemate phase. In the earliest part of this stage, small bands carry out armed resistance in rural areas characterized by rugged terrain and weak government control. If the guerrillas face significant government opposition, they have the option of reverting to stage one. The most likely considerations in the decision-making calculus of the guerrillas are the vitality of the incumbent regime, its projected capability against guerrilla warfare, and external political-military factors.

The insurgent aim in the initial part of stage two is to isolate the people from the government. The organization established in phase one begins to supply small guerrilla units, and full- and part-time personnel play a more prominent role. During the early part of stage two, there is still a lack of organization above the village level, and groups operate from shifting and remote bases. Military actions in early stage two are small hit-and-run attacks against convoys, military and economic installations, and isolated outposts. These scattered attacks are intended to goad the government into adopting a static defensive posture and dispersing its forces in order to protect many potential targets.[9]

If there is satisfactory progress during the early part of stage two, insurgents normally move into the second part of that stage and expand their organization in the regions they control. In addition, regional forces emerge, which, along with the full-time forces, enable the insurgents to join villages together into a political network that constitutes a major base area. At this point, the guerrillas step up the mobilization of the population by exploiting and satisfying (as best they can) popular aspirations. Meanwhile, there is usually an emphasis on ideology designed to supplant whatever type of legitimacy sustains the existing regime.[10]

During stage two, the parallel hierarchy is more visible than during stage one. Besides resembling the state apparatus, it also includes auxiliary organizations controlled by revolutionary cells linked to the central political structure. Moreover, a government-in-exile may be created.[11] Organizational evolution in late stage two includes the establishment of arsenals, arms production facilities, and hospitals. The logistics operation encompasses activities that range from procurement of basic foodstuffs and war supplies to acquisition of material aid from external sources. Once base areas are set up, the delivery of supplies from nearby friendly states becomes less risky and more likely.

In the military realm, emphasis turns to the recruitment of full-time guerrillas, the establishment of an extensive reserve system, and the creation and training of regular army units. If voluntary recruits are insufficient, there may be forced abductions. Since the latter often make poor fighters, voluntary enlistments are stressed. Three operational levels often constitute the military organization in late stage two: regional, district, and local. The regional troops, the best armed and trained, form the strike forces, which are the backbone of the movement. At the next level, full-time cadres lead district battalions, although subordinate companies are composed of part-time soldiers. The local forces are made up of both full- and part-time guerrillas, with the part-timers predominating. A central headquarters coordinates all three levels in pursuit of common military and political objectives.

Even though the parallel hierarchy and military organization may be relatively secure in late stage two, the guerrillas usually do not elect to fight positional battles or even defend their base areas, for they consider themselves to be in a position of strategic stalemate. Instead, the insurgents avoid large government sweeps and patrols in order to demonstrate the government's inability to destroy them and to contrast the regime's ephemeral authority with the guerrillas' permanency.[12]

While base areas are being constructed, the insurgents continue to establish bands of followers and send agents into contested or government-controlled areas to implant new cells, networks, and groups there. The insurgents make a major effort to deceive the government, hoping its response will be tardy, insufficient, and tactically misdirected. Military actions in late stage two are basically large-scale guerrilla attacks carried out from secure base areas. In addition to operations designed to acquire additional supplies and to reduce areas of government control, armed propaganda teams are dispatched to further undermine the enemy. In the terminal period of this stage, considerable attention is devoted to seizing and securing large areas and preparing the physical battlefield for mobile conventional warfare. Thus, military considerations receive as much attention as political calculations when it comes to target selection.[13]

The third and final stage of the protracted-popular-war strategy, the strategic offensive, is, as noted, characterized by the transformation of most guerrilla forces into regular, orthodox forces. Although regular units may engage in some positional warfare, primary emphasis is on mobile conventional operations, with small guerrilla bands supporting the main effort in an ancillary role. The principal military objective at this point is to destroy the government's main forces; the principal political aim is the displacement of the governing authorities. The scale of military operations usually requires high-level leadership skills (the command, control, and coordination of multiple operations by large units); effective communications; an efficiently functioning, complex logistical system; and external assistance—unless, of course, government forces quickly disintegrate.[14]

It is important to note that although the Maoist strategy of protracted popular war theoretically consists of an orderly progression through three phases, victory can come at any point if the government suddenly loses its will. Where a loss of will does not occur and the conflict proceeds as Mao envisaged, the insurgent leadership faces the need to assess the relative positions of the two sides and to make judgments concerning whether or not the conflict has entered into a new phase. Because such judgments may be erroneous, leaders must be ready, if necessary, to revert to the actions and policies appropriate to a previous phase.[15] This element of flexibility increases the attractiveness of Mao's approach and no doubt also explains its adoption by insurgents in many Third World states, such as Algeria, Vietnam, Malaya, the Philippines, Thailand, Oman, Portuguese Guinea, Mozambique, Peru, and Nepal.

It was probably inevitable that Mao's strategy would take on a number of variations as insurgents adopted and implemented it elsewhere. The Algerian insurgency against the French during the 1950s is a case in point. The Algerian insurgents, who were Arab nationalists and Muslims rather than Marxists, aimed to achieve independence from France by waging a protracted struggle that emphasized popular support and gradually escalating violence (i.e., guerrilla warfare followed by conventional operations). Their "oil spot" strategy was reminiscent of Mao's because it was based on the idea of gradually expanding political control in the countryside and surrounding the cities. Unlike the Chinese, the Algerians could never make the transition to the conventional warfare stage because the French were able to rectify early military deficiencies and defeat the insurgents. But while the French won on the battlefield, the Algerians won the war because they were able to maintain widespread popular support and wear down French resolve through skillful propaganda efforts at home and abroad, to exploit violent excesses by the French (torture and terrorism), and to pose the prospect of a costly and interminable struggle.

In the final analysis, the Algerian war showed that victory is possible without the structured phasing and military progression associated with the implementation of Mao's strategy. The key to overcoming the deficiencies of a more ad hoc approach (and military regression) was gaining and maintaining popular support through good organization and astute psychological warfare campaigns.[16]

Further variations from Mao's strategic thinking, which occurred in Algeria and elsewhere, are evident with respect to terrorism, significant activity in urban areas, the targeting of the economic infrastructure, and international policies. In contrast to Mao, who downplayed terrorism and concentrated almost exclusively on guerrilla warfare in the rural areas, the Algerians, as well as such groups as the Vietcong in Vietnam, the New People's Army (NPA) in the Philippines, and Sendero Luminoso (Shining Path) in Peru, concluded that greater violence in the cities and more extensive use of terrorism were necessary. Another twist added by the Algerians—and later by the Shining Path in Peru, the Farabundo Martí National Liberation Front (FMLN) in El Salvador (after 1985), and the Union for the Total Independence of Angola, among others—is the objective of destroying the national economy through sabotage as a major way to weaken and discredit the government. Finally, the Algerians, the Vietnamese, and a number of other groups sought to undermine support for their adversaries through propaganda campaigns directed at popular opinion inside the borders of either the colonial power (France in the Algerian and Vietminh cases) or the major outside benefactor of the government (the United States in the Vietnam War).

Whatever the variations in specific cases, the protracted-popular-war strategy is a demanding one because insurgents must obtain extensive popular support and create a complex organizational apparatus, tasks that usually require considerable time and secure base areas. The strategy calls for directly or indirectly engaging increasing numbers of people in a long-term conflict with the government in order to control the countryside, thereby isolating the urban centers and wearing down government resistance. Such an undertaking is vulnerable to determined government psychological, organizational, and military-police countermeasures at many points, as the British demonstrated in both Malaya and Kenya in the 1950s and in Oman in the 1960s. Moreover, many groups currently following the strategy find it more difficult to rally popular support than the Chinese or Algerians did because they have a narrower base. The Chinese and Algerians transformed resentment of political, social, and economic discrimination by foreigners into a widespread surge of nationalism directed at imperial and colonial ruling authorities (the Japanese and the French), but many of today's insurgents represent smaller segments of the population (class, ethnic, racial, or religious groups) and face an indigenous government rather than a foreign one. Under such circumstances, it is far more difficult to galvanize nationalist sentiments, even when an effort is made to depict governments as tools of neoimperialist foreign interests.

The successful application of the strategy by insurgents in today's world may also be impeded by unfavorable environmental factors and enhanced government capabilities. In China, Vietnam, and, to a lesser extent, Algeria, favorable topographical and demographic patterns (i.e., they were large, well-populated countries with inaccessible areas) enabled the insurgents to secure bases, then to consolidate and expand their organization and base of popular support in relative security. As we shall see later when further examining the environmental factor, several contemporary insurgent movements that subscribe to a strategy of protracted popular war operate in less-than-desirable physical and human settings. They must also confront and neutralize government forces' enhanced firepower, mobility, and intelligence capabilities, which are the outgrowth of technological developments in the areas of transportation, weaponry, detection systems, and information processing.

Under current circumstances, the kinds of obstacles just enumerated render the successful use of the strategy more difficult. As a result, many insurgents tend to place more emphasis on external assistance (moral, political, and material support and sanctuary) to compensate for weaknesses with respect to one or more factors, especially the environment and government response. In fact, with few exceptions—notably NPA in the Philippines and the Shining Path in Peru—most insurgent movements have cast aside the notion of following Mao's prescription for self-reliance.

Military-Focus Strategy

The military-focus strategy is similar to the strategy of protracted popular war in that it may involve a prolonged struggle. It is fundamentally different because it gives primacy to military action and subordinates political action. Though fully aware of the value of popular support, the insurgents make no systematic, sustained effort to acquire it through extensive political organizing efforts in the rural areas. Instead, proponents of the military focus believe that popular support either is already sufficient or will be a by-product of military victories. Moreover, widespread support may be unnecessary if the government's forces are defeated on the battlefield.

The American Civil War, during which the South adopted a military-focus strategy in pursuit of its goal of secession, is a case where adequate support from the population existed when hostilities commenced. Since political structures that extended down to the local level already existed, the Confederacy did not have to worry about creating political institutions to gain support. Furthermore, its secessionist aim obviated any effort to expand its control gradually over areas in the North. Under such conditions, the South could afford to concentrate most of its energy and resources on military affairs. Although the Confederacy did mount four sizable invasions of the North (the 1862 Antietam campaign in Maryland, an advance into Kentucky in 1861, the 1863 Gettysburg campaign in Pennsylvania, and Jubal Early's march to Washington's suburbs in 1864), and although some advocated a sustained offensive strategy of carrying the war to the North shortly after the early success of Bull Run, the South's overall strategy was to conduct a defensive conventional war that would gradually wear down the North's will to continue by increasing the human and material costs it would have to pay. But, the key point here is that throughout the war, the military dimension of the conflict received the main emphasis because, in contrast to insurgencies that adopt a strategy of protracted popular war, Southerners perceived no need to mobilize and gradually expand popular support or to make prolonged guerrilla warfare or terrorist operations the fulcrum of the struggle.

The Biafran civil war (1967–1970), a more recent case, was similar to the American Civil War in several ways. Despite a different human and physical environment, the principal goal of the dominant ethnic group in eastern Nigeria, the Ibo, was to secede, and the strategy clearly emphasized military activity. With the exception of a belated effort to conduct guerrilla attacks, military operations were essentially conventional, reflecting the training of the Ibo officers at Sandhurst in Great Britain. Moreover, aside from a bold, yet ultimately failed, attempt to seize the Midwestern region in the summer and fall of 1967, conventional military operations (many of them artillery and mortar duels) took place in the eastern region. Like the

South in the American Civil War, the Ibo relied on military successes to erode the federal government's will to continue the conflict by increasing its human and material costs and by creating political pressures through the acquisition of international recognition. In the end, the strategy failed, not only because the government was able to consolidate its position and exploit its considerable relative advantage with respect to resources but also because conventional operations and ideas were, in the view of John de St. Jorre, totally unsuited to the terrain, the ability of the Biafran military, and the superior firepower of the adversary.[17]

Not all insurgents who adhere to a military-focus strategy believe that conventional military operations are a viable option. Where a sharp asymmetrical balance of military force favors the opposition, immediate action is manifest in lesser forms of violence, that is, terrorism or guerrilla warfare. The most notable example in recent times is the Cuban insurrection, which provided an alternative to the strategy of protracted popular war and, hence, engendered acrimonious debate between Chinese and Cuban Communists who were involved in supporting or sponsoring insurgencies in the 1960s and 1970s.[18] Given its contemporary importance, the Cuban variation of the military-focus strategy deserves further comment.

Che Guevara, a much-publicized figure in insurgent folklore, opened his book *Guerrilla Warfare* with the following comments:

> We consider that the Cuban Revolution contributed three fundamental lessons to the conduct of revolutionary movements in America. They are: (1) Popular forces can win a war against the army. (2) It is not necessary to wait until all the conditions for making revolution exist; the insurrection can create them. (3) In underdeveloped America the countryside is the basic area for armed fighting.[19]

While one may debate the originality of the first and third points, the second claim merits attention because Guevara seems to give more scrutiny to the initial phase of insurgency than does Mao. John Pustay suggests that this may be because Castro and Guevara had to start by recruiting at the grassroots level, whereas Mao did not have to start from scratch. In Pustay's words,

> Castro, Guevara, and their eleven cadre men, on the other hand, were forced to form guerrilla insurgency units by drawing upon recruitment sources at the grassroots level. They had to start essentially from nothing and build a revolutionary force to achieve victory. It is reasonable, therefore, for Guevara to discuss in detail the initiatory steps in creating a viable guerrilla force. Of priority is the assembly of revolutionary leaders

> and cadre guerrilla fighters in exile or in some isolated spot within an object country "around some respected leader fighting for the salvation of his people." Guevara then calls for elaborate advanced planning, for the advanced establishment of intelligence networks and arsenals, and above all for the continued maintenance of absolute secrecy about the potential insurgency until overt resistance is actually initiated. Thus Guevara fills in the details, overlooked by Mao and slightly covered by Giap [the Vietnamese Communist strategist], of the initiatory phases of the first general stage of Maoist insurgency warfare.[20]

Guevara's discussion of strategy contains a number of ideas found in Mao's thinking. In addition to his previously mentioned point about situating the conflict in the countryside, Guevara stressed the importance of bases in inaccessible terrain and the need for popular support and civil organization after areas have been seized. Moreover, like Mao, he argued that complete victory would be achieved only when the guerrilla army had been transformed into a regular army.[21] While it is tempting to interpret this merely as Guevara's attempt to reiterate Mao's strategy, a closer look at the Cuban case reveals noteworthy digressions from the strategy of protracted popular war.

Guevara contended that insurgent leaders do not have to wait for the preconditions of insurgency to appear because they can act to catalyze existing grievances required for positive action. Thirty to fifty men, he believed, would be adequate to start an armed rebellion in Latin American countries, given conditions like their favorable terrain for operations, hunger for land, repeated attacks upon justice, and the like.[22] In other words, Guevara suggested that the mere act of taking up arms in situations where grievances exist would create suitable conditions for revolution. Guevara depicted the beginning of the insurrection as follows:

> At the outset there is a more or less homogeneous group, with some arms, that devotes itself almost exclusively to hiding in the wildest and most inaccessible places, making little contact with the peasants. It strikes a fortunate blow and its fame grows. A few peasants, dispossessed of their land or engaged in a struggle to conserve it, and young idealists of other classes join the nucleus; it acquires greater audacity and starts to operate in inhabited places, making more contact with the people of the zone; it repeats attacks, always fleeing after making them; suddenly it engages in combat with some column or other and destroys its vanguard. Men continue to join it; it has increased in number, but its organization remains exactly the same; its caution diminishes, and it ventures into more populous zones.[23]

Like Lenin and Mao, Fidel Castro believed that an elite vanguard was a necessary condition for a successful insurrection; unlike Lenin and Mao, he did not believe the vanguard had to be a Marxist-Leninist party. Historical circumstances, according to Regis Debray, determine the form of the vanguard. In his treatise on the Cuban insurrection, *Revolution in the Revolution?* Debray notes,

> Fidel Castro says simply that there is no revolution without a vanguard; that this vanguard is not necessarily the Marxist-Leninist party; and that those who want to make the revolution have the right and the duty to constitute themselves a vanguard, independently of these parties.
>
> It takes courage to state the facts out loud when these facts contradict a tradition. There is, then, no metaphysical equation in vanguard = Marxist-Leninist party; there are merely dialectical conjunctions between a given function—that of the vanguard in history—and a given form of organization—that of the Marxist-Leninist party. These conjunctions arise out of prior history and depend on it. Parties exist here on earth and are subject to the rigors of terrestrial dialectics. If they have been born, they can die and be reborn in other forms. How does this rebirth come about? Under what form can the historic vanguard appear?[24]

During the Cuban revolution, Castro dealt with the question about the form of the vanguard by rejecting the idea of subordinating the guerrilla force to the party. Instead, he placed primary emphasis on the guerrilla army as the nucleus of the party. Putting it another way, Debray argues that the guerrilla force is a political embryo from which the party can arise. While Mao stressed the leading role of the party and the need for substantial political preparation *before* the military struggle, Debray claims the Cuban case made it clear that military priorities must take precedence over politics.

Debray contends that it is an old obsession to believe revolutionary awareness and organization must and can, in every case, precede revolutionary action. Rather than wait for the emergence of an organization, it is necessary to proceed from what he calls "the guerrilla foco" (focus), the nucleus of the popular army. This foco is "the small motor" that sets "the big motor of the masses" in action and precipitates formation of a front as victories by the small motor increase.[25] Debray's belief in the widespread applicability of this strategy is obvious in this remark:

> The Latin American revolution and its vanguard, the Cuban revolution, have thus made a decisive contribution to international revolutionary experience and to Marxism-Leninism. *Under certain conditions, the*

> *political and the military are not separate, but form one organic whole, consisting of the people's army, whose nucleus is the guerrilla army. The vanguard party can exist in the form of the guerrilla foco itself. The guerrilla force is the party in embryo.* This is the staggering novelty introduced by the Cuban Revolution.[26]

For insurgents who see the Cuban experience as analogous to their own situation and believe Mao's strategy of protracted popular war is inappropriate in their environments, there is another way, the *military focus* emphasized in Cuba. In this approach the key ingredients are violence in the form of small to moderately sized guerrilla or terrorist attacks, limited political organization, and limited popular support. Although it is not a strategic assumption stressed by Castro or examined sufficiently by Debray, a weak government is closely related to Castro's version of the military-focus strategy. Indeed, it is questionable whether Castro could have achieved his aims if the Batista government had not been in a state of profound decay and its military weak and divided. As a matter of fact, a reasonably strong government will undoubtedly take resolute steps to eradicate any insurgency that threatens either the political community or the political system. On the other hand, where preservationist or reformist insurgents are operating, the military focus might prove effective even in the face of a strong government because government leaders might decide to reduce their losses by initiating policy changes that do not threaten the integrity of either the political community or the political system.

As is the case with the conspiratorial and protracted-popular-war strategies, the exhilaration of a historic victory (in Cuba) gave rise to claims that a military-focus strategy based on guerrilla warfare had widespread applicability, especially in the Latin American countries. In fact, Che Guevara's belief that the Cuban experience could be replicated in Bolivia led him to a fateful end in that country. Guevara's dismal failure, as well as the recognition that not all governments were as fragile as Batista's had been in Cuba, prompted insurgent Latin American intellectuals to reassess strategic approaches and develop what some of them believed to be a new strategy of urban warfare in which terrorism is prominent.[27] Although, as Thomas Marks has pointed out, urban warfare has increasingly been incorporated into the protracted-popular-war strategy in some situations, and in others it could be viewed as a subset or variation of the military-focus strategy, it seems prudent to acknowledge cases wherein urban warfare is conceptualized (wisely or not) as a separate strategy because of the distinctive, at times decisive, emphasis its proponents place on cities as the epicenter of insurgency.[28]

Urban-Warfare Strategy

Terrorist acts in support of political objectives are, as we know, hardly a new phenomenon. Although assassinations, kidnappings, and the slaughter of innocent people can be traced back to antiquity, our concern here is the articulation in recent times of an urban-centered strategy in which terrorist attacks play a preponderant role. The emergence of this strategy as an alternative to those discussed thus far is due not only to the resiliency and relative strengths of incumbent governments but also to increased urbanization in many parts of the world. In the modernized societies of Europe and North America, inaccessible rural areas where guerrillas may operate with impunity simply do not exist. Accordingly, insurgents who pursue political aims through violent acts have been compelled to locate in the cities and to operate on a small scale in order to survive. In less-developed countries, most especially in Latin America, the strategy of urban warfare has also been attractive. In some cases, such as in Venezuela, Argentina, and Uruguay, the situation is similar to Europe and North America; that is, the population is essentially urban rather than rural.

In other situations, where there is an urban-rural mix, as in many other Latin American countries, the failures of insurgents to establish footholds in the countryside in the 1960s led insurgent leaders to reassess social, political, and economic changes in the hope of uncovering new government vulnerabilities to exploit. One such change was increased migration from rural to urban areas, accompanied in most cases by the establishment of slums filled with poor, psychologically disoriented people whose search for a better life had yielded little more than bitter disillusionment. Insurgent leaders saw such conditions as presenting significant opportunities for carrying out, and gaining support for, insurrectionary activities. Consequently, the locus of potential for insurgencies shifted to the cities. Moreover, the socioeconomic differentiation of the urban centers provided ample targets for sabotage and terrorism, and the population density rendered unusable such government military assets as aircraft, artillery, mortars, and the like.

Although their ultimate goals may vary, insurgents engaged in urban violence all pursue the intermediate aim of eroding the government's will to resist. As with the protracted-popular-war and military-focus strategies, eventual mass support is considered important, but the process of achieving it is different. The essential strategy of the urban terrorist, according to Carlos Marighella, one of its foremost proponents, is to "turn political crisis into armed conflict by performing violent actions that will force those in power to transform the political situation of the country into a military situation. That will alienate the masses, who from then on will revolt against the army and police and thus blame them for this state of things."[29] To cause this transformation, urban insurgents engage in various actions, including armed propaganda; strikes and work interruptions; ambushes; assassinations; kidnappings; temporary occupation of schools, factories, and radio stations; assaults on fixed targets (e.g., banks, businesses, military camps, police stations, and prisons); and sabotage of economic assets. In addition, they usually want to infiltrate the police and military to foster a breakdown from within. The organization responsible for these actions is basically a small one with cells that each contain a "link man."[30] Cumulative acts of violence wreak havoc and create insecurity, which will eventually produce a loss of confidence in the government.

For some Latin American theorists like Marighella and Abraham Guillen, action in the cities is crucial but not decisive because the struggle must eventually be transferred to the countryside. According to Marighella, the function of urban terrorists is to tie down the government forces in the cities, thus permitting the emergence and survival of rural guerrilla warfare, "which is destined to play the decisive role in the revolutionary war."[31] Accordingly, the major question is how effective urban warfare is in undermining the government and in gaining popular support, not whether urban warfare alone can be successful.[32] The perceived need to transfer the conflict to the rural areas stems from the belief that widespread popular support will be needed to defeat an adversary that controls the state apparatus and is unlikely to remain passive in the face of a challenge to the political community or the regime.

Initiating an insurgency by means of urban warfare and eventually transferring it to the countryside is a Latin American notion that not all urban insurgents subscribe to. During the 1970s and 1980s, Irish Republican Army (IRA) leaders believed that violence in the cities and abroad directed at British officials and military personnel, as well as unarmed civilians, would eventually wear down British will and lead to a withdrawal from Ulster. Likewise, organizations like Action Direct in France, the Red Brigades in Italy, the Fighting Communist Cells in Belgium, the Japanese Red Army, and Basque Homeland and Liberty (ETA) in Spain have pursued their goals (which, except in the case of ETA, are somewhat ambiguous) through urban violence, giving little or no indication of plans eventually to carry out a rural struggle. In effect, this means that there are really two variations of the urban-warfare strategy: one that calls for a move to the countryside and one centered solely on the cities.

With the exception of South Yemen in 1967, the urban-warfare strategy has been ineffective.[33] While the Tupamaros in Uruguay and the Monteneros in Argentina succeeded in provoking a heavily militarized government response, the brutal repression it generated crushed the insurgent movements. As a result, insurgents in places like El Salvador, Guatemala, and Peru returned to either the rural-based protracted-popular-war or the military-focus strategies discussed earlier. Others, like the previously mentioned groups in Europe, continue to carry out urban terrorist actions but appear to have little prospect of achieving their ultimate goals.[34]

ASSESSING STRATEGIC APPROACHES

The preceding section does not aim to suggest that all past and present insurgent strategies fit precisely into four perfectly distinct categories. It does suggest, however, that differences between strategic approaches are discernible. We have suggested four strategic approaches that have guided and inspired many insurgent leaders. These four approaches stand out, among other reasons, because their original proponents and adherents claimed that they had widespread, if not universal, applicability. Despite the fact that ex post facto conceptual codifications of these strategies involve oversimplifications, idealization, selective history, and, perhaps, distortion with respect to what really transpired, it is nonetheless true that many others have adopted these strategies.

The adoption of the strategic approaches is not always clear-cut, and this in turn leads to several important points. First, in some cases the adopted strategies are emulated in a careful and specific way; in other cases, they are loosely articulated and applied. For example, the adoption and implementation of the strategy of protracted popular war by the NPA in the Philippines and the Vietcong in Vietnam was effected in a programmatic way, with great attention to the political and military requisites associated with that strategy. In contrast, some Palestinian groups claiming to follow the Maoist version of the strategy have been far less attentive to details, particularly with respect to stages and their sequencing. Thus, an important question for the researcher is how, and to what degree, groups diverge from the specifics of whatever strategy they have adopted. An examination of writings and pronouncements of insurgent leaders, as well as their plans and operational directives, can yield some answers that may help explain insurgent fortunes. Insurgent failures and shortcomings, for instance, might be traced to an incomplete understanding and application of the particular facets of the strategy they profess to be following.

Second, the analyst should keep in mind that divided insurgent movements frequently have independent groups pursuing several strategies simultaneously. A case in point was the FMLN in El Salvador prior to 1985: the People's Revolutionary Army of Joaquín Villalobos was clearly following a military-focus strategy, while the Popular Liberation Forces, led by Leonel González, favored the protracted-popular-war approach.

Another example is the Palestinian resistance from 1968 to 1990: the Popular Democratic Front followed a Maoist protracted-popular-war strategy, Fatah subscribed to a less rigid scheme akin to the Algerian protracted-popular-war experience, and the Popular Front for the Liberation of Palestine–General Command and the Abu Nidal Organization adopted the military-focus approach (principally terrorist actions).

The effects of such strategic dissonance are of no small consequence. For instance, precipitate violence (terrorist, guerrilla, or conventional attacks) in keeping with the military-focus strategy can undercut the strategic and tactical aims of groups following the protracted-popular-war strategy because it risks galvanizing major government countermeasures. Since they perceive themselves to be in a weak position relative to the government during the earliest stage of insurrections, adherents of the protracted-popular-war strategy want the government to remain relatively inactive and complacent while they are gradually establishing their insurgent infrastructure. Cultivating inaction and complacency, however, is very difficult when other groups disagree with that strategy and carry out acts of violence against government forces. The key questions for the analyst are whether there is a lack of consensus on strategy, what the conflicting strategies are, what actions take place, and what the effects of the discordant behavior are.

Both the choice of a strategy and its effectiveness are related to the criteria used to evaluate the progress of insurgencies. Although the links between factors will be drawn at various points in subsequent chapters, it may be helpful to illustrate this general point before proceeding. Two factors that can have a major impact on the choice of a strategy are the environment and government response. Some groups have chosen an urban-warfare strategy (e.g., the IRA and the Red Brigades in Italy) because they operate in an environment that is largely urbanized rather than a backward rural area with inaccessible regions and because the balance of coercive force decidedly favors the government.

None of this should lead to the assumption that all insurgents correctly assess the overall situation when choosing a strategic approach. To the contrary, in some cases insurgents badly misread the situation. Regardless of whether they chose a military-focus or protracted-popular-war strategy, Palestinian groups committed to the liberation of all Palestine in the late 1960s and early 1970s accurately assessed Israel's advantageous position but deluded themselves when it came to the physical and human environment. As time passed, they came to recognize that acquiring mass popular support and setting up bases in both Israel and the occupied territories was difficult, if not impossible, because the area was relatively small, had little natural cover, and had a highly developed road and communications system. Furthermore, the population inside Israel was composed of a Jewish majority and a relatively tranquil Palestinian Arab sector. By the mid-1970s, the recognition that the physical environment left much to be desired could be seen in references to the "jungles of the people," an oblique acknowledgment that real jungles did not exist. Moreover, a growing understanding that the physical and human environment inside Israel and the occupied areas was simply not conducive to any of their strategies probably influenced the 1974 decision by pragmatic elements of the Palestinian Liberation Organization to concentrate on liberating the occupied West Bank and Gaza Strip rather than destroying Israel.

THE TRANSNATIONAL STRATEGY OF AL QAIDA: EPHEMERAL OR ENDURING?

The reality that some insurgents have not explicitly adopted one of the four strategies discussed thus far does not necessarily mean they have no strategy. Al Qaida, for instance, may be formulating a new strategy that will have lasting and widespread appeal. Whether that is so remains uncertain, given the absence of a clear and comprehensive articulation of the overall strategy and our dearth of knowledge about strategic discussions among its leaders. Nonetheless, given the magnitude of the threat posed by Al Qaida, it is worthwhile to sketch out some preliminary thoughts on the matter.

To begin with, Al Qaida certainly engages in strategic thinking. This much is obvious, given the use of all instruments of power at its disposal. Through its diplomatic efforts, it has forged alliances with like-minded Islamic militants in all corners of the world. Relying on its economic capability, it has acquired support by bribing individuals (e.g., leaders of tribes in Afghanistan) and dispensed economic assistance for basic social services to many disadvantaged groups and people in various locales. Al Qaida's well-known and extensive information campaigns include books, pamphlets, formal religious decrees (fatwas), Internet chat rooms and Web sites, and the carefully timed release of videos and press communiqués, often in conjunction with guerrilla and terrorist attacks. The explicit synchronization of the information and military instruments is designed to achieve various political objectives. For instance, the purpose of the Madrid bombing in March 2004 was to influence the national elections so that a new government would be installed that would withdraw Spanish troops from Iraq.

Even though Al Qaida may not have fully developed an overall strategy for conducting an insurgency, several tenets of its thinking, as well as its behavior, suggest a gradually evolving, coherent approach. Al Qaida's clearly articulated long-term goal is, as we have noted previously, to establish a global political system (caliphate) based on its version of Islamic law, an outcome that would, by its very nature, remove the threat of Western secularization once and for all. To achieve this, Al Qaida believes it must eliminate American influence and presence in the Middle East by undermining U.S. alliances and draining its human and economic resources through continuous attacks and threats. Destruction of the American economy is central in this regard. Once the will of the United States is broken, so the reasoning goes, it will withdraw its forces; that, in turn, will lead to the demise of "apostate" regimes that depend on it (e.g., in Egypt, Jordan, and Saudi Arabia). This will then open the door for the establishment of pure, Islamic political systems.

In a major break with past insurgencies, Al Qaida's main focus is not concentrated within the borders of a given country. Instead, the entire globe is considered a battlefield, with attacks possible anywhere. This transnational campaign is envisaged as a long struggle that emphasizes violent attacks carried out by Al Qaida's own agents and various regional affiliates and local mavericks. It is not conceptualized within the framework of progressive stages, as is the case with the protracted-popular-war strategy. Nor does it stress the establishment of complex shadow governments. It does, however, envisage the need to takeover at least one key country early in the struggle, preferably Saudi Arabia, which can then be used as a base to continue the global insurrection. Accordingly, the strategy of Al Qaida is best viewed as a military-focus one with a global theater of operations.[35]

SUMMARY

Before making a systematic appraisal of the strengths and weaknesses of an insurgency, it is important to have as clear a picture as possible of the goals, forms of warfare, and strategy of the insurgents. With these firmly in mind, it is possible to set forth the things insurgents need to do to be successful. As far as strategies are concerned, four general approaches have been popular in recent and present times—conspiratorial, protracted popular war, military focus, and urban warfare. Each places a different combination of requirements on insurgents. The conspiratorial approach emphasizes an elite small-scale organization and low-level violence; protracted popular warfare stresses political primacy, mass organization, and gradually escalating violence; the military-focus approach emphasizes military primacy and concentrates on either guerrilla or conventional warfare; urban warfare involves small-scale organization and low to moderate terrorist or guerrilla attacks in urban centers, with some proponents envisaging an eventual transition to warfare in the rural areas. Insurgents may follow these approaches exactly or adopt them more loosely. In some cases, they may underplay or overplay aspects of the strategy or blend in new dimensions. But even where this is done, the general strategy is recognizable. The key questions for the analyst are, what approach, if any, is being followed, and what are the divergences and their implications? As for gauging the effectiveness of various strategies, it is essential to identify those factors that experts deem crucial for their success and then assess how the insurgency is progressing, if at all, with respect to each. That process will be the subject of subsequent chapters.

NOTES

1. John Shy and Thomas W. Collier, "Revolutionary War," in *Makers of Modern Strategy*, ed. Peter Paret (Princeton, N.J.: Princeton University Press, 1986), 829. Lenin's crucial assumption concerning a general governmental crisis is set forth in "Left-wing Communism—An Infantile Disorder," in *The Lenin Anthology*, ed. Robert C. Tucker (New York: W. W. Norton Co., 1975), 602. An example of the successful use of the conspiratorial strategy was the April 1978 coup in Afghanistan by the People's Democratic Party of Afghanistan. See Abdul Samad Ghaus, *The Fall of Afghanistan* (McLean, Va.: Pergamon-Brassey's, 1988), 187–208. On the strategy of the Islamic Organization in Egypt see Barry Rubin, *Islamic Fundamentalism in Egyptian Politics* (New York: St. Martin's Press, 1990), 43. A new twist to the conspiratorial strategy is provided in the Republic of South Africa by the Boer Force (Boeremag), which believes that it can carry out terrorist attacks against Muslims, who will provoke blacks to attack whites, who, in turn, will act defensively and thus trigger a coup. See *Johannesburg SAPA*, Internet Version-WWW, in English, October 31, 2003, in *FBIS-Terrorism (INE)*, October 31, 2003. Those interested in a detailed analysis of coups, especially the tactical and operational aspects of strategy, should read Edward Luttwak, *Coup d'État* (New York: Alfred A. Knopf, 1969).
2. "Left-wing Communism," 572.
3. "Left-wing Communism," 550–618, contains a vigorous defense of united-front tactics by Lenin.
4. Robert H. McNeal, *The Bolshevik Tradition* (Englewood Cliffs, N.J.: Prentice-Hall, 1963), 45. For Lenin's major work on the question of seizing power and the role of the party, see his *What Is to Be Done*, trans. S. V. Utechin and Patricia Utechin (London: Oxford University Press, 1963). Needless to state, volumes have been written about Lenin and the Bolshevik coup; for a brief summary account, see David Shub, *Lenin*, abridged ed. (New York: Mentor Books, 1950), especially 76–139; and Alan Moorehead, *The Russian Revolution* (New York: Bantam Books, 1959), 132–260. For a more detailed, systematic analysis of the Bolsheviks, see Bertram D. Wolfe, *Three Who Made a Revolution* (New York: Delta Books, 1948).
5. See Mao Tse-tung, *Selected Military Writings of Mao Tse-tung* (Beijing: Foreign Language Press, 1967), 92–98, on the characteristics of China's revolutionary war that made it different from the Russian experience. To better understand the evolution of Mao's thinking, it is useful to put it in its sociopolitical context. See, for instance, Stuart Schram, *Mao Tse-tung* (Baltimore: Pelican Books, 1966), especially chs. 5, 6.
6. Mao Tse-tung, *Selected Military Writings of Mao Tse-tung*, 210–219, deals with the stages of a protracted armed struggle. For a succinct account of Mao's strategy, see Benjamin

I. Schwartz, *Chinese Communism and the Rise of Mao* (Cambridge, Mass.: Harvard University Press, 1951), 189–204, and John J. McCuen, *The Art of Counter-Revolutionary War* (Harrisburg, Pa.: Stackpole Books, n.d.), 31.

7. Mao Tse-tung, *Selected Military Writings of Mao Tse-tung*, 228. On the first phase of protracted popular war, see McCuen, *The Art of Counter-Revolutionary War*, 31.
8. John S. Pustay, *Counterinsurgency Warfare* (New York: Free Press, 1977), 54–59.
9. Pustay, *Counterinsurgency Warfare*, 59–71; McCuen, *The Art of Counter-Revolutionary War*, 33.
10. Pustay, *Counterinsurgency Warfare*, 71–72; McCuen, *The Art of Counter-Revolutionary War*, 34. On types of legitimacy, see Charles F. Andrain, *Political Life and Social Change*, 2nd ed. (Belmont, Calif.: Duxbury Press, 1974), 153–57.
11. Ted Robert Gurr, *Why Men Rebel* (Princeton, N.J.: Princeton University Press, 1970), 294–95; Pustay, *Counterinsurgency Warfare*, 36, 72; McCuen, *The Art of Counter-Revolutionary War*, 34–35.
12. Pustay, *Counterinsurgency Warfare*, 72–74; McCuen, *The Art of Counter-Revolutionary War*, 34, 36.
13. Pustay, *Counterinsurgency Warfare*, 75–76.
14. Pustay, *Counterinsurgency Warfare*, 76–78; McCuen, *The Art of Counter-Revolutionary War*, 37–40.
15. The notion of reversion to previous stages (i.e., from conventional to guerrilla war and then later from guerrilla to conventional) can be seen in Mao's discussion of strategic changes during the anti-Japanese War. See Mao Tse-tung, *Selected Military Writings of Mao Tse-tung*, 277–79.
16. On strategy in the Algerian war, see Joan Gillespie, *Algeria: Rebellion and Revolution* (London: Ernest Benn Limited, 1960), ch. 9; Edgar O'Ballance, *The Algerian Insurrection, 1954–1962* (Hamden, Conn.: Archon Books, 1967), 42, 62–63, and especially 205–10; and Alf Andrew Heggoy, *Insurgency and Counter-insurgency in Algeria* (Bloomington: Indiana University Press, 1972), ch. 5, particularly pp. 90–91, 95–100.
17. John de St. Jorre, *The Nigerian Civil War* (Toronto: Hodder and Stoughton, 1972), 125–231, and especially 273–82. Jefferson Davis called the South's strategy in the American Civil War "offensive-defensive." See James M. McPherson, *Battle Cry of Freedom* (New York: Ballantine Books, 1988), 338; Clement Eaton, *A History of the Southern Confederacy* (New York: The Macmillan Co., 1958), 124–25; Archer Jones, *Civil War Command and Strategy* (New York: The Free Press, 1992), 143–45, 151–54; and Gary Gallagher, ed. *Fighting for the Confederacy: The Personal Recollections of General Edward Porter Alexander* (Chapel Hill: University of North Carolina Press, 1989), 415.
18. For a succinct account of the differences between the Maoist and Debray schemes, see Arthur Jay Klinghoffer, "Mao or Che? Some Reflections on Communist Warfare," *Mizan* (March–April 1969): 94–99.
19. Che Guevara, *Guerrilla Warfare* (New York: Vintage Books, 1961), 1.
20. Pustay, *Counterinsurgency Warfare*, 112.
21. Guevara, *Guerrilla Warfare*, 3–12, 80–86.
22. Guevara, *Guerrilla Warfare*, 112.
23. Guevara, *Guerrilla Warfare*, 71, and Brian Crozier, *The Study of Conflict* (London: Institute for the Study of Conflict, 1970), 7.

24. Regis Debray, *Revolution in the Revolution?* trans. Bobbe Ortiz (New York: Monthly Review Press, 1967), 20–21, 95–105; Crozier, *The Study of Conflict,* 8.
25. Debray, *Revolution in the Revolution?* 83–84.
26. Debray, *Revolution in the Revolution?* 106. Italics are from Debray. Despite Debray's claims, the idea of military action preceding popular support was already present in the literature on insurgency. It was one of several possibilities raised in "La guerre revolutionaire et ses donnes fundamentales," *Revue militaire d'information* (February–March 1957): 9–29.
27. On the failure of Castroism in Latin America, see Douglas S. Blaufarb, *The Counterinsurgency Era* (New York: Free Press, 1977), 280–86; John Pimlott, ed., *Guerrilla Warfare* (New York: Bison Books, 1985), 108–15.
28. Thomas A. Marks, "Urban Insurgency," *Small Wars and Insurgencies* (autumn 2003): 100–142.
29. Carlos Marighella, "On Principles and Strategic Questions," *Les tempes modernes* (November 1969).
30. Robert Moss, *Urban Guerrilla Warfare,* Adelphi Paper no. 79 (London: The International Institute for Strategic Studies, 1971), 3.
31. Carlos Marighella, "Minimanual of the Urban Guerrillas," appendix to Moss, *Urban Guerrilla Warfare,* 26.
32. The rural-urban linkage within the framework of a protracted war of liberation is perhaps best illustrated in the writings of Abraham Guillen, one of the major revolutionary thinkers in Latin America; see his *Philosophy of the Urban Guerrilla,* ed. and trans. Donald C. Hodges (New York: William Morrow, 1973), 229–300. Although Guillen allows for the possibility of a Leninist type of takeover under certain conditions, the essential thrust of his argument concentrates on prolonged conflict. Guillen, it should be noted, focuses on Latin America. While he believes that armies of liberation must be created in each country, he contends that they must be part of a larger continental strategic command that could orchestrate the liberation of all Latin America.
33. For a succinct, incisive critique of the urban terrorist approach, see Anthony Burton, *Revolutionary Violence* (New York: Crane, Russak, 1978), 130–44; Walter Laqueur, *Guerrilla* (Boston: Little, Brown, 1976), 403–4; Jennifer Morrison Taw and Bruce Hoffman, *The Urbanization of Insurgency* (Santa Monica, Calif.: The Rand Corporation, 1994), 7–22. Insurgents' success in South Yemen is noted in John Pimlott, ed. *Guerrilla Warfare* (New York: Bison Books, 1985), 136. One might also make a case that Palestine in the 1940s and Cyprus in the 1950s were also examples of what, on balance, was an urban-warfare strategy. If one accepts this, the common denominator in the Yemen, Palestine, and Cyprus cases is a weakened imperial power desiring to cut its losses. In today's world, those using an urban-warfare strategy face indigenous governments, none of which has succumbed.
34. It is clear that terrorism may achieve short-term objectives such as extracting ransom, publicizing the movement, solidifying existing support, and provoking overreaction by the government. It is not clear that relying on terror as the primary form of warfare can be strategically decisive. Where it has contributed to success, terrorism has been one of several forms of warfare. While it is tempting to ascribe the British withdrawal from Palestine to dramatic terrorist actions by Jewish extremist groups like the Irgun and

Stern Gang, this ignores the guerrilla warfare and small-scale conventional operations by the major Jewish military force, the Haganah, and its elite strike force, the Palmach.

35. As of this writing, there is no definitive treatment or systematic evaluation of Al Qaida's strategy. In part, this may be due to the absence of a clear, holistic strategy to begin with. The elements suggested in the text above are drawn from a wide range of sources that, inter alia, include Daniel Benjamin and Steve Simon, *The Age of Sacred Terror* (New York: Random House, 2002), 134, 156; Rohan Gunaratna, *Inside Al Qaeda* (New York: Columbia University Press, 2002), 54–94; Yassin Musharbash, "Change of Strategy: The New Al-Qaida Doctrine," *Hamburg Spiegel Online*, March 18, 2004, in *FBIS-NESA (INE)*, March 18, 2004. Richard A. Clarke, *Against All Enemies* (New York: The Free Press, 2004), 280, argues Pakistan would be a desirable country for Al Qaida to control and use as a base given the popular support for fundamentalism and nuclear capability.

4

THE ENVIRONMENT

The first major criterion for evaluating an insurgency is the environment. It has two general components. The first is the physical aspect, which refers to the terrain, climate, and transportation-communications system. The second, the human dimension, focuses on demography, socioeconomic conditions, political culture, and the political system. Both physical and human aspects of the environment are important because they provide opportunities for insurgents and place constraints on insurgent strategies as well. In many cases, success or failure can be traced to the way insurgent and government strategies, plans, and policies are related to environmental characteristics.

THE PHYSICAL ENVIRONMENT

Terrain

The physical setting plays a significant part in insurgent conflicts. To begin with, it can have a major impact on the choice of a strategy. Small, urbanized countries, for instance, are unsuitable for strategies that call for substantial guerrilla warfare. It comes, therefore, as no surprise to find that groups like the Irish Republican Army (IRA) in Northern Ireland have opted for an urban-warfare strategy. Simply put, the reality is that any thought of adopting either a protracted-popular-war or a military-focus strategy stressing guerrilla warfare would be a mistake because armed insurgent units could easily be detected and attacked during the beginning stages of the conflict, except in those rare instances where the government demonstrated little, if any, will to resist. It has yet to be determined whether a prolonged military-focus strategy that involves considerable terrorism in urban centers across the world, such as the novel one pursued by Al Qaida, can succeed.

We do know, however, that the physical environment plays a key role in those situations where the government is assumed to enjoy political-military supremacy at the beginning of hostilities and insurgents adopt a protracted-popular-war or military-focus strategy emphasizing guerrilla warfare. Rugged terrain—vast mountains, jungles, swamps, forests, and the like—is usually related to successful guerrilla operations because it hinders movement by government troops and provides inaccessible hide-outs for the guerrillas' main bases. A. H. Shollom explains it thus:

> One of the main factors contributing to the development of a partisan movement was the presence of suitable terrain in which to operate. We include in such terrain: swamps, mountains and forests where mobility is limited to movement on foot and in light vehicles. The fact that the partisan operates in such terrain will be to his advantage, for in an environment of this nature, the regular forces lose the use of their vehicles and artillery as well as the ability to mass superior members. In essence, the terrain reduces the better equipped, better trained, and better armed regular force to a level where the partisan is its equal. It has been estimated that approximately 5,000 Communist partisans in Malaya were being hunted by 230,000 regular soldiers and police, a seemingly overwhelming majority, but the jungle is the equalizer. In this jungle it took 1,000 man-hours for each partisan killed. In open terrain the future of these partisans would be something less than secure.[1]

The triple-canopied jungles of Indochina, a tremendous asset to the forces of Ho Chi Minh in two wars, are another example of good terrain for guerrilla operations and bases. Until the introduction of large numbers of American troops into Vietnam in the mid-1960s, heavy jungles such as the U Minh forest south of Saigon and War Zone D to the north were well-nigh impregnable.

Unlike areas with heavy foliage, open spaces (e.g., deserts) are normally unfavorable for guerrillas; air surveillance and attack make insurgents susceptible to detection and destruction. In Arthur Campbell's words,

> Open plains are obstacles to guerrillas because they have to concede mastery of the air to their opponents. Before the onset of air power, Lawrence and his Arabs were able to retreat at will into the Arabian deserts, but the FLN [National Liberation Front] in Algeria, opposed by a powerful French air force, were denied access to the vast reaches of the Sahara.[2]

A more recent illustration can be seen in the differing approaches Egypt and the Palestinian Liberation Organization (PLO) adopted to combat Israel following the June 1967 war. Not long after the cease-fire, Mao Tse-tung sent President Gamal Abdel Nasser of Egypt a military plan of action inspired by China's experience; it called for breaking the Egyptian army into guerrilla units to fight the Israelis in the occupied Sinai Peninsula. Nasser rejected this course, pointing out that because the Sinai had a sparse population, was arid, and allowed visibility of thirty to forty miles, guerrilla forces would stand no chance.

Unlike Egypt, the PLO believed there was merit in Mao's thinking. Accordingly, it mounted a guerrilla campaign against Israeli military outposts and settlements in the West Bank from 1968 to 1970. The West Bank is small and has little vegetation; even a few people can be seen for miles, so the Palestinians could neither move in large numbers nor set up permanent or semipermanent bases without being detected and attacked by the Israeli Defense Force. As a result, Palestinian guerrilla raids originated from across the borders of Lebanon and especially Jordan. And given the paucity of vegetation in Jordan (except for a limited area along the Jordan River), guerrilla bases across the borders also proved vulnerable to detection and attack, especially from the air.[3] It is worth noting, however, that where effective air power like Israel's is lacking, insurgents who are intimately familiar with the terrain may successfully exploit vast expanses of desert. Effective attacks by Front for the Liberation of Rio d'Oro and Saguia el-Hamra (Polisario) guerrillas in both the western Sahara and southern Morocco from 1977 to 1984 are a case in point.[4]

Even when the terrain is favorable for guerrilla warfare, its effects may be limited by size and proximity. Small areas can be cordoned off, isolated, turned into free-fire zones, and penetrated. By contrast, where guerrillas take advantage of extensive good terrain by expanding their operations, the government will find it more difficult to maintain and defend its civilian administration, to supervise the populace, and to concentrate troops and firepower.[5] This is precisely the predicament the Soviets confronted in Afghanistan, where the sheer size of the country would have required an enormous commitment of resources to pacify the countryside. Considerations such as these led Mao to believe that a vast countryside is a sine qua non of successful protracted war.[6]

As for proximity, it is preferable to have areas with good terrain reasonably close to one another in order to facilitate planning, command, control, and communications and to gradually establish and integrate a logistical structure to support intensified hostilities. Conversely, widely separated areas make it extremely difficult, if not impossible, for insurgents to contemplate sustained large-scale guerrilla or mobile conventional operations. Such a situation would seem to exist in the Philippines: there are plenty of jungle areas conducive to guerrilla warfare; however, since the

Philippines is an archipelago, and the insurgents' operational areas are thus separated from one another, the military operations of the New People's Army (NPA) have been localized. Whether the NPA could move beyond decentralized local operations and adopt and implement a coordinated nationwide strategy involving large-scale military operations remains doubtful.

One important benefit that favorable topography bestows on insurgents (which merits closer attention at this point) is the seclusion of base areas. Bases are necessary for guerrilla warfare, particularly in the earliest phases, when, as Che Guevara pointed out, the essential task of the guerrilla fighter is to avoid elimination by taking up positions out of reach of the enemy.[7] Maintaining a strong base of operations as the war progresses is no less important. In his *Selected Military Writings,* Mao wrote of the crucial role of bases:

> Without such strategic bases, there will be nothing to depend on in carrying out any of our strategic tasks or achieving the aim of the war. It is a characteristic of guerrilla warfare behind the enemy lines that it is fought without a rear, for the guerrilla forces are severed from the country's general rear. But guerrilla warfare could not last long or grow without base areas. The base areas, indeed, are its rear.
>
> History knows many peasant wars of the roving rebel type, but none of them ever succeeded. In the present age of advanced communications and technology, it would be all the more groundless to imagine one can win victory by fighting in the manner of the roving rebels. However, this roving rebel idea still exists among many impoverished peasants, and in the minds of guerrilla commanders it becomes the view that base areas are neither necessary nor important. Therefore, ridding the minds of the guerrilla commanders of this idea is a prerequisite for deciding on a policy of establishing base areas. . . . Only when this ideology is thoroughly overcome and the policy of establishing base areas is initiated and applied will there be conditions favorable for the maintenance of guerrilla warfare over a long period.[8]

Concealed, permanent base areas allow the insurgents to plan, train, rest, recuperate, marshal equipment, and organize the people in relative security. A case in point was the network of bases set up by one of Afghanistan's most notable guerrilla leaders, the late Ahmed Shah Masoud, in the mountains overlooking the Panjshir Valley. Reports by observers and several major Soviet campaigns in the valley that failed to locate and dislodge his forces made clear the positive contribution of those bases to Masoud's successful guerrilla attacks against the Russians. Likewise, Jonas

Savimbi's forces in southern Angola expanded operations and proved a tenacious foe of the government because, among other things, they had a solid and secure basing structure. Prior to September 11, the growing effectiveness and menace of Al Qaida was due in large measure to a series of major bases in Afghanistan that served as training camps, planning and communications facilities, and supply areas.

An absence of permanent bases inside a country means that insurgent units cannot generate a steadily increasing level of guerrilla warfare. The Polisario guerrillas' experience during the 1980s in the western Sahara is instructive here. While the Polisario was able to establish temporary facilities in certain areas and to carry out periodic and sometimes quite successful raids, the overall capability of the insurgents was—and remains—limited. All things considered, Polisario's fighters resemble what Mao called "roving bands" because they have had no permanent bases inside the western Sahara.

One final note with regard to bases is that whether bases are permanent or semipermanent, there is a natural temptation to defend them against major government assaults. Such a course invites disaster when the insurgents are not ready to confront the government in set-piece battles. An example is the attempt and subsequent costly failure of guerrillas to defend their Grammos and Vitsi bases during the Greek civil war.[9] This obviously suggests that by throwing prudence to the winds, guerrillas in such circumstances simply go from a bad to a worse situation.

The specific issue of bases underscores the more general connection between insurgencies' success and topography. This does not imply that favorable topography is necessary in all insurgencies, for there are exceptions, such as the Jewish and Cypriot revolts against the British and Lenin's seizure of power in Russia. In these cases, topography played no significant role; the insurgents succeeded because they had enough popular support, and the government was weak and wavering. When, as in most cases, governments evince a strong commitment and are able to prevent a deterioration of morale in the military and police forces, topographical features and base areas become vital for insurgents who emphasize rural guerrilla warfare.

For insurgents who opt for urban warfare, base areas and topography are not major concerns. As we have learned, however, urban areas have not been decisive in situations where governments demonstrate a reasonable commitment to the struggle. Although the complex and functionally interdependent nature of large urban centers yields tempting targets and provides concealment for insurgents, groups that have relied almost exclusively on terrorism as a form of warfare (notably the Baader-Meinhof group in Germany, the Japanese Red Army, Basque Homeland and Liberty in Spain, the IRA, the Red Brigades in Italy, the Tupamaros in Uruguay, and the Monteneros in Argentina) have not come close to achieving their long-term aims and, in most cases, have been dealt severe losses, if not destroyed. The reasons for this have been noted by Ted Robert Gurr, who points out that police and military forces are usually concentrated in cities and that, unless the insurgents include most of the urban population and have the sympathy of the security forces, a rare set of conditions, they are easily dispersed.[10] Hence, while cities may provide opportunities for terrorists whose operations are ancillary to rural warfare (e.g., Afghanistan), they have not, by themselves, proven to be areas where decisive strategic successes can be achieved against committed governments with adequate resources.

Climate

In writings on insurgency, the effect of climate has not received anywhere near the attention that terrain has received, perhaps because climate can help or hinder both sides, depending on the strategic and tactical circumstances. When insurgents conduct small guerrilla attacks, heavy rain or snow makes it difficult for governments to exploit their advantages with respect to equipment and transportation both on the ground and in the air. While guerrillas can move on foot, government forces tend to rely on aircraft, armored personnel carriers, jeeps, trucks, and tanks for transportation. Since bad weather and resulting mud, snowdrifts, and the like impede the maintenance and movement of machines, the guerrilla has a relative advantage, in part because lulls in government operations are common during periods of bad weather. In Oman, for example, the activity of the Sultan's Armed Forces in Dhofar Province dropped off noticeably during the rainy season, and in Afghanistan, Soviet military activity decreased during the winter months. Although guerrilla attacks also tend to decrease, insurgents can use bad weather to regroup and reorganize in relative security.

When the fighting in an insurgency escalates to the mobile conventional level, the greater transportation and logistical needs of both sides are hampered by bad weather. Whether the insurgents or the government can benefit varies. It depends on short-term calculations about enemy troop dispositions and the ability to overcome adverse weather. As the 1954 battle of Dien Bien Phu in the first Indochina war and various attacks on U.S. Special Forces camps in the second Indochina war showed, bad weather can be used to tactical advantage. In both cases, assaults were timed to coincide with heavy cloud cover that prevented or interfered significantly with government efforts to provide close air support and to resupply beleaguered garrisons. Despite these situations, it would be an overgeneralization to argue that, over the long term, climate is a factor that favors one side or the other in any critical way.[11]

Transportation-Communications Infrastructure

One aspect of the physical environment that can have considerable bearing on the fortunes of an insurgency is the state of the transportation-communications systems, especially in large countries experiencing rural guerrilla warfare. Under those circumstances, the responsibility of government forces to provide security for many areas (i.e., cities, towns, military installations, and so forth) puts great strain on manpower and resources. Government strategies usually emphasize mobile-reaction units to compensate for shortcomings associated with the need to provide sufficient static defenses throughout the country. If transportation and communications systems are highly developed, the missions of mobile-reaction teams can be carried out more easily and expeditiously. Conversely, poor roads, rail networks, and river transport systems and inadequate communications make mobility difficult and therefore favor the insurgents.[12] Gurr comments on this point:

> Guerrilla war is common in underdeveloped countries because of poor transportation and communication networks and the isolation of rural areas, which facilitate guerrilla incursions. Free access to rural people enables guerrillas to propagandize, control, and secure support from them. The relatively dense road and rail networks of the Congo helped make it possible for United Nations and Congolese forces to suppress a number of regional rebellions between 1961 and 1966; the lack of comparable facilities has contributed to the inability of the Sudanese army to control the Anya-nya rebellion in the southern Sudan. The insulation of the American colonies from Britain by 2,000 miles of ocean facilitated a successful revolt; a comparable geographic separation has been of little value to rebels in Portuguese Angola and Mozambique. The Castro guerrillas were able to sustain themselves in the Sierra Maestra against a much larger army that lacked surface or aerial mobility; Spanish-American dissidents in the more rugged terrain of northern New Mexico had no such chance, in June 1967, against police helicopter patrols.[13]

Although a well-developed road and communications system is generally favorable to governments in a strategic sense, it should be noted that there is a tactical downside with regard to roads because dependence on roads for transportation and communications presents tempting targets. Just as convoys and the like were incessantly ambushed along major arteries in Vietnam and Afghanistan, so they are today in Iraq, where improvised explosive devices have extracted a disturbing human toll.

THE HUMAN ENVIRONMENT

Demographic Distribution

Although students of insurgency have devoted substantial attention to the physical attributes of the environment, the human dimension is even more important. Indeed, it is here that one uncovers the causes, or so-called roots, of insurgencies. Of primary interest are demography, social structure, economics, and the political culture and system. Demography, for instance, can have a major impact on the course of events. Where the population is small and concentrated, it is easier for the government to control the people and sever its links with the guerrillas. When most of the people live in cities, the situation does not appear as favorable to insurgent movements as when the population is concentrated in rural areas, although some contemporary insurgent strategists believe otherwise. As suggested earlier, if a society is highly urbanized, the government can control and monitor the people more easily and minimize the role and effects of rural guerrilla bases. But if the government is weak and the insurgents have a significant degree of international support, it is possible for the insurgents to advance or achieve their aims. Again, an example is Palestine from 1947 to 1948, when Jewish attacks combined with external moral, political, and material support for the Zionists forced the British government, weakened by World War II and beset with economic problems, to retreat. When the authorities demonstrate both the resolution and the competence to combat the insurgent threat and thus compel the insurgents to opt for prolonged warfare, an urban environment, although conducive to terrorist activities, hardly suffices; an underdeveloped rural society is more promising.

Social Structure

To better understand insurgencies, we need to go beyond the basic demographic attributes of a population and inquire about the impact of its social structure. Societies may be divided vertically by race, ethnicity, and religion, or horizontally by class or caste. While vertical cleavages are self-explanatory, a few remarks about class and caste are in order before proceeding. Although the criteria for distinguishing social classes vary somewhat and remain the subject of academic debate, I view classes as differing according to wealth (and the various benefits derived from it) and occupation. Both wealth and occupation confer status. Castes are extremely rigid groups divided by economic and occupational differences and explicit privileges, all of which are legitimized by theological or philosophical ideas. While there is mobility between classes (at least theoretically), membership in castes is static. Since caste systems are rare, we will focus once again on classes when we consider economic factors.

Societal cleavages along racial, ethnic, and religious lines are frequently among the root causes of insurgency and can be either helpful or detrimental to the progression of an insurrection. When one group enjoys disproportionate political and economic power and benefits relative to other groups, insurgents often find an opportunity to gain support from the disadvantaged groups. If the relatively deprived group constitutes a majority of the population, the possibilities for gaining support are naturally greater. Colonial governments are especially vulnerable, as the French found out in Algeria and Vietnam. The same is true of minority-based governments, such as Ian Smith's in white-ruled Rhodesia (now Zimbabwe), which deny the majority political participation and practice economic discrimination. Even if disadvantaged groups do not constitute a majority, they can still provide the foundation for a serious insurrection if they are sizable: witness the Kikuyu in Kenya in the 1950s, the Ovimbundu tribesmen in Angola in the 1980s and 1990s, the Kurds in Iraq and Iran, and the Eritreans in Ethiopia.

The above comments do not suggest that all situations in which minorities experience political and economic deprivation are advantageous for insurgent movements. In circumstances in which the disadvantaged groups are minorities, governments may garner support against them by emphasizing ancient antagonisms and the threats that the minorities pose to the privileges of the majority. When this transpires, insurgents (such as those in northern and northeastern Thailand or the Tamils in northern Sri Lanka) find it very difficult, if not impossible, to attract wide popular support because their identification with minorities undercuts their appeal to the majority. The reliance on minorities for support is especially precarious for insurgents when topographical features can isolate groups they represent. A striking example is the case of Oman, where support for the Popular Front for the Liberation of Oman came primarily from the *jebali* ("mountain people") of Dhofar Province. With the coastal area to the east and an inhospitable desert (the Rub al-Khali) to the west, the government was able to separate the guerrillas from the rest of the country by constructing military interdiction barriers across the insurgents' north-south lines of transportation. Insurgents who confront conditions such as these (as we shall see in later chapters) compound their problems if they pursue far-reaching goals that threaten either the political community or system. If they are less ambitious and seek only reforms, they may have some success.

Two final points should be made about societal divisions and insurgencies. First, rival groups may have a deleterious impact on an insurgent movement, the government, or both. Where more than one disadvantaged group is incorporated into insurgent ranks, the size and capability of the movement may increase. Sometimes, however, it creates problems with respect to cohesion. In Afghanistan, for instance, all ethnic and religious groups were engaged in the struggle against the Soviets and the Afghan government. At the same time, however, ancient animosities between groups, most notably Hazara, Tajik, Uzbek, and Baluchi resentment of the Pashtuns, were a source of disunity, fragmented political-military strategies and operations, and internecine strife. Such rivalries also present the government with opportunities to infiltrate insurgent ranks and play one group off against another. But, as the Afghan case also shows, the government can suffer the same malady: witness the endemic strife inside the People's Democratic Party of Afghanistan, which resulted in no small part from the different ethnic composition of its Khalq and Parchamite wings (the former is Pashtun-based; the latter is composed largely of Tajiks and other minorities). In the Iraqi insurgency, the underlying social cleavages and distrust among Kurds and Arabs and Sunnis and Shiites are also a problem for both sides, although their affect on the political outcome is unclear as of this writing.

The second point about societal groups relates to their internal structure of authority. The essential question is how conducive the structure is to organization and discipline. Three general structural configurations of power provide a useful frame of reference: hierarchical, pyramidal, and segmented. Hierarchical power structures have clearly delineated lines of authority from top to bottom (e.g., the Roman Catholic Church). Pyramidal structures may have an authority figure that is first among equals, but there are multiple centers of more or less equal power (e.g., the Shiite grand ayatollahs in Iran and Iraq). Segmented structures are marked by a diffusion of power to local groups that act autonomously (e.g., *jebali* tribes in Oman). While all power configurations can accommodate conspiratorial and urban-warfare strategies, segmented structures are not as favorable for military-focus and especially protracted-popular-war strategies because they obstruct the organizational development associated with those strategies. Disunity, in particular, is often the natural by-product of insurgencies waged by groups with segmented structures. By way of illustration, many observers believe that Ahmed Shah Masoud's creation of a sophisticated organization in the Panjshir Valley in Afghanistan was facilitated by the fact that the Tajiks are not a tribally oriented people. In contrast, the segmented society of the Pashtuns has impeded organizational development.

This brief discussion of societal factors should make one thing clear: it would be a great mistake to focus simply on the more familiar economic and political dimensions of the human environment of insurgencies.

Although the relationships between societal divisions and the fortunes of insurgent movements are various and complex, they cannot be passed over lightly because they may provide key explanations of insurgencies' successes or failures. Moreover, in some situations, like Afghanistan, where there is shared poverty, they are the central dynamic, not economics. As later chapters will show, popular support, organization, unity, and government response can be affected in very important ways by societal factors. That said, in many cases, their impact is an outgrowth of their interplay with economic factors.

Economic Factors

As even a cursory look at insurrections makes clear, in most cases, economic factors of one sort or another do in fact play a key part in the outbreak and endurance of political violence.[14] Accordingly, it is necessary to assess trends related to familiar economic measurements, such as gross national product, growth rates, inflation, employment, productivity, and, especially, income distribution. While both stagnation and sudden downturns in the economy after a period of growth have been associated with insurgencies, violence may also occur during periods of prosperity and growth. In light of this, it is necessary to relate economic indicators to the expectations of various groups within the society to find out whether social groups or classes have come to believe that they are victims of institutionalized discrimination related to socioeconomic benefits (i.e., income, jobs, education, housing, health services, and so on).

Numerous past and current cases provide ample evidence that economic inequities that create a perception of relative deprivation are a major cause of insurrectionary violence. In some situations, such as in El Salvador in the 1980s, in Nicaragua under the Somoza regime, and in the Philippines and Nepal today, where small ruling elite and capitalist classes deny the peasant and working classes a fair share of the wealth, economic considerations are a primary motive for violence; in many other cases, they are interwoven with, and reinforce, other grievances. During the nationalist, anti-Japanese conflict in China, for instance, Mao consciously and successfully exploited the economic plight of the peasantry. Likewise, FLN in Algeria made flagrant economic discrimination by French settlers an integral part of its overall nationalist appeal.

Many current conflicts that seem on the surface to be based on communal rivalries turn out, upon closer inspection, to have significant economic dimensions. For example, no serious commentator would deny that the IRA's ability to take advantage of Catholic-Protestant differences in Northern Ireland during the 1970s and 1980s was related to actual and perceived economic discrimination against the Catholics. Nor could the actions against the Maronite Christian political and economic establishment in Lebanon by the Shiites in Hezbollah and other groups be explained without taking into account the long-standing relative impoverishment of the Shia community.

Institutionalized economic discrimination is often a main (if not the main) underlying cause of insurgency, as demonstrated by the preceding examples and a plethora of others, such as insurrections involving the Kurds in Iran, Turkey, and Iraq; blacks in southern Sudan; ethnic or tribal minorities in Oman and Malaya; and Muslim religious groups in southern Thailand today. Furthermore, some groups in relatively advantageous economic circumstances may also resort to illegal political violence to prevent the loss of their privileged status. To some degree, this is one motive behind the actions of Protestant preservationist groups in Northern Ireland and right-wing organizations in some Latin American countries. Where previously held privileges are eliminated and groups suffer a consequent relative economic decline, they may also turn to violence to restore their position. In Sri Lanka, minority-based Tamil insurgents took advantage of the Tamil community's decline in wealth, which resulted from losing a disproportionate share of coveted civil service positions it held by virtue of its superior educational achievements. Among these educational achievements was command of the English language. When Sinhalese politicians mandated their language as the official one (in lieu of English), a key advantage conferred by the superior education of the Tamils was swept away. The resultant anger and frustration provided the potential for political violence, which was soon actualized by Tamil militants, and a long and bloody war of secession followed.

In calling attention to the importance of economic factors in many insurgent conflicts, we do not wish to imply their primacy in all cases. As noted above, economic factors were inconsequential in the Afghan insurrection against the Soviets. The Afghan conflict was fueled by three noneconomic factors, all of which were deeply rooted in history. The first was ethnic resentment, in this case based on Uzbek, Tajik, and Hazara rejection of a new and assertive government controlled by Pashtuns who dominated the Khalq faction of the ruling Marxist party. The second was religious and nationalist resentment of foreign rule that began to take hold after the Soviet invasion in 1979. The third was resistance by local tribal chiefs and mullahs who stood to lose power as a result of centralizing efforts and reforms by the Marxist government in Kabul. While it is true that land, marriage, and educational reforms had economic implications, the real threat perceived by the insurgents was not the economic impact per se but rather the loss of local political influence they entailed.

Exceptions like Afghanistan notwithstanding, economic factors are frequently crucial to understanding an insurgency. Therefore, it behooves the analyst to ask whether, and in what way, they account for the development of the insurgency. The question of whether economic or social conditions and trends give rise to insurgent activity is closely related to the existing political culture and system and the nexus between the two. An examination of the political setting furthers our understanding of why some people and societal groups are more inclined than others to create, join, and otherwise support insurgent movements.

Political Culture

Political culture refers to the salient and enduring attitudes or orientations of people toward aspects of politics that are observable. More specifically, it encompasses their knowledge, feeling, and judgments about aspects of politics. Although studies of political culture cover a vast range of orientations toward politics, we shall limit our attention to those with noteworthy implications for insurgency.

In their pioneering cross-national study of political culture, *The Civic Culture,* Gabriel A. Almond and Sidney Verba develop three concepts—parochial, subject, and participant—to characterize the differences between people in terms of their awareness of the political process and their feelings and judgments about their ability to influence it.[15] These differences help us further understand the opportunities insurgent leaders have to mobilize support from societal groups.

Those citizens who have little or no awareness of the political system at the national level and no perception of their ability to influence it are referred to as *parochials.* They are generally illiterate, live at a subsistence level, and are located in isolated areas. Although relatively deprived and neglected, they eschew involvement in political activity, including insurgencies. The rural Indian population of Guatemala during an insurrection in the 1960s is an example. Despite their poverty and insurgent overtures, the Indians remained passive and indifferent, thus preventing the insurgent movement from developing a much-needed base of mass support among them. Simply put, groups like the Guatemalan Indians do not provide much in the way of support for insurgents unless governments intrude significantly into their areas and affairs. They simply prefer to be left alone.[16]

Subjects have become part of the political system and are aware of its impact on their lives but are not directly active in shaping policy. Normally, subjects are not inclined to join insurgent movements, as the conservative orientations of slum dwellers in many countries, especially

Latin America, have shown. This does not mean that they will tolerate adverse treatment and discrimination by the government ad infinitum. Skillful propaganda and organizing by insurgent cadres can change orientations by creating a new awareness. But since such a process may take years, governments have the time and opportunity to respond. The nature of the government's response will obviously affect the magnitude of change in popular attitudes. Where the response is poor, erstwhile loyal subjects may become alienated from the system, authorities, and policies. Once that happens, they may support insurgent movements in order to effect changes in policies they consider illegitimate.[17] Although this may also involve support for a change of regime or authorities, subjects are not motivated to become active participants in day-to-day political processes. They want better judicial, economic, and social treatment. If this is achieved by astute government reforms, they may defect from the insurgency and revert to their more passive roles. Not surprisingly, the rank-and-file members of many insurgent organizations in the Third World fall within this category.

Participants are generally educated citizens who are cognizant of national political institutions and policies and wish to engage actively in the decision-making process. Normally members of the educated strata, they are confident they can impact national events and policies effectively. With such an orientation, they are vulnerable to recruitment by insurgents if their desire to participate is blocked and if they become alienated from both the political system and authorities. Alienation of elites, as Jack Goldstone has pointed out, is a fundamental condition for revolution.[18]

Besides these three basic orientations, other attitudes rooted in more general societal values and norms may be politically relevant to insurgencies. Given the vast range of social values and norms in the world, it exceeds our purposes here to identify and classify all of them. Instead, we will suggest a few possibilities that analysts need to be aware of, with the caveat that the consideration and assessment of other values and norms may be necessary on a case-by-case basis.

In this context, attitudes and orientations involving acceptance of authority, interpersonal and intergroup trust, and tolerance of violence and foreigners can be quite important with respect to the other major factors used to analyze insurgencies. While resistance to the imposition of authority beyond immediate social groups (e.g., tribes) and low interpersonal and intergroup trust may be a major cause of violence, especially if the imposition is perceived as humiliating, the same disdain for authority and distrust can undercut the effectiveness of organized violence. In fact, it is a more important reason for the divisiveness that plagues so many insurgent movements than any temporary ideological, strategic, and tactical disputes. Such an attitude toward authority may also undermine government efforts, no matter how benign, to organize and gain support from the people.

Where there is a low tolerance for violence, insurgent recruitment will suffer, and violent acts, particularly dramatic, terrorist ones, will probably be considered repugnant, if not counterproductive. The negative reaction of Italians to the Red Brigades and the Egyptians to Islamic militant violence during the 1980s reflected their generally nonviolent cultures. In fact, in both cases, major terrorist attacks (the execution of Prime Minister Aldo Moro in Italy and the indiscriminate killing of foreign tourists in Luxor in Egypt in 1997) created revulsion toward the insurgents. Where there is a high tolerance for violence, however, the potential for the existence and growth of insurgencies is greater. This was certainly true of the Apaches, whose militant culture and socialization processes played a significant role in the persistent insurrection they waged against far superior forces in the American Southwest and parts of Mexico in the latter part of the nineteenth century.[19]

Finally, the attitude toward foreigners may be important. This is especially so when the foreigners have historically been rivals or the object of long-standing dislike, if not hatred. In such cases, involvement by foreigners can undermine whichever side they are supporting. Ostensibly, this is the case in Iraq where insurgents of all types have successfully tapped historical antipathy towards foreign occupation forces to oppose the U.S. coalition, and foreign jihadis like Abu Mussab al-Zarqawi have incurred the wrath of a number of indigenous insurgents because of the ideological threats they pose to both secularists (Saddam elements) and the Shiites.

The Afghan resistance to the former Soviet Union demonstrates how important deeply rooted sociopolitical orientations can be in providing a better understanding of the flow of events in an insurgency. The tenacity of the guerrillas in the face of the vastly greater resources of their adversary was due, in large part, to the attitudes of the various ethnoreligious groups, particularly the Pashtuns. Age-old resistance to authority in defense of tribal autonomy and individualism created stiff opposition to the extension of central government authority and a high tolerance for violence; and the emphasis on vengeance in the *Pashtunwali,* or code of conduct, contributed to an upsurge of support for the guerrillas in the wake of indiscriminate attacks by government and Soviet forces. Moreover, historical animosities toward Russians exacerbated this tendency, producing a clear target for popular wrath. Islamic religious values and norms, such as those promising eternal rewards for martyrs who fell defending Islam against nonbelievers (infidels), further reinforced these trends. On the negative side of the ledger, attitudes indicated low intergroup trust, which militated against cooperation and unity among insurgent groups. This all suggests that any analysis of the strengths and weaknesses of the two sides in Afghanistan—or elsewhere, for that matter—that ignores the country's political culture will be seriously deficient. Hence, an effort to understand and profile the political culture carefully is very important; in doing so, students of insurgency need to rely on the expertise of regional and country specialists, particularly historians, anthropologists, and sociologists.

Political System

To obtain a profile of the political system, one can consult area experts, along with political scientists specializing in the country. Since the stage of analysis that examines societal groups and their interplay will have already determined the composition of the political community, the focus at this point should be on the system, authorities, and general policies and their relationship to the political culture. As noted in chapter 2, a number of useful and readily available classification schemes in the literature on comparative politics delineate basic differences between political systems. Some of the schemes are quite detailed, others more general.[20] Regardless of which the analyst chooses, he or she must answer some basic questions.

With respect to the political system, one must ascertain the dominant values, rules, and structures involved in the political process and whether they are congruent with the political culture. In addition, one must look at subcultures (groups with orientations toward politics that deviate in various ways from overall orientations). For example, consider a traditional autocracy where, as shown in chapter 2, the values tend to be elitist and ascriptive, and structures are limited and controlled. This means that final decision-making authority at the national level is the exclusive domain of a select group deemed to have the right to rule by virtue of heredity (e.g., members of royal families in places like Morocco, Saudi Arabia, Persian Gulf sheikdoms, and Ethiopia under its former emperor, Haile Selassie). While other groups such as the military, the clergy, landowners, and businessmen are influential, their role supports existing arrangements from which they benefit. To the extent that political structures beyond the decision and support elites (e.g., parties, interest groups, and the media) are allowed to exist, their activity is controlled and carefully circumscribed. Any independent and organized opposition is prohibited, and general participation is discouraged. More often than not, religious values and norms play a key part in legitimizing a traditional autocracy.

While a number of traditional autocracies are remarkably stable, they are nonetheless vulnerable to global socioeconomic forces (the so-called process of social mobilization), such as increased media exposure, education, and geographic mobility. Such forces often heighten people's awareness of politics. This in turn can reduce parochialism and lead to demands for government services and even participation. Such changes in the political culture can be a source of trouble for traditional autocracies, particularly those with limited resources. Increased socioeconomic demands arising from formerly parochial groups that have made the transition to a subject orientation (e.g., many Indians in Guatemala in the 1980s) and demands from existing subject-orientated groups place great stress on leaders to alter the distribution of benefits. The central political question is whether the decision makers and key supporting elites are willing to share the wealth or are intransigent. For traditional autocracies like Saudi Arabia and Kuwait, excess petrodollars make it much easier to cope with such demands. For others who are less fortunate, the problem may become acute because economic stagnation or regression means that a transfer of resources is the only option, and this usually meets with resistance on the part of privileged elites who stand to lose part of their wealth.[21]

Demands for participation create even greater dilemmas for traditional autocracies or other authoritarian political systems because, as we have seen, the political values and structural makeup of such systems do not allow for broadened participation. It is precisely this situation that creates incongruence between the political culture and the political system. In some cases, leaders (e.g., the late King Hassan of Morocco and his successor, Muhammad) may buy time by establishing constitutional monarchies that permit selected oppositional parties and interest groups (e.g., unions) to function in a limited and controlled way. The long-term viability of such arrangements, however, remains questionable because the numbers of people with participatory orientations may increase. Failure by leaders to open channels to participation may then lead to insurgent activity.

Exactly the kind of political participation desired will vary. The essential questions are, who wishes to participate, and what kind of participation do they have in mind? In general, the larger and more educated the groups seeking participation, the greater the problem they can pose. Smaller groups are easier to manage. The kind of participation desired is also important. Not all demand Western-style formulas of participation. In the context of Middle Eastern political culture and style, for instance, participation is more apt to mean playing a role in the consultative process than in "one man, one vote" open elections, political parties, and so on. Where professional middle classes increasingly demand participation, careful, empirical investigation is needed to discern whether desired participation is an adaptation of local institutions or the fashioning of new ones. Whatever the case, denial of participation, especially when the authorities have already granted it, can be a major factor leading to violence. We need look no further than the years of savage terrorism that followed a January

1992 decision by Algerian authorities to terminate the second stage of national elections and to circumscribe political reforms previously enacted in response to social, economic, and political turmoil. The decision was based on the fear that the Islamic Salvation Front, which, surprisingly, had won victories, first in municipal elections in July 1990, then in the first stage of parliamentary elections in December 1991, was poised to take over parliament. The effect of the cancellation of the elections was to disenfranchise and disillusion nonviolent Islamic activists, many of whom turned to terrorist violence, which became virulent.[22]

Dynamics of Change

The preceding analysis of the impact of social, economic, and political factors is necessary, but not sufficient, for understanding the context of an insurgency, which requires, in addition, an assessment of the disruptive psychological effects of socioeconomic change in each situation.[23] In particular, we need to look at the relationship between two things: first, the ability of governments to meet rising material expectations generated by steadily growing informational awareness, elite promises, and increased education; and second, the disorientation caused by a shift from rural, traditional, social settings—in which birth determines one's station in life (ascription), benefits depend on loyalty, and religious norms restrain behavior—to impersonalized urban centers where social mobility is deemed possible, advancement depends on achievement, merit determines reward, and secularism and materialism increasingly govern behavior. The essential problem is that too many of those caught up in such a process discard their old values but end up with little material compensation. Often unemployed or underemployed, restless and psychologically cut off from the old social setting, they become rootless in the new one. Humiliated, alienated, and hopeless, they become vulnerable to insurgent recruiters who promise to return their souls, empower them, give them meaning, and lead them to a brave new world.

SUMMARY

A careful examination of the physical and human dimensions of the environment is a good starting point for analyzing an insurgency. An assessment of topography and transportation-communications systems can reveal a good deal about the potential or actual effectiveness of the strategy and forms of violence used by insurgents, particularly guerrilla warfare, whereas a careful look at demography, social groups, the economy, and the political culture and political system will shed light on the causes underlying insurgencies. It is particularly important to understand the political culture and system and how they relate to one another because political shortcomings may lead to the emergence—and intensity—of insurgencies. While social, economic, and psychological factors may be primary motivations for insurrections, the decisions and policies of political leaders may exacerbate or ameliorate situations. As chapter 8 on government response will show, many things can be done to mitigate, diminish, or eliminate insurgencies. But, whether they are likely or feasible courses of action relates closely to the calculations of political elites, whose range of choices is affected by values, ideologies, and the extant internal power structure (i.e., the system).

In the final analysis, no matter how favorable the physical milieu or how bad the social, economic, and political conditions, a serious insurgent threat will not emerge without determined opposition leaders who have the requisite skills to exploit potential opportunities and to organize at least some popular support. We now turn to the subject of what these skills are and how they are acquired.

NOTES

1. A. H. Shollom, "Nowhere Yet Everywhere," in *Modern Guerrilla Warfare*, ed. Franklin Mark Osanka (New York: The Free Press of Glencoe, 1962), 19. Numerous other authors have called attention to the importance of rugged terrain in an insurgency. See, for instance, Virgil Ney, "Guerrilla Warfare and Modern Strategy," in Osanka, *Modern Guerrilla Warfare*, 28; Brooks McClure, "Russia's Hidden Army," in Osanka, *Modern Guerrilla Warfare*, 87–91; Roger Trinquier, *Modern Warfare* (New York: Frederick A. Praeger, 1964), 16–17; and Otto Heilbrunn, *Partisan Warfare* (New York: Frederick A. Praeger, 1962), 39, 160.
2. Arthur Campbell, *Guerrillas* (New York: The John Day Co., 1968), 283.
3. On the Mao-Nasser exchange of views, see Muhammad Haykal, *The Cairo Documents* (Garden City, N.Y.: Doubleday, 1973), 312. The effect of the terrain on Palestinian operations is summarized in Bard E. O'Neill, *Armed Struggle in Palestine* (Boulder, Colo.: Westview Press, 1978), 103.
4. Numerous observers have noted the ability of the Polisario insurgents to conduct guerrilla attacks in the desert. See, for instance, Tony Hodges, *Western Sahara* (Westport, Conn.: Lawrence Hill & Co., 1983), 279–91; *New York Times*, March 15, 1977; *Washington Post*, May 29, 30, 1977; *Los Angeles Times*, November 15, 1977; and *The Age* (Melbourne), August 3, 1978.
5. C. E. S. Dudley, "Subversive Warfare—Five Military Factors," *Army Quarterly and Defence Journal* (July 1968): 209.
6. Mao Tse-tung, "On Protracted War," in *Selected Military Writings of Mao Tse-tung* (Beijing: Foreign Language Press, 1963), 200–201.
7. Che Guevara, *Guerrilla Warfare* (New York: Vintage Books, 1961), 9. On the importance of bases, see Heilbrunn, *Partisan Warfare*, 45; McClure, "Russia's Hidden Army," 90; Boyd T. Bashore, "Dual Strategy for Limited War," in Osanka, *Modern Guerrilla Warfare*, 197; Anthony Crockett, "Action in Malaya," in Osanka, *Modern Guerrilla*

Warfare, 312; George B. Jordan, "Objectives and Methods of Communist Guerrilla Warfare," in Osanka, *Modern Guerrilla Warfare,* 406; and John J. McCuen, *The Art of Counter-Revolutionary War* (Harrisburg, Pa.: Stackpole Books, n.d.), 69. An excellent recent analysis relates the limited military capabilities of Egyptian militants to their inability to establish a permanent base in Upper Egypt because of unfavorable topography. See Chuck Fahrer, "The Geography of Egypt's Islamist Insurgency," *The Arab World Geographer* 4, no. 3 (2002): 174–77.

8. Mao Tse-tung, "Strategy in Guerrilla War against Japan," *Selected Military Writings of Mao Tse-tung,* 165–66.
9. Heilbrunn, *Partisan Warfare,* 46, and Edward R. Wainhouse, "Guerrilla Warfare in Greece, 1946–1949: A Case Study," in Osanka, *Modern Guerrilla Warfare,* 226.
10. Robert Ted Gurr, *Why Men Rebel* (Princeton, N.J.: Princeton University Press, 1970), 266; Campbell, *Guerrillas,* 283.
11. Ney, "Guerrilla Warfare and Modern Strategy," 28–30, cites climate as a consideration in his discussion of environment but does not explain its relationship to guerrilla fortunes; Shollom, "Nowhere Yet Everywhere," 18, calls attention to logistical needs caused by severe weather; Bernard B. Fall, "Indochina: The Seven Year Dilemma," in Osanka, *Modern Guerrilla Warfare,* 258, cites the Vietnamese tactic of hitting the French during inclement weather to deny the latter effective air support.
12. Campbell, *Guerrillas,* 252–53, and Gene Z. Hanrahan, "The Chinese Red Army and Guerrilla Warfare," in Osanka, *Modern Guerrilla Warfare,* 159.
13. Gurr, *Why Men Rebel,* 263–64.
14. Jack A. Goldstone, "An Analytical Framework," in *Revolutions of the Late Twentieth Century,* ed. Jack A. Goldstone et al. (Boulder, Colo.: Westview Press, 1991), 37–40. An excellent discussion of the nexus between militant Islam and economic inequity and deprivation may be found in Alan Richards, *Socio-Economic Roots of Radicalism: Towards Explaining the Appeal of Islamic Radicals* (U.S. Army War College, Strategic Studies Institute, July 2003), 1–26.
15. Gabriel A. Almond and Sidney Verba, *The Civic Culture* (Princeton, N.J.: Princeton University Press, 1963). A more succinct treatment of political culture that provides the basis for our coverage of the subject is Gabriel A. Almond and G. Bingham Powell Jr., *Comparative Politics,* 2nd ed. (Boston: Little, Brown, 1978), ch. 2.
16. Vincente Collazo-Davila, "The Guatemalan Insurrection," in *Insurgency in the Modern World,* ed. Bard E. O'Neill, William R. Heaton and Donald J. Alberts (Boulder, Colo.: Westview Press, 1980), 121.
17. A recent report of cautious, conservative peasants gradually giving assistance to insurgents as a result of the latter's exploitation of socioeconomic problems may be found in the *Christian Science Monitor,* April 14, 1987. A year later, James LeMoyne observed that much of the support for the rightist Nationalist Republican Alliance during National Assembly elections had come from peasants and slum dwellers. See *New York Times,* March 24, 1988.
18. Goldstone, "An Analytical Framework," 37–47.
19. Robert N. Watt, "Raiders of a Lost Art? Apache War and Society," *Small Wars and Insurgencies* (autumn 2002): 4–17.
20. For typologies of political systems, see Almond and Powell, *Comparative Politics,* 71–76; David E. Apter, *The Politics of Modernization* (Chicago: University of Chicago

Press, 1965), 28–42, 357–421; and Charles F. Andrain, *Political Life and Social Change*, 2nd ed. (Belmont, Calif.: Duxbury Press, 1974), 188–292.

21. The problem of reconciling the interests of key elites with necessary reforms is discussed in D. Michael Shafer, *Deadly Paradigms* (Princeton, N.J.: Princeton University Press, 1988), 120–22.
22. Joachim Tzschanschel, "Algeria Torn between Fundamentalism and Democracy," *Aussenpolitik* (English ed.) (January 1993): 23–29; John P. Entelis, "The Crisis of Authoritarianism in North Africa: The Case of Algeria," *Problems of Communism* (May–June 1992): 75–81. On the complex nature of terrorism perpetrated by both the government and Islamic militants, see Report by Ahmad al-Hawwari in *Al-Watan al-Arabi* (Paris), January 23, 1998, in *FBIS-NES (INE)*, January 26, 1998.
23. Steven Metz, *The Future of Insurgency* (Carlisle Barracks, PA: Strategic Studies Institute, December 10, 1993), 2–5.

5

POPULAR SUPPORT

Most insurgent leaders know they risk destruction by confronting government forces in direct conventional engagements. Instead, they opt to erode the strength of the government through the use of terrorism or guerrilla warfare, not only to increase the human and material cost to the government but also to demonstrate its failure to maintain effective control and provide protection for the people. Eventually, according to the insurgent's logic, the authorities will grow weary of the struggle and seek to prevent further losses by either capitulating or negotiating a settlement favorable to the insurgents.

The recourse to terrorism and guerrilla warfare reflects the inferiority of insurgent organizations vis-à-vis governments, which are initially in an advantageous position because they control the administrative apparatus of the state and, most important, the army and police. To offset the superior resources of the government, many insurgent leaders stress the critical strategic role of popular support. In the words of Mao Tse-tung, "The richest source of power to wage war lies in the masses of the people." Echoing this sentiment, Bernard Fall suggests that the evidence amassed on guerrilla battlefields on three continents over three decades indicates that civilian support is the essential element of successful guerrilla operations.[1] The constant reiteration of the need for popular support, in one form or another, in the written and spoken commentaries of countless insurgent leaders demonstrates its centrality to insurgent thinking in the twentieth and twenty-first centuries, as does the attention that it receives in counterinsurgency literature and thinking. Government campaigns to "win the hearts and minds of the people" acknowledge it explicitly, and it is implicit in the often-misleading rule of thumb that governments need a favorable ten-to-one ratio of military forces to subdue guerrillas. The unspoken assumption underlying this ratio is that despite their inferiority in numbers and resources, insurgents' hit-and-run tactics, dispersal, frequent ability to exploit advantageous terrain, and ability to gain support from segments of the population make them hard to subdue and control.

Many assume that popular support must be extensive if insurgents are to succeed, due in part to the importance ascribed to popular support and a tendency to equate insurgency with the protracted-popular-war strategy. There is a twofold problem with this. First, the other strategies we studied do not emphasize extensive mass support. Second, and more important, some insurgents, like Lenin and Castro, seized power with moderate to minimal support.

As important as popular support may be, most analysts and practitioners treat it in rather general terms. The fact of the matter is that precise calculations of popular support are impossible, given the absence of careful and systematic survey research in countries where insurgencies are taking place (because of prohibitions by one or both sides and security considerations). Nevertheless, estimates can be made based on a number of sources: documents and statements by the parties to the conflict, independent observers who are able to visit insurgent or government areas, accounts of defectors, and the behavior of the people. Government analysts have the added advantage of access to highly classified data from agents, intercepted electronic communications, and the like. Since information from any single source can be distorted or completely erroneous, corroboration from several sources is necessary. In the case of Afghanistan, for instance, inadvertent statements by the Russians and Afghan authorities, reports by journalists from all parts of the world who visited guerrilla zones, and information supplied by Russian defectors all validated the proposition that the insurgents enjoyed widespread support. It could also be inferred from Russian efforts to move or destroy elements of the population in key areas, particularly along lines of communications.

To better understand the role of popular support in an insurgency, available data needs to be structured, interpreted, and related to other aspects of insurgency. To facilitate this undertaking, we discuss the notion of popular support here in terms of (1) its two types (active and passive), (2) the role of intellectuals and the masses, and (3) the various techniques that insurgents use to gain support. As we proceed, we will link the various aspects of popular support to other relevant factors of the analytical framework.

TYPES OF POPULAR SUPPORT

Passive

Passive support includes individuals who quietly sympathize with the insurgents but are unwilling to provide material assistance. Although at first glance passive supporters may seem inconsequential, they are not. At a minimum, they are not apt to betray or otherwise impede the insurgents, and this is important because the acquisition of information from the people is a key aspect of counterinsurgency strategy for government units combating elusive terrorists and guerrillas. Thus, passive support is a valuable commodity for insurgents.

Active

The most important kind of support the people can render to the insurgents is, of course, active. *Active support* encompasses those who are willing to make sacrifices and risk personal harm by either joining the movement or providing the insurgents with intelligence information, concealment, shelter, hiding places for arms and equipment, medical assistance, guides, and liaison agents. It also includes people who, in some cases, carry out acts of civil disobedience or protest that may result in severe punishment by the government. The Vietminh manual on guerrilla warfare aptly summarizes the vital part active support plays:

> Without the "popular antennae" we would be without information; without the protection of the people we could neither keep our secrets nor execute quick movement; without the people the guerrillas could neither attack the enemy nor replenish their forces and, in consequence, they could not accomplish their mission with ardour and speed. . . .
>
> The population helps us to fight the enemy by giving us information, suggesting ruses and plans, helping us to overcome difficulties due to lack of arms, and providing us with guides. It also supplies liaison agents, hides and protects us, assists our actions near posts, feeds us and looks after our wounded. . . . Cooperating with guerrillas, it has participated in sabotage acts, in diversionary actions, in encircling the enemy, and in applying the scorched earth policy. . . . On several occasions and in cooperation with guerrillas, it has taken part in combat.[2]

The importance the Vietminh ascribed to active popular support was consistent with their adherence to a protracted-popular-war strategy in which, as we saw in chapter 3, popular support is the most vital element. This does not mean active popular support is irrelevant when it comes to other strategies. Insurgents following the military-focus approach assume that substantial—but not necessarily widespread—support either exists already or will be acquired as a consequence of military success. Those following conspiratorial, urban-warfare, and transnational approaches do not require extensive mobilization of active support; yet, even here, active support does have a role. Conspirators, it will be recalled, benefit from a context of generalized discontent and seek to energize selected segments of the population at particular times. Even proponents of urban warfare with small-scale operations and organization need at least some active support to survive. Moreover, those urban-warfare strategists who envisage a transition to rural warfare believe that increased active support will eventually become necessary. As for the transnational strategy, the jury is still out since firm conclusions regarding the scope and extent of active popular support are premature and the cellular structure of Al Qaida is not conducive to mass mobilization. Whatever the case, the fact that at least some degree of active popular support is important in all insurgencies is evident from accounts of many past cases—for instance, the Boer War in South Africa and insurgencies in Greece, the Philippines, Malaya, Indochina, Algeria, Cuba, Cyprus, Kenya, China, and Sarawak.[3]

A striking contemporary example of the contribution of both passive and active popular support for an insurgent movement is Afghanistan, where poorly trained and severely divided rebels with uneven leadership and external support fought Soviet and Afghan government forces to a stalemate, even though their enemies were superior in terms of men and equipment. Almost every observer who visited the area pointed to two factors: a physical environment with many features conducive to guerrilla warfare and, more important, support for the insurgents from the vast majority of the people. As suggested above, the critical role of popular support was also acknowledged by the Soviets, occasionally in words but very clearly in their deliberate strategy of neutralizing the populace through indiscriminate attacks and forcible displacement of large numbers of people.

On the other side of the balance sheet are examples of insurgencies that have failed, owing in part to an inability to obtain at least a modicum of popular support. Che Guevara's ill-fated movement in Bolivia and the insurgency in Guatemala in the 1960s are cases in point. In both instances, efforts to entice backing from poverty-stricken peasants did not succeed, and the resulting stagnation of the insurgent groups rendered them vulnerable to government campaigns to isolate and cripple them.

Intellectuals and Masses

Populations from which insurgents seek support are not always homogeneous. As indicated in chapter 4, some or all of the following divide them: education level, socioeconomic class, race, ethnicity, and religion. These distinctions are important to bear in mind when analyzing popular support.

Educational level is especially significant and provides the basis for dividing insurgents into two general categories, the intelligentsia and the masses, each of which plays a different role. In developed countries, the terms *intelligentsia* and *intellectual class* are usually associated with leading thinkers who normally, but not exclusively, have completed graduate training at the university level. In Third World countries, the *intelligentsia* includes those with at least some undergraduate or equivalent training and, in rare cases, those who are self-taught.

Intellectuals are particularly crucial with respect to active popular support because they constitute the principal source for recruitment to both high- and middle-level leadership positions (i.e., commanders of guerrilla units, terrorist networks, and political cadres).[4] Both Ted Robert Gurr and Jack Goldstone have noted the part that intellectuals play in catalyzing insurrections, pointing out that their desertion from the government has repeatedly been a harbinger of revolution.[5] The existence of intellectual leadership is necessary for an insurgency's success because it provides strategic vision, organizational know-how, and technical competence. Conversely, insurgent movements without leadership by intellectuals, such as peasant uprisings, are, in the words of David A. Wilson, "notoriously ineffective."[6] Although support from the intellectuals is vital to an insurgency's success, the picture with respect to mass support can vary considerably, for, as noted in chapters 2 and 3, conspiratorial insurrections stress small, cohesive, elite groups. But, aside from coups, successful conspiratorial insurgencies require at least selective support from the mass population, especially if their goals call for changes in the political system or withdrawal from the political community, both of which tend to generate considerable government resistance.

The social composition of the political community affects the acquisition of popular support from both intellectuals and the masses. In my discussion of the human environment in chapter 4, I suggested that if distinct cleavages along racial, ethnic, religious, or class lines coincide with economic and political disparities, there is fertile ground for obtaining at least some popular support for an insurgency. The larger the groups that feel relatively deprived, the greater the possibilities for mobilizing mass support and sustaining a widespread insurgency (e.g., the black population in Rhodesia at the time of the Ian Smith government, the Eritrean insurrection in Ethiopia, and Angola's Union for the Total Independence of Angola insurgency, which drew its strength from the largest tribal group, the Ovimbundu). The smaller the disadvantaged groups, the smaller also the potential, since governments can deal with them more easily by encapsulating, perhaps even exiling or exterminating, them. At this juncture, an earlier point bears repeating: insurgencies based on minority groups stand a much better chance of accomplishing their aims if they are reformists, rather than secessionists, traditionalists, pluralists, egalitarians, or anarchists, because reformists generally do not require much support that cuts across group lines.

TECHNIQUES FOR GAINING POPULAR SUPPORT

While a review of the sociological composition of a political community will greatly increase understanding of an insurgency's potential for popular support, the actual level of support depends on insurgent leaders' organizational skills and techniques. Chapter 6 treats the question of organization, so my comments here are confined to methods or techniques used to gain support.

In the most promising of all insurgent environments, community support and security are "safeguarded best when the native population identifies itself spontaneously with the fortunes of the guerrilla movement."[7] But, since spontaneity is rare, insurgent movements must actively proselytize among the people. Insurgents generally employ one or several of the following methods to gain the desired support and recruits:

- charismatic attraction
- esoteric appeals
- exoteric appeals
- terrorism
- provocation of government repression
- demonstrations of potency
- coercion

All except the last of these methods aim to convince the people to render support because the insurgents' goal is just and achievable.

Charismatic Attraction

In certain cases, assertive individuals emerge as the clearly identifiable leaders of insurgent movements. When they are perceived to have supernatural qualities or when they manifest captivating oratorical skills and a dynamic, forceful personality, such leaders can frequently motivate others to join their cause through their example and persuasiveness. This is especially true in political communities where a tradition of heroic leadership is highly valued (e.g., many Middle Eastern and African states). While the process of "great men" inspiring sizable numbers to follow them may unfold in an unpremeditated and natural way, in some instances the insurgent movement may deliberately exaggerate the prowess and attributes of its leader in order to attract adherents. In these cases, the individual leader becomes the principal reason why some people support insurgent movements. The following individuals exemplify the phenomenon of charismatic attraction: Mao Tse-tung, Fidel Castro, Vladimir Lenin, and, more recently, Jonas Savimbi (Angola), Abimael Guzman (Peru), and Osama bin Ladin. In the absence of survey data, it is impossible to specify exactly how many people have joined these men's causes because of charismatic attraction, as opposed to other factors, but many observers of the insurgencies led by these men have indicated that the force of their personalities was or remains important. In view of this, we must be alert to the possible importance of charisma in any case under investigation.[8]

Esoteric Appeals

Esoteric appeals directed primarily at the intellectual stratum provide a second way to obtain popular support—one frequently associated with charismatic leadership. Esoteric appeals seek to clarify environmental conditions by putting them in a theoretical context that has neat, orderly interpretations and explanations for all perceived social, economic, and political "realities." The theoretical contexts are ideological in nature in that they set forth systematic, interrelated ideas that purport to explain the past and present and to predict the future (albeit in general terms).

Ideologies can be either secular or sacred. While both types claim to provide the truth about the destiny of man, their basis for doing so differs fundamentally. Secular ideologies limit their analyses to the observable, concrete world. They further claim that their formulations about mankind's behavior constitute scientific, or lawlike, explanations. A classic example is Marxism-Leninism, which depicts history as progressing through a series of class struggles, the last of which will result in an inevitable victory of the proletariat (working class) over the capitalist class, which will eventually lead to a utopian future devoid of exploitation and alienation forever after. Gabriel Almond captures the powerful role of political ideologies like Marxism-Leninism in the political arena:

> An ideology imputes a particular structure to political action. It defines who or what the main initiators of action are, whether they be individuals, status groups, classes, nations, magical forces, or deities. It attributes specific roles to these actors, describes their relationships with one another, and defines the arena in which actions occur.[9]

Marxist revolutionaries, for example, have found Lenin's thesis on the exploitative nature of imperialism especially persuasive in Third World countries because it provides a coherent, logical, and comprehensive explanation of the poverty, illiteracy, and oppression that often characterize the local political, economic, and social environment. Furthermore, by pointing a finger at indigenous feudal or capitalist classes and their links with foreign imperialist elements, it provides an identifiable target for the frustrations of intellectuals, especially those who are either unemployed or underemployed.[10]

Sacred ideology, or theology, also lays claims to the truth about man's past and future. It differs from secular ideology in its assertion that truth reposes in sacred revelations by a supreme being and comes to lay persons through the interpretation of those revelations by a privileged class of men (learned religious leaders). Although associated with the spiritual, rather than the material, realm, the metaphysical belief systems articulated by religious thinkers usually possess a compelling logical consistency, especially for those in search of higher meaning. In recent and current times, the sacrifices of Islamic insurgents across the world exemplify dramatically the role of theology in inspiring active popular support.

While the belief systems underlying esoteric appeals are directed primarily at the intellectuals, other aspects of ideology are important in gaining and maintaining support from both the intellectuals and the masses. Where frustrated by perceived deprivations, the people need to focus their discontent on a villain if they are to be energized to carry out or support violence. One of the functions of ideology, the explicit identification of friend and foe, meets this need. Identifying the source of frustration and grievances is important because, as Gurr notes, "discontented people act aggressively only when they become aware of the supposed source of frustration, or something or someone with whom they associate frustration."[11] In Marxist thought, poverty, repression, alienation, and the like are the natural result of rule by members of feudal or capitalist classes who exploit workers and peasants. For Islamic insurgent thinkers, the source of trouble is a ruling group that has deserted the path of Islam either by establishing a secular political system or by allowing conspicuous deviations from prescribed Islamic behavior; in other words, they blame discontent and deprivation squarely on the sinful or lax beliefs and behaviors of specific ruling authorities deemed guilty of apostasy, which is punishable by death.

The attraction of esoteric appeals based on ideology is even greater where foreign countries impose their authority directly (imperialism), exert tremendous influence through international economic networks (neoimperialism and globalization), or intervene in support of local authorities, because nationalist feelings can be evoked by depicting the outside power—along with the local authorities—as the source of deprivation. Of course, Marxist-Leninist theories that accent the intimate connection between international imperialism and indigenous capitalist or feudal ruling classes use just this tactic. The linking of foreign and domestic forces of exploitation to create a clear target for popular wrath is also evident in the cosmology of Islamic extremists, who portray the West, and particularly the United States ("the Great Satan"), as the source of evil and disintegrative moral and social changes that have led Islamic countries to humiliation and to a loss of their collective souls.[12]

Aside from this essentially nationalist variation, the general effectiveness of esoteric appeals as a method for gaining popular support should not be overemphasized. While some intellectuals may be attracted by the belief systems, in the Marxist cases that Almond examines, many people, especially among the rank and file, paid little attention to ideology at the time they joined political movements.[13] Ideology may be important, however, in determining which insurgent groups people join (i.e., choosing one group instead of another because it is more intellectually compelling). Theology seems a more important means of recruitment than secular ideology because those who join insurgencies led by religious leaders already have some familiarity with the basic beliefs and behavioral norms of the faith. But, even here, the decision to engage in, or support, violence may not spring from beliefs alone, for, as Gurr points out, men's susceptibility to beliefs that rationalize violence is a function of their discontent.[14] Discontent presupposes concrete, existing grievances.

Exoteric Appeals

Exoteric appeals focus on the concrete grievances of both the intelligentsia and the masses. In the case of the intellectuals, unemployment or underemployment can lead not only to an inadequate supply of material necessities but also to psychological dissatisfaction (i.e., lack of recognition, status, and self-worth). Exoteric appeals are essential for the acquisition of popular support from the masses. Using Communist groups to illustrate this point, Almond notes,

> The masses are only capable of registering their grievances; they cannot grasp the shape and form of the historical process in which those grievances are merely incidents. Hence, at the level of mass appeals, the Communist movement portrays itself in ways that are adapted to specific social and political settings. Persons attracted to these external representations may later be systematically exposed to the esoteric or internal doctrine in the training schools and in the higher echelons of the movement.[15]

The adaptation to specific social and political settings involves the identification of existing grievances. Since specific grievances, such as conspicuous corruption, repression by local officials, and insufficient land, food, jobs, health services, schools, and so forth, vary from case to case, both analysts and parties to the conflict must exercise care in determining exactly what the problems are. Astute insurgent leaders, most notably Mao, have stressed the need first to go among the people and find out what their grievances are in order to formulate propaganda appeals that will fall on receptive ears. Mao summarized this process as follows:

> In all practical work of our Party, correct leadership can only be developed on the principle of "from the masses to the masses." This means summing up (e.g., coordinating and systematizing after careful study) the views of the masses (i.e., views scattered and unsystematic), then taking the resulting ideas back to the masses, explaining and popularizing them until the masses embrace the ideas as their own, stand up for them and translate them into action by way of testing their correctness. Then it is necessary once more to sum up the views of the masses, and once again take the resulting ideas back to the masses so that the masses give them their whole-hearted support.[16]

As sensible as Mao's prescription may seem, it is frequently ignored by both insurgents and government leaders, who presume a priori that they understand the people's mind. A misreading of the content, extent, and intensity of popular grievances can have costly, sometimes fatal, consequences. Two contemporary examples, one involving an insurgent group, the other a government, illustrate this point. The Popular Front for the Liberation of Oman (PFLO) rightly identified government neglect as a source of discontent among tribesmen in Dhofar Province but wrongly assumed that the tribesmen wanted—or would accept—reforms in the areas of property ownership, religion, and traditional authority patterns. When PFLO leaders tried to solidify and expand support by implementing a program consisting of communal property, the elimination of Islamic influences, and centralized control in "liberated zones," they met with stiff resistance from tribesmen, who highly valued private ownership, individualism, and tribal autonomy. When the PFLO reacted to the resistance with harsh repression, defections from the rank and file ensued, rendering the insurgency more vulnerable to government reforms directed at popular demands for better administration and social services.

The second contemporary example illustrates how governments sometimes misconstrue popular demands and thereby create exoteric grievances that insurgents can exploit. Witness the urbanized Marxists who seized power in Afghanistan in April 1978 and proceeded to promulgate land, educational, and marriage reforms that they mistakenly assumed would meet with popular approval. Instead, they found spreading opposition among tribal and religious leaders, as well as rank-and-file Afghans, who perceived themselves as losers under the new arrangement. Ironically, the government's reforms proved to be the major impetus behind the insurrection in its early phase (1978–1979). Hence, what at first appeared to be popular measures designed to address exoteric grievances actually became the source of exoteric grievances that fueled an insurrection. The lesson is clear: assumptions about popular grievances that do not have a solid empirical basis can be quite erroneous, since the source of exoteric grievances is the people, not what elites, however well disposed, presume.

Terrorism

Where esoteric and exoteric appeals do not yield expected support (because they are defective or because of effective government action or environmental disadvantages), insurgents may turn to terrorism to obtain popular support by demonstrating the government's weaknesses in the face of insurgent initiatives.[17] Insurgents' success in this undertaking depends in large part on two factors: the target of terror and the length of terrorist campaigns.[18]

If insurgents target individuals or groups disliked by the people, terrorism may lead oppressed and exploited people to identify with them. By manipulating resentment (based on grievances) and using selective terror against hated individuals and groups, insurgents may well increase popular support. Such was the case during the Cypriot insurrection against the British and in the Algerian war against France, where colonial officials and Muslims who sympathized with the French were targeted. This tactic is also evident today in Al Qaida's attacks against Western secularists, who are referred to as Crusaders and Jews, both of whom are explicitly identified as oppressors.[19]

Relying on terrorism as a means to garner popular support runs the risk of its prolongation and intensification, which may be counterproductive for two reasons: first, it can disrupt traditional lifestyles, making life increasingly miserable for the general population; second, failure to replace terrorism with more effective military operations can create the impression that insurgents have lost the initiative and that their chances of success are remote. Even worse, there is a danger that as it continues, terrorism will become indiscriminate. If this occurs, insurgents can end up alienating potential domestic and international supporters. Both the experts and our own case studies suggest that the Malayan Communist Party, Mau Mau in Kenya, the Irish Republican Army (IRA) in Ulster, the Red Brigades in Italy, and the Shining Path in Peru all suffered both defections and decreased popular support because of their indiscriminate actions. The precariousness and uncertainty surrounding indiscriminate terrorism was clearly evident during the rocket attacks by insurgents against the Afghan capital of Kabul in the summer of 1988. Although one observer indicated that the solidarity between the people and the mujahedin led some to ascribe the attacks to the government side (specifically, to the Russians), the leader of the Jamiat-i-Islami ("Society of Islam") forces was concerned that the ultimate impact would be counterproductive. Hence, he ordered his fighters to ensure that the rocket attacks focused on military and government targets, not civilian areas.[20]

As for transnational terrorism, there is little to suggest that it was a significant means of acquiring popular support in the twentieth century. If anything, the decision by groups like the Popular Front for the Liberation of Palestine (PFLP), Black September, and the Abu Nidal Organization to engage in transnational terrorism was generally associated with three things: a marginal capability to operate inside the target area (in this case, Israel and the Occupied Territories), questionable or shaky domestic support, and a desperate need to demonstrate that the insurgent movement was neither defunct nor impotent. As dramatic and newsworthy as transnational terrorist acts like bombings and skyjackings may have been, there is no evidence that any groups that carried them out in the past three decades gained any appreciable degree of popular support through such actions. In fact, the PFLP and Black September eventually terminated such acts in part because they tarnished the image of the Arabs. Inconsistent statements by Palestinian Liberation Organization (PLO) public relations spokesmen and other officials alternately bragged about and took responsibility for such acts and disavowed them altogether, showing that the PLO understood the negative perception of transnational terrorism both internationally and within parts of the Palestinian community.[21]

Whether the relationship between popular support and transnational terrorism will change in the years ahead remains an open question. Although Al Qaida believes that such actions will increase support by demonstrating the ability of jihadis to strike the hated sources and symbols of oppression where they are supposedly most secure, repeated, indiscriminate attacks against civilians could have the same negative effects they have had in other cases, namely, by engendering opposition among erstwhile sympathizers and potential recruits.

Provocation of Government Repression

A fifth means that insurgents utilize in winning popular support is the age-old tactic of "catalyzing and intensifying counter-terror which further alienates the enemy from the local population."[22] Basque Homeland and Liberty (ETA) in Spain has made the most explicit commitment to this tactic, referring to it as the "action-reaction spiral theory." Insurgents carry out attacks to provoke arbitrary and indiscriminate government reprisals against the population, calculating that this will increase resentment and win the insurrectionary forces more support. The nature of the government response and the social groups involved affect the success of such an insurgent ploy. Excessive violence by military and police units—an all-too-frequent occurrence in insurrections—and government-sponsored vigilantes (death squads) is generally recognized as a factor accounting for increased support for insurgents in many cases, such as Bangladesh in 1971 and El Salvador in the late 1970s and early 1980s. Even where ruthless methods by the government restore law and order in the short term, the long-term effect may be, as Richard Clutterbuck indicates, to sow the seeds of further insurgency. A good example is Guatemala, where indiscriminate violence by right-wing death squads helped quell an insurrection by the late 1970s but created resentment that led to a renewal of insurgent activity in the early 1980s.[23]

The importance of social heterogeneity as a factor in examining popular support is less clear in the context of harsh government repression. Jerry Silverman and Peter Jackson have argued that group solidarity between the insurgents and the people may lead the population to forgive the violent excesses of insurgents but not those of government forces drawn from rival racial, ethnic, or religious groups.[24] That insurgent leaders believe ruthless violence against the people by governments controlled by rival groups can be instrumental in obtaining support is obvious in their propaganda and information campaigns, which seek to dramatize "massacres," "slaughters," and the like and to associate them with the different social composition of the ruling authorities.

Efforts to exploit intergroup differences, distrust, and dislike in this way have had mixed results. On the one hand, there have been numerous reports of indiscriminate government crackdowns and violence leading to increased popular support for insurgents (e.g., the upswing in support for Tamil insurgents in Sri Lanka in the late summer of 1984 after uncontrolled attacks by Sinhalese army units and Russian excesses in Chechnya); on the other hand, there are instances in which such behavior has actually led to animosity directed at the insurgents. In Vietnam, for example, the Vietcong ploy of provoking American air attacks against villages by firing at aircraft from nearby areas sometimes led local Vietnamese to blame the guerrillas. Similarly, in southern Lebanon, there were cases in 1969 in which Israeli attacks in Shiite Muslim areas in retaliation for PLO raids led the Shiites to petition the government in Beirut to remove the Palestinians, who are fellow Arabs.

While a definite answer as to why these and other differential reactions occurred requires more careful and systematic inquiry, a few propositions may be useful. To begin with, indiscriminate violence by government forces seems to provide the greatest impetus for supporting insurgencies among uncommitted persons who have lost close friends or especially relatives because of such violence, as well as among those who were already contemplating supporting the insurgents because of other grievances. Those who have lost friends, relatives, parents, and so forth to government violence seem more inclined to render support to insurgents if they live in cultures like Chechnya's, where vengeance is customary and expected. It was certainly true in Afghanistan, where, as mentioned before, the code of conduct stresses, besides other things, blood vengeance (*badal*). In such contexts, where loss of life is concerned, it is desirable to kill a member of the offender's group. Accordingly, it was hardly surprising that visitors to guerrilla areas in Afghanistan reported that revenge for indiscriminate violence was a key factor generating support for the resistance against the Soviets. In the words of one Afghan guerrilla, "Every time a Russian helicopter gunship strafes a village, every man in it will not rest until he has drawn Russian blood." On another occasion, Abdul Haq, one of the leading field commanders, explained the tenacious resistance to the Russians with one word—"revenge."[25]

Demonstrations of Potency

The sixth technique insurgents may rely on to obtain support, demonstrations of potency, has two dimensions: meeting the needs of the people through an administrative apparatus (shadow government) that provides social services (e.g., schools, health clinics), and gaining the military initiative. The first aspect manifests not only the insurgents' presence but also the corresponding government failure to deal with shadow-government political cadres. Besides governing, guerrilla political operators normally seek to meet some of the people's basic needs and cooperate with them in such mundane affairs as harvesting crops and building schools. Of this, Andrew Molner and his associates, write,

> The agent, much like a ward or precinct politician, surveys the needs, likes and dislikes of the people in his district. He may keep individual records on all who live in his area of responsibility. He may find jobs for the unemployed, arrange housing for those who do not have shelter, or assist farmers with their crops.
>
> In rural areas and small villages, where the close personal contacts among the villagers make it difficult to organize secret cells, a special technique is used. An insurgent force marches into and takes over a village. They assist the farmers in the fields in this way to develop close contacts in spite of having come uninvited.[26]

Quite often, the extension of such aid to people will be the first step in involving them with the insurgent movement, either actively or passively. This would seem to be especially true where the government has been delinquent in meeting the people's needs. The social services provided by

Hamas in the West Bank and Gaza Strip over the past two decades provide a striking illustration.

The second means of demonstrating potency, gaining the military initiative, is designed in part to create the impression that the insurgency has momentum and will succeed. A number of writers have stressed the important part initiative plays in acquiring new recruits and boosting and sustaining morale within insurgent organizations. "Units that are active and successful in the accomplishment of assigned missions build up a high esprit de corps and attract followers; success is contagious." Put another way, "No guerrilla movement in the field can afford to remain inactive for long; by so doing, it loses its morale and sense of purpose."[27] Al Qaida's recognition of this principle is without doubt a motivating force for many of its terrorist attacks.

In his quest to gain the initiative, the insurgent has at his disposal a flexible arsenal of tactics—ambushes, sabotage, kidnapping, assassinations, mass attacks, bombings, and so on. In order to maximize the effectiveness of such diverse methods, however, insurgents must have a coordinated strategy, which in turn requires cohesion. Although chapter 6 addresses the question of cohesion, a few comments about its relationship to popular support are necessary at this point. In insurgent movements, not only will competing centers of loyalty raise command and control problems that undercut military operations and initiative, but they may also lead some potential supporters to believe the resistance is in a state of confusion. The corresponding picture of weakness may dissuade many from joining. Moreover, violent conflict between insurgent groups may appear to be a demonstration of impotency that saps the movement's overall strength, diverts it from the main enemy, and denies it a positive public image. The spectacle of various insurgent organizations criticizing each other in order to enhance their stature is bound to bewilder potential recruits.

Military initiative requires continuous victories. Since guerrillas are usually weak at the start of hostilities, these may be small successes initially. But such tactical self-sacrifices at the beginning may be necessary for eventual victory.[28] Local victories in guerrilla war, however, are heavily dependent on popular support; hence, initiative and popular support are interdependent.

Initiative requires freedom of action. As Mao wrote, "Freedom of action is the very life of an army and once this freedom is lost, an army faces defeat or annihilation."[29] Although normally associated with operations in the target country, freedom of action is at times related to sanctuaries outside the country. These sanctuaries, which involve external support, are of great importance if, during the incipient stages of the conflict, the resistance movement has difficulty operating within the target country's borders. In such circumstances, the attitude of contiguous states will assume a major role in the conflict since the territory of such states constitutes the insurgent's last fallback position. One should not conclude from this, however, that guerrillas can operate indefinitely from outside the target state. At some point, they must establish a popular base within the target country. Douglas Hyde has called attention to the fact that guerrillas in Sarawak found that operating from bases across the border in Indonesia had a deleterious effect on the insurgent movement because it prevented direct and continuous contact between leaders and guerrillas. As a result, the insurgents had to make an effort to set up bases in Sarawak itself.[30]

A final aspect of initiative that deserves mention is what Hyde has called the dramatic gesture. Insurgents employ this tactic, which may involve guerrilla, conventional, or terrorist acts, to convince world and domestic opinion that they are not just rabble but are active and fighting for a worthwhile goal. Along these lines, Shadi Abdullah, an Islamic militant, revealed that the leader of Al Tawhid wa al-Jihad ("Monotheism and Holy War"), Abu Mussab al-Zarqawi, planned major attacks in Germany in 2002 that, in Abdullah's view, would have made the organization "very famous." As he put it, "It would have had the same message as the attacks of Al Qaida on Sept. 11, namely that our organization is as active in other parts of the world."[31]

The problem with dramatic gestures, of course, is that they frequently indicate not only that other techniques for gaining popular support have failed but that their effects will be short-lived if they are not followed by the skilled use of the other techniques. Moreover, terrorist acts may have the effect of alienating the people if they are repugnant. As mentioned before, a case in point was the backlash from the general population and even some insurgents when the Red Brigades murdered Aldo Moro, the former Italian prime minister, in 1978. The infamous seizure of the school in the Russian town of Beslan by Chechen secessionists in September 2004 may have a similar midterm, negative effect for the Chechens, and perhaps for Islamic militants in general, if the immediate outpouring of criticism and indignation by Muslim intellectuals is any indicator. Whether it does will depend on government reforms and enlightened policies that take advantage of the psychological fallout. By contrast, reliance on counterforce and revenge will simply neutralize anti-insurgent feelings and, thus, eliminate an opportunity to reduce popular support for the insurgents.[32]

Coercion

Despite their best efforts, insurgents may still find major segments of the population unresponsive. When this happens, there is a great temptation to turn to the final technique for gaining support, coercion. This is the least effective because of the resentment it causes and the weak commitment of those who are directly victimized. The situation in insurgent-controlled areas of El Salvador during 1984 amply demonstrated this point. Frustrated by a lack of support, the insurgents pressured peasants to collectivize plots of land to feed the rebel forces, to send their children to insurgent-run schools, to form labor gangs to repair roads and carry wounded guerrillas, and to join military units as fighters. Young men who did not respond favorably were abducted and compelled to join. The bitterness that resulted was obvious to visiting journalists and acknowledged by insurgent cadres. One leader of the Popular Liberation Forces said, "We do not renounce our right to recruit from the population, but we realize that our image has been damaged by the recruitment. It is better to build the consciousness of the people to induce them to join us."[33]

The negative impact of coercion on attempts to gain popular support raises the larger question of insurgent rectitude in dealing with the population. Simply put, actions that victimize the population can undermine painstaking efforts to acquire support by relying on various combinations of techniques other than coercion. Mao recognized this and clearly articulated it in a code of conduct for dealing with the people. In what he referred to as "Eight Points of Attention," he admonished his military forces to do the following:

- Speak politely.
- Pay fairly for what you buy.
- Return everything you borrow.
- Pay for anything you damage.
- Do not hit or swear at people.
- Do not damage crops.
- Do not take liberties with women.
- Do not ill-treat captives.[34]

As chapter 3 points out, some contemporary insurgents who subscribe to the protracted-popular-war strategy have deviated from Mao's admonitions, incorporating economic sabotage and terrorism into their strategic approach (i.e., the New People's Army in the Philippines, the Shining Path in Peru, and the Farabundo Marti National Liberation Front in El Salvador). In each case, such actions weakened the government's capabilities but also led to popular resentment, thus undercutting the insurgents' quest for active support.[35] Economic sabotage and terrorism can have different effects over the long term, depending on the government response. If governments under attack do not rectify their own deficiencies and begin to address socioeconomic problems seriously, the insurgents may succeed, despite their excesses. But if governments do begin to turn things around, such insurgent excesses may prove fatal mistakes.

SUMMARY

Of all the factors influencing the progression of insurgencies, popular support probably receives the most attention in the literature and oratory of the participants. This is to be expected, in view of its critical role in offsetting government strengths. Because acquiring popular support, especially active support, is not an easy task, it requires considerable effort on the part of the insurgents. The choices they make from among the seven methods for inducing support and the skill and wisdom they show in applying the methods will influence their success or failure. Whether those choices and the quality of their effort will prove beneficial depends, in turn, on the judgments and assessments insurgents make vis-à-vis the other elements of the larger strategic equation. This is especially true regarding such variables as the environment, organization, cohesion, external support, and the government response because each of these will present various opportunities and obstacles. Attention to the broader strategic perspective also permits sounder judgments about how much popular support is needed. A strong organizational effort is called for when that need is considerable, a point to which we now turn.

NOTES

1. Bernard B. Fall, *The Two Viet-Nams,* 2nd rev. ed. (New York: Frederick A. Praeger, 1967), 345. The quote from Mao may be found in Mao Tse-tung, *Selected Military Writings of Mao Tse-tung* (Beijing: Foreign Language Press, 1967), 260.
2. Cited in Otto Heilbrunn, *Partisan Warfare* (New York: Frederick A. Praeger, 1962), 87. The Vietminh directives quoted by Heilbrunn were first published by the État-Major de la Force Publique in Leopoldville in *Bulletine Militaire* (June and August 1955) under the title "Guerrilla selon l'ecole Communists."
3. See, for example, John J. McCuen, *The Art of Counter-Revolutionary War* (Harrisburg, Pa.: Stackpole Books, n.d.), 30, 53, 55–56; Arthur Campbell, *Guerrillas* (New York: John Day Co., 1968), 4, 279–81; Julian Paget, *Counter-Insurgency Campaigning* (New York: Walker & Co., 1967), 22–23, 27–28; Virgil Ney, "Guerrilla Warfare and Modern Strategy" in *Modern Guerrilla Warfare*, ed. Franklin Mark Osanka (New York: The Free Press of Glencoe, 1962), 31–34; Douglas Hyde, *The Roots of Guerrilla Warfare* (Chester Springs, Pa.: Dufour Editions, 1968), 53, 55, 104–8, 122–23, 131–32; Roger Trinquier, *Modern Warfare* (New York: Frederick A. Praeger, 1964), 8, 55; Peter Paret and John W. Shy, *Guerrillas in the 1960s,* rev. ed. (New York: Frederick A. Praeger, 1962), 45–51; Heilbrunn, *Partisan Warfare,* 16, 34, 36, 86–87.
4. For an analysis of the role and traits of the intelligentsia in the Third World, see Harry J. Benda, "Non-Western Intelligentsias as Political Elites," in *Political Change in*

Underdeveloped Countries, ed. John H. Kautsky (New York: John Wiley and Sons, 1967), 235–51. On their role in insurgencies, see David A. Wilson, *Nation Building and Revolutionary War* (Santa Monica, Calif.: The Rand Corporation, 1962), 7; Gil Carl Alory, *The Involvement of Peasants in Internal Wars,* Research Monograph no. 24 (Princeton, N.J.: Center for International Studies, Princeton University, 1966), 16–19.

5. Ted Robert Gurr, *Why Men Rebel* (Princeton, N.J.: Princeton University Press, 1970), 337, and Jack A. Goldstone, "An Analytical Framework," in *Revolutions of the Late Twentieth Century*, ed. Jack A. Goldstone et al. (Boulder, Colo.: Westview Press, 1991), 37–47.
6. Wilson, *Nation Building and Revolutionary War,* 7; Alroy, *The Involvement of Peasants in Internal Wars,* 16–19.
7. Ney, "Guerrilla Warfare," 34.
8. Suggestive analyses of the psychological foundations of the leader-follower relationship may be found in Bruce Mazlish, *The Revolutionary Ascetic* (New York: Basic Books, 1976), especially 22–43; E. Victor Wolfenstein, *The Revolutionary Personality* (Princeton, N.J.: Princeton University Press, 1967), 174–239. Both Mazlish and Wolfenstein limit their focus to revolutionary leaders. For a more general and historical examination of leaders that distinguishes between eventful and event-making men, see Sidney Hook, *The Hero in History* (Boston: Beacon Press, 1943), 151–83.
9. Gabriel A. Almond, *The Appeals of Communism* (Princeton, N.J.: Princeton University Press, 1954), 62. On the basic distinction between esoteric and exoteric appeals, see Almond, *Appeals of Communism*, 65–66; and Morris Watnick, "The Appeal of Communism to the Underdeveloped Peoples," in Kautsky, *Political Change in Underdeveloped Countries.* The same dichotomy is implicit in Peter Van Ness, *Revolution and Chinese Foreign Policy* (Berkeley: University of California Press, 1970), 118–19; and Gurr, *Why Men Rebel,* 195. Many scholars have discussed the functions of ideology; among them, David Apter stands out. As Apter maintains, an ideology imparts a sense of solidarity and self-esteem to followers; see his *The Politics of Modernization* (Chicago: University of Chicago Press, 1965), 354–70. An excellent example of esoteric appeals in a particular case may be found in G. L. Vasquez, "Peruvian Radicalism and the Sendero Luminoso," *Journal of Political and Military Sociology* (winter 2003): 197–216
10. V. I. Lenin, *Imperialism: The Highest Stage of Capitalism* (New York: International Publishers, 1969), 1–128. Other aspects of Leninist thought, such as the leading role of the intellectuals within the revolutionary party, enhance its attractiveness for many intellectuals. See John H. Kautsky, *Communism and the Politics of Development* (New York: John Wiley and Sons, 1968), 77. Van Ness, *Revolution and Chinese Foreign Policy,* 118, notes one effect of the Chinese revolutionary model was to provide revolutionary cadres with a theoretical plan or practical ideology for making a revolution.
11. Gurr, *Why Men Rebel,* 119.
12. The effectiveness of nationalist appeals based on resistance to outsiders is summarized in an astute comparative analysis of the Spanish resistance to Napoleon and the Afghan resistance to the Soviets by Anthony James Joes, "Continuity and Change in Guerrilla War: The Spanish and Afghan Cases," *The Journal of Conflict Studies* (fall 1996): 64–74. Thomas H. Greene has argued that "an ideology that appeals to national identity is the most powerful symbolic means of mobilizing revolutionary support." See his *Comparative Revolutionary Movements* (Englewood Cliffs, N.J.: Prentice-Hall, 1974),

52. Also see Carl Leiden and Karl Schmitt, *The Politics of Violence* (Englewood Cliffs, N.J.: Prentice-Hall, 1968), 107–8. The depiction of the West and especially the United States as the enemy of Islam is well known by now. See Roland Jacquard, *In the Name of Osama bin Laden* (Durham, N.C.: Duke University Press, 2002), 73–85; Daniel Benjamin and Steven Simon, *The Age of Sacred Terror* (New York: Random House, 2002), 117–20; Rohan Gunaratna, *Inside Al Qaeda* (New York: Columbia University Press, 2002), 28–29.
13. Almond, *Appeals of Communism*, 65. The failure of the masses to perceive the larger ideological aims of insurgent leadership elites is a major conclusion of Haim Gerber, *Islam, Guerrilla War and Revolution* (Boulder, Colo.: Lynne Rienner, 1988). Also see Stathis N. Kalyvas, "New and Old Civil Wars: A Valid Distinction?" *World Politics* (October 2001): 106–7.
14. Gurr, *Why Men Rebel*, 208.
15. Almond, *Appeals of Communism*, 66.
16. Mao Tse-tung, "On Methods of Leadership," in *Selected Works* (New York: International Publishers, 1958), 4:113, quoted in McCuen, *The Art of Counter-Revolutionary War*, 55–56.
17. McCuen, *The Art of Counter-Revolutionary War*, 32, and Paget, *Counter-Insurgency Campaigning*, 28, see terror as a response to government action; Gurr, *Why Men Rebel*, 236, views terror as systematically related to the balance of coercive control and believes it is likely when dissidents are very weak relative to the regime.
18. The impact of terrorism has led some scholars and practitioners to contend that terror is the most powerful weapon for establishing community support. Roger Trinquier, for example, calls it the principal weapon of modern warfare (revolutionary warfare) and suggests that by making people feel insecure, it leads them to lose confidence in the government and draws them to the guerrillas for protection; see his *Modern Warfare*, 16–17. It has been argued that the Chinese Communists' ability to get popular support without large-scale terror is atypical because most insurgents start without the degree of popular backing that Mao had and therefore must resort to terror. See, for example, Brian Crozier, *The Study of Conflict* (London: The Institute for the Study of Conflict, 1970), 7.
19. Alf Andrew Heggoy, *Insurgency and Counterinsurgency in Algeria* (Bloomington: Indiana University Press, 1972), 114; Jerry M. Silverman and Peter M. Jackson, "Terror in Insurgency Warfare," *Military Review* (October 1970): 62–64; Paget, *Counter-Insurgency Campaigning*, 65; Benjamin and Simon, *The Age of Sacred Terror*, 117, 256–57.
20. Silverman and Jackson, "Terror in Insurgency Warfare," 64–67; McCuen, *The Art of Counter-Revolutionary War*, 33. In the fall of 1951, the insurgents of the Malayan Communist Party realized that intimidation was not gaining popular support, so they issued a directive prohibiting attacks on innocent people. See Richard L. Clutterbuck, *The Long, Long War* (New York: Frederick A. Praeger, 1966), 63. Paget, *Counter-insurgency Campaigning*, 29, 93, points out that the Mau Mau in Kenya retained a degree of popular support until they alienated the population with the massacre of Kikuyu tribesmen in the village of Lari in March 1953. Ironically, the Kikuyu were the main base of support for the Mau Mau. Heilbrunn, *Partisan Warfare*, 89, points out that the Vietminh were concerned about the effects of terror on the people and, there-

fore, argued that sabotage was important but should serve the interests of the people by not interfering with the lifestyle and production of the region. On the Afghan rocket attacks, see the *Washington Times*, August 1, 24, 1988. On Sendero Luminoso, see Cyrus Ernesto Zirakzadeh, "From Revolutionary Dreams to Organizational Fragmentation: Disputes over Violence within ETA and Sendero Luminoso," *Terrorism and Political Violence* (winter 2002): 79–81; Gordon H. McCormick, *The Shining Path and Peruvian Terrorism*, Rand Report, 1987, 20; James Ron, "Ideology in Context: Explaining Sendero Luminoso's Tactical Escalation," *Journal of Peace Research* 38, no. 5 (2001): 588.

21. Until the Jordanian civil war of 1970, Fatah, the largest and most important organization in the PLO, saw little to be gained from transnational terrorism. After 1970, Fatah secretly backed the operations of Black September. By the end of 1973, Fatah had pulled back from transnational terrorism. Since that time, it has been critical of transnational terrorism and ambivalent about terrorism inside Israel and the occupied territories. My own discussions with Palestinians over the past two decades revealed considerable disenchantment with, and criticism of, transnational terrorist attacks.
22. J. K. Zawodny, "Unconventional Warfare," in *Problems of National Strategy*, ed. Henry A. Kissinger (New York: Frederick A. Praeger, 1965), 340–41. Peter Braestrup, "Partisan Tactics—Algerian Style," in Osanka, *Modern Guerrilla Warfare*, 393, argued that such was the case with the French in Algeria; see also Fall, *The Two Viet-Nams*, 348–52.
23. Clutterbuck, *The Long, Long War*, 178–79. On the effects of death-squad activity in El Salvador, see T. David Mason and Dale R. Krane, "The Political Economy of Death Squads: Toward a Theory of the Impact of State-Sanctioned Terror," *International Studies Quarterly* (1989): 175–98. On the action-reaction spiral theory of ETA, see Francisco J. Llera, Jose M. Mata, and Cynthia L. Irvin, "ETA: From Secret Army to Social Movement—The Post Franco Schism of the Basque Nationalist Movement," *Terrorism and Political Violence* (autumn 1993): 16.
24. Silverman and Jackson, "Terror in Insurgency Warfare," 67; *Washington Times*, August 24, 1988.
25. See *New York Times*, March 22, 1982; *Washington Times*, October 25, 1988.
26. Andrew R. Molner, James M. Tinker, and John D. LeNoir, *Human Factors Considerations of Underground in Insurgencies* (Washington, D.C.: American University, Center for Research in Social Systems, 1966), 109; also see Vo Nguyen Giap, *People's War, People's Army* (New York: Bantam Books, 1968), 50.
27. George B. Jordan, "Objectives and Methods of Communist Guerrilla Warfare," in Osanka, *Modern Guerrilla Warfare*, 404, 409, and Paget, *Counter-Insurgency Campaigning*, 22. Other writers also stress the importance of initiative in guerrilla warfare; see, for instance, McCuen, *The Art of Counter-Revolutionary War*, 20, 35; Hyde, *The Roots of Guerrilla Warfare*, 123; Campbell, *Guerrillas*, 26; Heilbrunn, *Partisan Warfare*, 60–61, 67–68. Trinquier, *Modern Warfare*, 52, argues somewhat differently in that he believes the goal of guerrilla warfare is the creation of insecurity rather than local success. In this formulation he appears to overlook the fact that the two are compatible because local success can create insecurity as well as achieve other guerrilla aims, such as obtaining popular support and boosting insurgent morale. On the provision of services by Hamas, see Ilana Kass and Bard O'Neill, *The Deadly Embrace* (Lanham, Md.: National Institute for Public Policy and University Press of America, 1997), 260–61.

28. Edward L. Katzenbach Jr. and Gene Z. Hanrahan, "The Revolutionary Strategy of Mao Tse-tung," in Osanka, *Modern Guerrilla Warfare*, 144–45.
29. Mao Tse-tung, "On Protracted War," in *Selected Works* (London: n.p., 1954), 2:211ff., quoted in Heilbrunn, *Partisan Warfare*, 56.
30. Hyde, *The Roots of Guerrilla Warfare*, 86–88. He also cites his conversations with Huk leaders in the Philippines who said the government's ability to sever the leaders from the rest of the movement was a key reason for their downfall.
31. Hyde, *The Roots of Guerrilla Warfare*, 36–37, 43. Abdullah is quoted by Faye Bowers and Peter Grier in the *Christian Science Monitor*, May 11, 2004.
32. While the Aldo Moro assassination is generally viewed as the Red Brigades' most impressive operation, it was also a turning point. The operation caused a rift in the brigades, alienated the public, and provided an impetus to improve counterterrorist policies. According to one former brigade member, it also led less competent and more unsavory elements to enter the organization. See *New York Times*, January 29, 1982; *Christian Science Monitor*, May 11, 1982, and March 27, 1987; and *Washington Post*, June 1, 1983. On the Beslan incident, see *New York Times*, September 9, 2004.
33. Christian Science Monitor, August 27, 1984. Also see Christian Science Monitor, August 28, 1984.
34. Mao Tse-tung, *Selected Military Writings of Mao Tse-tung* (Beijing: Foreign Language Press, 1967), 343.
35. *New York Times*, March 24 and June 5, 1988; *Washington Post*, May 20 and July 26, 1988; *Christian Science Monitor*, June 17, 1988.

6

ORGANIZATION AND UNITY

The ability of insurgent movements to compensate for the material superiority of their opponents by acquiring popular and external support depends on their organizational skills. Indeed, when analysts and observers emphasize the point that insurgency is more a political phenomenon than a military one, they usually have in mind the great amount of time and effort insurgents devote to organizational matters. Three structural dimensions—scope, complexity, and cohesion—and two functions—instrumental services and channels for expressive protest—are of primary interest when examining an insurgent organization.[1]

SCOPE

Scope refers to the numbers and kinds of people across the political spectrum either playing key roles in the movement (political cadres, terrorists, guerrillas, and regular soldiers) or providing active support. As might be expected in light of the clandestine nature of much insurgent activity, most attempts to tabulate insurgent numbers yield rough estimates. Because of this and because of variations among insurgencies with respect to goals, strategies, forms of warfare, environmental conditions, external support, and government responses, there are no precise numerical thresholds that correlate with success or failure. Consequently, upward or downward trends need to be assessed in terms of the overall situation. Noticeable single-direction increases or decreases in insurgent numbers over the course of several months or longer can suggest the trends of an insurgency. Particularly important are continuing defections from insurgent ranks since they usually indicate hard times, if not failure. It was not happenstance that the setbacks and containment of the Popular Front for the Liberation of Oman in the mid-1970s followed steadily increasing desertions during the early 1970s.[2] The same could be said of the diminishing effectiveness of the Thai Communist insurgents after significant defections among Thai intellectuals following a return to civilian rule and an amnesty program in 1982. Many of the defectors had at one time bolstered the insurgency after fleeing repression by a military government.[3]

COMPLEXITY

Parallel Hierarchies

Whatever the scope of the insurgency, the effective use of people will depend on the skill of insurgent leaders in identifying, integrating, and coordinating the different tasks and roles essential for success in combat operations, training, logistics, communications, transportation, and the medical, financial, informational, diplomatic, and supervisory areas. The complexity of the organizations designed to perform these functions reflects insurgent strategies.

Insurgents who subscribe to conspiratorial and urban-warfare strategies stress small, closely knit, and secretive organizations with minimal complexity. In fact, a few, notably anarchists, hardly wish for any organization at all. By contrast, those who adopt military-focus or protracted-popular-war strategies require more sophisticated organizational structures because they normally anticipate a long struggle that will involve support for substantial military activity.

As pointed out before, some insurgents follow a military-focus strategy because they are not concerned with creating political structures since they already exist. During the American Civil War, for example, the Confederacy simply used existing state and local government structures to perform various functions in support of the war. But not all insurgents who opt for a military-focus strategy inherit organizational structures. Although they may emphasize fighting, rather than waiting for political structures to take shape, the insurgents cannot, as Che Guevara and Regis Debray have both argued, ignore organization altogether. Indeed, structural development is necessary in order to take advantage of military success and further escalate the struggle.[4] Insurgents who follow a protracted-popular-war strategy not only share this view but go a step further by stressing party primacy and assiduous political organizing prior to hostilities. The complex organizations that emerge are commonly referred to as parallel hierarchies or shadow governments in the literature on insurgencies.[5]

The parallel hierarchy can take several forms. One is the use of existing government political-administrative institutions through the infiltration of insurgent agents. If infiltration is widespread, the insurgents can not only obtain information about government plans and impending actions but also expand their influence by exercising de facto control over parts of the population. Moreover, if the ruling authorities begin to lose their grip on power and confront a crisis, the infiltrators stand ready to take the reins of government.

A more prevalent and familiar form of parallel hierarchy, one that goes beyond infiltration, is the creation of political structures or institutions to administer, organize, and rule the population in areas controlled by the insurgents ("liberated zones"). In a few cases, like that of various right-wing paramilitaries in Colombia in 2004, insurgents aim to preserve or expand existing political and economic control, including, in this case, the drug trade. In most situations, however, the purpose of implanting such structures is to commence the process of changing the political community, system, or policies. The initial step is to challenge the government in contested areas by establishing small, secretive cells that assess the insurrectionary potential of the people and recruit followers and supporters. If all goes well, the insurgents will seek to create a more sophisticated and centralized organization.[6]

While the details of shadow governments vary at the central level, each typically consists of a small executive committee comprising the top leaders; departments responsible for governmental functions such as finances, diplomacy, the military, information, and the like; and a large assembly of representatives from the broader ranks of the movement. The larger assemblies meet infrequently and usually confine their activity to ratifying and applauding policies already decided upon at the higher levels. Communist insurgent movements with politburos, central committees, administrative offices, and popular congresses are typical examples; in fact, non-Communist insurgents have often emulated them in whole or in part, albeit with varying degrees of success.

In his insightful and balanced portrait of the Algerian nationalists, Alf Andrew Heggoy points out that they borrowed organizational methods from both the Communist Party and the French colonial administration, pragmatically adapting them to local needs. However, during the early years of the conflict, the functioning of the organization was anything but smooth, largely because military officers in charge of local commands tended to act as independent warlords and to ignore orders from the central political leadership, which was based outside the country in Egypt and Libya. Despite the problems between the exterior and interior commands, political assistants in the local commands nevertheless provided effective political leadership in such areas as propaganda, financial affairs, and the establishment of political-administrative cells that were to gradually undermine and replace the authority of the French administration. Heggoy concludes that the insurrection essentially succeeded because the shadow government represented the rebellion directly to the rural peasantry.[7]

The National Union for the Total Independence of Angola (UNITA) provides another example of non-Communist insurgents adopting Marxist-Leninist organizational ideas. Even though external assistance from South Africa and elsewhere was no doubt very important to UNITA (especially in offsetting generous Soviet and Cuban aid to the government), the political controversy surrounding such aid obscured reports of the contribution of UNITA's organization to its survival and successes. Visitors to UNITA areas in the southeast consistently reported a smoothly functioning central governing apparatus, which extended its authority to the village level and managed to provide basic services. UNITA's government had various ministries (e.g., health, information, natural resources) and a radio station (Voice of the Resistance of the Black Cockerel) that broadcasted in several languages. UNITA's ministries also managed more than nine hundred primary and secondary schools and the export of diamonds, ivory, timber, and other resources.[8]

The Algerian and UNITA examples raise a very important point worth underscoring: creating central structures that perform various governmental functions is necessary, but in itself insufficient, to acquire and expand popular support; rather, the organization must extend to lower levels and various sectors of a society. To do this, regional and local administrative structures must be established. Villages or small towns in liberated areas will thus have a leader (e.g., chief, commissar) and officials in charge of various functions (e.g., health, education, law enforcement, tax collection) who receive directions from the central apparatus. To further the mobilization of support, insurgents may also establish auxiliary organizations, or "fronts," based on various segments of the population, such as youth, peasants, workers, women, fishermen, and artists.[9] For instance, in the late 1940s and early 1950s, many people joined the Huk insurgency in the Philippines through front organizations.[10] The ability to extend organizational structures such as these was also instrumental in creating nationwide popular support in Algeria. In Angola, by contrast, the shadow government was limited to the southeast; thus, most of UNITA's active support was confined to that area.

In acknowledging the tremendous impact of Communist organizational formats on insurgent leaders, I do not mean to suggest they are the only basis for parallel hierarchies. Religious groups with hierarchical or pyramidal structures are, by their very nature, complex and, hence, can be used for planning, coordinating, and executing political and military activities. Where the religious groups are a minority, good organization will enhance their ability to consolidate support and use whatever resources are available to them. Yet, while this may enable them to cause serious problems for the government, their nationwide potential is low. Such is not the case with large religious groups, especially those that constitute a majority of the population. Although, strictly speaking, it was not an insurgency (because of its emphasis on nonviolence), the political uprising against the shah in Iran demonstrated the efficacy of religious organizational structures; Ayatollah Khomeini and his followers galvanized and directed opposition to the shah by using the extensive network of mosques throughout the country. In the final analysis, organization proved crucial to the success of the Iranian revolution.[11]

Of course, most insurgencies against governments as powerful as the shah's do not succeed without recourse to greater and more prolonged violence. Consequently, their leaders find it necessary to devote considerable attention to establishing a sophisticated military apparatus. In highly developed insurgent movements, guerrillas are usually divided into full- and part-time units operating at the central, regional, and local levels. The full-time guerrillas operate from secure bases, carrying out attacks against government military units and installations on a continuous basis, and will constitute the core of regular military formations if the movement progresses to mobile conventional warfare. For the most part, full-time guerrillas operate in specific areas, examples being the Q761, Q762, and Q763 Vietcong regiments in the areas north, east, and west of Saigon during the 1960s in the Vietnam War. Part-time or local guerrillas, meanwhile, stay in their communities and provide a number of invaluable services, such as collecting intelligence, harassing the enemy, storing supplies, and providing a coercive arm to protect political organizers. In addition, the local guerrillas can attach themselves to main-force units for specific operations, either as combatants or as scouts and guides.

Organized full- and part-time guerrilla units are only part of the story, for military successes also depend on the performance of an array of combat support tasks—command, control and communications, planning, training, medical care, finances, logistics, and so forth. The performance of such tasks becomes vital when insurgents engage in orthodox, conventional operations. Accordingly, organizational development must accompany the escalation of violence. Mao aptly summarized the indispensable role organization plays in the transition to mobile conventional warfare:

> In order to ensure the development of guerrilla hostilities into mobile warfare of an orthodox nature, both the quantity and quality of guerrilla

> troops must be improved. Primarily, more men must join the armies; then the quality of equipment and standards of training must be improved. Political training must be emphasized and our organization, the technique of handling our weapons, our tactics—all must be improved. Our internal discipline must be strengthened. The soldiers must be educated politically. There must be a gradual *change from guerrilla formations to orthodox regimental organization. The necessary bureaus and staffs, both political and military, must be provided.* At the same time, attention must be paid to the *creation of suitable supply, medical, and hygiene units.* The standards of equipment must be raised and types of weapons increased. Communication equipment must not be forgotten. *Orthodox standards of discipline must be established.*[12]

Few examples better illustrate Mao's insight into the crucial need for adequate organizational development during the transition from guerrilla to conventional warfare than the battle of Jalalabad in early 1989 following the Soviet exodus from Afghanistan. In that episode, disappointing setbacks and high casualty rates were attributed to, among other things, insufficiencies in certain types of conventional warfare equipment, poor training, a lack of discipline, and deficient coordination and command unity.[13]

Even more demanding than the organizational requirements of the protracted-warfare-strategy are those associated with the kind of transnational strategy adopted by Al Qaida. It is one thing to conduct a long struggle within the borders of a particular country and quite another to conduct one on a global scale. In pursuit of its aim to create a worldwide caliphate, Al Qaida has created an extensive, but essentially cellular, organization that emphasizes family connections and focuses on supporting and conducting military operations rather than gradually expanding a parallel hierarchy. As described by Jessica Stern, Rohan Gunaratna, and others, it consists of a central structure led by the emir-general (bin Ladin), a consultative council (*majlis al-shura*) made up of key elites appointed by bin Ladin, and four operational committees responsible for various functions: the military, finance and business, fatwa and Islamic study, and media and publicity. The military committee is in charge of combat support and operations, including an extensive training program. The financial committee oversees and coordinates various sources of income such as private and state charities, individual benefactors (especially in Saudi Arabia, the United Arab Emirates, Kuwait, and Qatar), banks, investments and small businesses, an informal *hawala* exchange system, and credit card fraud. The fatwa and Islamic study committee attends to ideological preparation and explanations, while the media and publicity committee directs and coordinates informational efforts of various kinds. The inner core plans and directs guerrilla and terrorist attacks of its own and in this sense is somewhat akin to the regular forces in the Maoist format. Through "connectors," it also coordinates with, inspires, and sometimes instigates attacks by independent—but like-minded—outer core groups across the world, some of which have closer ties with Al Qaida than others (e.g., Jamaa al-Islamiyya in Southeast Asia). As of 2005, Al Qaida's relations with the outer core have become increasingly diffuse as a result of the successful security and military operations of its adversaries.[14]

Functional Aspects of Organizations

By increasing the complexity of their organization, insurgents are better able to demonstrate potency by performing the instrumental and expressive functions that attract new followers. As Ted Robert Gurr has noted, the most immediate reason for a disgruntled individual to join an organization is to increase his options for attaining the things he values or desires. Participation can provide psychosocial satisfactions, such as companionship, self-definition, and reinforcement of shared beliefs, as long as members follow the normative prescriptions for conduct in the organization. An illustration of the psychological aspect inherent in Gurr's argument is the profile of young Germans who joined insurgent organizations in the 1970s. For the most part, they were alienated loners who had entered their adult years with low self-esteem, no money, and no power because of failures at school or work or because they had come from broken or unstable families. As both Jerrold Post and Konrad Kellen have noted, by joining an insurgent organization, they acquired a sense of belonging after a life of rejection, and the organization became the family they did not have.[15]

Besides a sense of self-worth, membership in insurgent groups, especially effective and stable ones, can provide security from external interference. And, as a bonus, organizations with the resources can enhance the material welfare of their members. Nevertheless, the fact remains that many dissident organizations lack the capability to meet psychosocial needs for status, communality, and ideational coherence. Where these needs go unfilled and where there is a general lack of progress and organizational conflict, division and desertion become more likely.

We should not conclude that a general lack of progress will doom insurgent movements since significant numbers of members of dissident groups may be intensely hostile to the government and intrinsically value opposition to it. Islamic militants come readily to mind in this regard. Providing ways to express this hostility can thus be an important function performed by insurgent organizations. In Gurr's words,

> Members of dissident organizations are therefore most likely to want means that satisfy both instrumental and expressive functions. The failure of instrumental means should not necessarily be expected to weaken the organization. Lack of success in obtaining demanded values is more likely to intensify than to reduce dissident opposition, because initial hostility not only persists, it is intensified by the effort expended in what was thought to be value-enhancing action. . . . The fact that external groups—the regime or political competitors—are responsible for not responding to the demands makes it likely that hostility will continue to be focused on them, not on the dissident leaders who specified the unsuccessful mode of action. Expressive protest also is intrinsically satisfying, hence reinforcing for the discontented, even in the absence of other value gains.[16]

Since the relative effects of instrumental and expressive functions vary from case to case, we can only ascertain their importance through careful empirical inquiry.

Complexity and Success or Failure

As noted above, the progress of insurgent movements facing resolute governments is closely tied to their organizational achievements. Although environmental conditions may be conducive to active support for insurgents, whether such popular support materializes through the use of the various techniques discussed in chapter 5 depends on the creation and extension of a complex political and military apparatus. In China, Vietnam, and Algeria, the ability to mobilize support through a complex organization was a major factor enabling insurgents to defeat a strong adversary. Without an extensive apparatus, the insurgents would probably have met the same fate as the Monteneros in Argentina, the Tupamaros in Uruguay, the Red Brigades in Italy, the Red Army of Japan, and other groups that have relied on small-scale, cellular structures and eschewed complexity.

Cases in which insurgents have considered complexity important, but failed in one way or another to bring it to fruition, may also illustrate its importance; take, for instance, the Afghan resistance. On the one hand, insurgents were able to sustain what could best be described as a low-to-moderate level of guerrilla warfare against superior Soviet forces because the vast majority of the people opposed both the Russians and the government; on the other hand, uneven organization undercut full exploitation of popular sympathies. Where there were regional shadow governments, like the one established by Ahmed Shah Masoud in the Panjshir Valley and throughout the northeast, training, logistics, and intelligence functions were performed efficiently, and operational coordination was more extensive and effective. It is no small wonder that Masoud was able to withstand several major Russian search-and-destroy operations and then return his guerrillas to the battlefield. While Masoud's regional shadow government, together with a few others in places like Wardak Province, the Hazarajat, and Nuristan, were instrumental in mujahedin successes, in areas where insurgents did not benefit from a complex political apparatus, observers reported that insurgent training left much to be desired, coordination and planning was rudimentary, and activity was small in scale.

Taken as a whole, the Afghan resistance was not well organized because, despite the pretensions of political parties based in Pakistan, there was no centralized political apparatus to give it a common sense of direction, integrate plans and strategy, standardize training, collect and disseminate intelligence, or provide a balanced and rationalized flow of materials. As a result, guerrilla activity leveled off, and the full potential of the resistance, which enjoyed either passive or active support from an estimated 90 percent of the people, was never realized.[17] Fortunately for the mujahedin, the Afghan government was inept and divided, and Russian counterinsurgency policies were poorly conceived and implemented. In the final analysis, the Russians' decision to withdraw in 1988 is best explained by their own blunders, environmental factors, external support, and, perhaps most important, a changed Soviet leadership with new and different priorities. To attribute that withdrawal to the organizational accomplishments of the Afghans would be an exaggeration, if not a clear mistake.

Much like the Afghan resistance, the Palestinian Liberation Organization (PLO) was strongest in places where parallel hierarchies existed. During the high point of Palestinian guerrilla activity in 1969 and 1970, active support came primarily from refugee camps in Lebanon and Jordan that were under the political control of resistance organizations. In the area the resistance considered most vital, the West Bank, active support was meager, in spite of general antipathy toward the Israelis, largely because there was no functioning parallel hierarchy. When a similar situation emerged in Jordan after the expulsion of the insurgents in the fall of 1970 and spring of 1971, Palestinian violence was reduced to transnational terrorism and an occasional guerrilla attack. With the Palestinians' military effectiveness at such a low point, observers puzzled at the seeming paradox of the PLO's success in the diplomatic arena as the 1970s unfolded. While this success could be partially attributed to perceived moderation on the part of Fatah and some other groups, one should not overlook the fact that the PLO had a central apparatus that included an efficient political department in charge of foreign affairs. Without this central apparatus, the PLO would have been reduced to impotence, a point it came perilously close to reaching by 1985 as a result of the Israeli invasion of Lebanon in 1982, the ejection of the PLO from that country, and its subsequent dispersal throughout the Arab world.[18]

Likewise, the absence of central political structures would have prevented the PLO from taking political advantage of the uprising (intifada) in the Gaza Strip and the West Bank that began in 1987. These accomplishments notwithstanding, all but the most biased observers see clearly that "armed struggle"—within the framework of a protracted-popular-war strategy—was a failure. Although both the physical environment and effective Israeli countermeasures militated against the strategy's success, the PLO's own organizational drawbacks also played a major role. In addition to deficiencies related to complexity, especially the failure to implant a shadow government in the occupied areas, another organizational shortcoming was responsible, namely, endemic disunity, something that has plagued many other insurgent movements.

COHESION

The presence or absence of cohesion, or unity, among insurgents can profoundly affect the developments and outcomes of insurgencies. One analyst puts it thus:

> The problem of unity is a particularly acute one for guerrilla forces. Technological powers, in possession of regular armed forces which boast long traditions of discipline and loyalty, rarely, if ever, experience open conflict within their military establishments; unity of command in wartime is no problem for them. But guerrilla movements, especially those in technologically less advanced societies, invariably are rent by factionalism.[19]

Few, if any, experts on and practitioners of insurgency have not stressed the importance of unity within insurgent ranks. John J. McCuen, for example, contends that unifying the effort is the basic principle behind effective strategy, planning, tactics, and organization. "This has been so ever since 1902 when Lenin's *What Is to Be Done?* made revolution into a science."[20] Although it may delegate the conduct of operations and responsibility to local leaders, a general headquarters that exercises authoritative control over policy, discipline, ethics, and ideology is indispensable.[21]

The absence of unity undermines authoritative control and can create a host of problems for insurgents, not the least of which is a lack of direction. Debray has noted,

> The lack of a single command puts the revolutionary forces in the situation of an artillery gunner who has not been told in which direction to fire, of a line of attack without a principal direction of attack: the attackers are lost on the field, they shoot at random, and die in vain. The amount and strength of firepower mean nothing without a plan, without assigning a fire or cross fire. The absence of a centralized executive leadership—a political-military leadership—leads to such waste, such useless slaughter.[22]

Moreover, as Mao pointed out in *The Strategy of Partisan Warfare*, "Without centralized strategic command the partisans can inflict little damage on their adversaries, as without this, they can break down into roaming, armed bands, and then find no more support by the population."[23]

Although unity is usually important for insurgent movements, its absence has not always resulted in failure since other factors may offset the problems disunity creates. Disunity need not preclude eventual success by insurgents where governing authorities lose the will to persevere, as the French did in Algeria; where they see their advantage undercut by widespread popular support for the insurgents, as happened in Angola in the 1960s during the uprising against the Portuguese; or where they face severe, long-term, geographic and demographic asymmetries in favor of the guerrillas, as was the case in white-ruled Rhodesia. But, if offsetting conditions such as these do not exist and if the government is strong, insurgents court disaster by fighting among themselves and failing to coordinate their efforts. This being the case, it is important to take a closer and more specific look at the effects of disunity.

Effects of Disunity

The disunity of insurgents can have many adverse consequences. First, it can undercut both political and military organizational efforts. Witness the example of the Vietminh guerrillas operating in the Mekong Delta in Vietnam during the war with the French. Their internecine conflict, rooted in different religious and political outlooks, hindered their organizational efforts and precluded the establishment of a cohesive political network. As a result, insurgent activity was confined to terror and low-level guerrilla operations. This situation contrasted starkly with that in the Red River Delta in the north, where the unity of the revolutionary forces made it possible for the insurgents to gain momentum and even to make the transition to mobile conventional warfare.[24]

A second and more specific result of disunity can be conflicting political and military policies, especially during the execution phase. Typically, this involves either inadvertent or deliberate military actions that undercut political endeavors. A case in point would be an attack by one insurgent group occurring while negotiations are impending or taking place between the government and the top leadership of the insurgent movement or a designated intermediary. For instance, terrorist attacks against civilians—both Jews and non-Jews—by hard-line groups such as the Abu Nidal Organization, the Popular Front for the Liberation of Palestine–General Command and, more recently, Hamas and Palestinian Islamic Jihad have usually aimed principally to prevent any dialog that could lead to a compromise. By blowing up school buses, bombing synagogues, and attacking buses, airliners, terminals, and ships, the hard-line groups have sought (with frequent success) to undermine any chance for negotiation by inflaming tensions and provoking Israeli retaliation.[25]

A third negative result of disunity is deficiency in combat support. As the Afghan guerrillas discovered, where insurgent groups insist on autonomy and distrust one another, intelligence collection, analysis, and dissemination are fragmented and unsatisfactory; the flow of logistical supplies is generally unbalanced; training is inadequate and unstandardized; and systematic communications are lacking. An even worse situation prevailed among the Palestinians during the 1990s. Despite creating a so-called Front of Ten for confronting their Zionist enemies, the distrust and ideological antipathy between the secular and religious rejectionist groups was so deep that they only succeeded in issuing wordy but meaningless communiqués.[26]

A fourth disadvantage is the inability to plan, orchestrate, and integrate multiple military operations, which seriously erodes, if it does not preclude altogether, any potential for sizable campaigns involving attacks in many areas. Again, the experience of Afghan guerrillas (especially at Jalalabad in 1989) illustrates the point. This was also true in Iraq as of 2005, where various secular and *jihadi* insurgents had not established a central command.

The fifth deleterious effect of disunity is the diversion of personnel and materials from attacks against the main enemy to attacks against opponents inside the insurgent movement. Internecine violence involving losses of personnel and materials plagued most Palestinian and Afghan factions at one time or another, as well as the Eritrean Liberation Front and the Popular Front for the Liberation of Eritrea, rival Kurdish groups in Iraq, and the Popular Movement for the Liberation of Angola (MPLA) and UNITA during the anti-Portuguese war. Even more astounding and very costly is intergroup fighting on the battlefield during confrontations with government forces. Although this may seem hard to believe, it has occurred. During one major Soviet campaign against Masoud's guerrillas in the Panjshir Valley, for example, rival insurgents belonging to Gulbudin

Hekmatyar's Hezb-i-Islami ("Party of Islam") actually attacked Masoud's forces in an effort to wrest control of areas from Masoud because of his affiliation with a rival insurgent organization, Jamiat-i-Islami ("Society of Islam").[27]

A sixth, very damaging outcome of disunity is the undermining of external support. The Islamic Conference Organization made it quite clear that greater largesse to Afghanistan depended on the unification of the various groups, demonstrating the reluctance of outside states to commit themselves to fragmented insurgents.[28] If insurgent movements contain groups that pose threats to actual or potential external supporters, the problem is even greater. A classic example was the Jordan-PLO relationship in 1969 and 1970. Since guerrilla bases in Jordan had become essential for the Palestinians following their organizational failures in the West Bank, the pragmatic elements of the PLO favored, and worked for, a compromise with King Hussein, only to see their efforts undermined by the Marxist Popular Front for the Liberation of Palestine (PFLP) and Popular Democratic Front (PDF) for the Liberation of Palestine, which carried out acts of sabotage as part of a campaign to overthrow the "feudal" regime. When the king moved forcefully against the PFLP following a multiple skyjacking in 1970, the pragmatists felt compelled to join the fighting on the side of their Palestinian brothers. Once the dust had settled, the PLO found that it had been badly beaten, suffered substantial losses in people and materials, and been expelled from its self-proclaimed "pillar base" in Jordan. Unquestionably, disunity in PLO ranks had played a key part in provoking this disastrous turn of events.[29]

The chronic disunity of the PLO also illustrates the seventh problem to be discussed in this context—outside interference. When insurgent leaders engage in conflicts among themselves, they open the doors to undesirable involvement by both their adversaries and states supporting the insurgent movement. The lack of discipline and unity and competition for recruits among insurgent factions often give governments opportunities to infiltrate the groups and sow the seeds of greater dissension. In a conversation with the French writer Alain Chevalerias, a captured secret police agent indicated that one of the purposes of infiltrating Afghan insurgent groups was to exacerbate differences between factions. Those who follow Palestinian affairs have long recognized the ability of Israel's security agencies (Mossad and Shin Bet) to do precisely this.[30]

The multifaceted, shifting alliances of the Arab states with different PLO groups illustrate dramatically the disruptive effect of outside influence. These alliances contributed to fighting among the Palestinians both in the Middle East and abroad because the provision of weapons, intelligence, planning assistance, and, in some cases, actual military support often came with strings attached. For instance, Syria supported and, thereby, periodically manipulated the Palestine Liberation Army (PLA) brigade in Syria for its own purposes. It also used its own Palestinian guerrilla organization, Saiqa, and various other Palestinian factions, such as Abu Musa's Fatah–Revolutionary Council, against its Palestinian adversaries, mainly Fatah.[31]

An eighth troublesome effect of disunity sometimes occurs when insurgents eliminate their rivals by killing them or providing information about them to the government in the hope that the authorities will apprehend or eliminate them. An example of the former was Osama bin Ladin's elimination of his former mentor and colleague, Abdullah Azzam, in November 1989. As for informing the authorities about rivals, one need look no further than the actions of the venerable Ho Chi Minh in the early, formative stages of his resistance to the French.[32] As perfidious as such behavior may seem, it may not always have a negative impact on the insurgency as a whole. In fact, over the long term, it may contribute to cohesion if rival factions are expunged.

Whether the effects of betraying rivals are good or bad will depend largely on the size and social composition of the victimized groups and the credibility of explanations given for such acts. Where betrayed groups or individuals are from small factions, especially when they are from minority groups, the damage is likely to be smaller than when the victims are from large, more important groups. The rationale for betrayal is also important; hence, the betrayer will frequently characterize those who are betrayed as traitors, government agents, spies, or the like. In other cases, such as bin Ladin's betrayal of Azzam, the victim may continue to be praised! For the analyst, the key questions are whether betrayal has occurred and, if so, what its impact is.

As the foregoing discussion makes clear, disunity can be a source of many difficulties for an insurgent movement. Accordingly, where disunity is obvious, a careful analysis of its specific effects is imperative since it may reveal some of the major explanations for the course of events in an insurgency.

Causes of Disunity

Since most insurgent leaders recognize the deleterious impact that disunity can have on their fortunes, they normally adopt organizational, coercive, and other policies designed to prevent or quickly end it. But such efforts are often futile if the causes of disunity are ignored or misunderstood.

Our studies of insurgent movements suggest seven causes of disunity—social, political-cultural, personal, teleological, theoretical, strategic, and tactical. Social and cultural causes of disunity are, as chapter 4 shows, rooted in the environment. Social factors include group cleavages based on race, ethnicity, religion, and sometimes regionalism. Where such cleavages exist, and particularly where they are cumulative, creating and unifying insurgent movements composed of multiple groups is very difficult. The lack of cohesion in the Afghan insurgent movement reflected, in part, historical animosities and rivalries among ethnic and, in the case of the Hazara (who are Shiites), religious groups. The resentment of the largest group, the Pashtuns, by the smaller groups was the most salient. Hence, not surprisingly, most guerrilla units inside Afghanistan were composed of members of a single group. The same situation existed in the Rhodesian insurgency, where the Zimbabwe African People's Union (ZAPU) was drawn from the dominant Mashona ethnic group, while the membership of the rival Zimbabwe African National Union (ZANU) drew from the Matabele peoples. Likewise, in the Angolan insurrection against Portugal, the tripartite division of the insurgents was based on ethnicity, with the Ovimbundu supporting UNITA, the Bakongo backing the Front for the National Liberation of Angola, and the coastal peoples sustaining the MPLA. In Rhodesia and Angola, the strife between groups precluded unity, and even when the insurgencies succeeded because of other factors, the newly independent states were quickly engulfed by renewed hostilities involving the rival groups. During the war against the Russians, common forecasts of a similar future for Afghanistan were more than vindicated by the subsequent endemic strife among mujahedin organizations, most notably the Pashtun-dominated Hezb-i-Islami and the Tajik-led Jamiat-i-Islami.

The political culture of a country may also be a source of fissiparous tendencies in an insurgent movement. This is especially so where there is low interpersonal and intergroup trust, combined with an aversion to centralized authority. In chapter 4, we noted this with respect to the Afghan case. It is also prevalent among Kurdish secessionists and in Arab insurgent movements like the Muslim Brotherhood in Syria and the Palestinian resistance, which are marked by splits. Although other factors often play a role in such divisiveness, the suspicion, conflict, secrecy, and conspiracy that have characterized authority relationships in Arab political cultures for centuries are often overlooked.[33] That they should be prevalent in insurgent movements like the PLO comes as no surprise to students of the area; it would be surprising if they were not.

Personal ambitiousness—that is, a straightforward struggle for control of an insurgency among individual leaders—can also cause disunity, particularly when resources are dispersed and no single group is strong enough to eliminate its rivals. With the passage of time, the leaders of various groups become more convinced that they, rather than their rivals, should become first among equals, if not the only authority figure. The bitterness and hatred that come to characterize such rivalries are recognizable to all analysts of politics. The questions with reference to an insurgent movement are whether such a situation—say, for instance that between Osama bin Ladin and his nominal subordinate Abu Mussab al-Zarqawi—has emerged and how it contributes to disunity.

Disunity may also be caused by teleological, theoretical, or strategic differences. Although often intertwined, the three are distinct. Teleological differences—that is, discord over the ultimate political goal that insurgents ought to be pursuing—can be profoundly unsettling, as the admixture of reactionary and moderate traditionalists and egalitarians in both the Afghan and Palestinian cases has shown.

Deep divisions over goals are frequently the outgrowth of theoretical disagreements, which, as we saw in discussing esoteric appeals in chapter 5, involve ideology and theology. The problem is that different ideological and theological assumptions about man and society can yield quite different prescriptions with respect to required actions, potential friends and enemies, and desired outcomes. While a combination of cultural, personal, and strategic differences clearly contributed to the previously noted disunity that led to the 1970 civil war in Jordan, it would be an oversight to ignore the part that theoretical divisions played. Put briefly, the Marxist ideology of the PFLP and PDF led the two groups to conceptualize the conflict with Israel in class terms. As they saw it, there was an unholy alliance of international imperialism, Zionism, and what they referred to as "Arab reaction," by which they meant Arab states with leaders who were considered either feudal-traditionalist or petit bourgeois. Since they assumed that the class interests of such leaders benefited from the status quo, the PFLP and PDF concluded that those leaders and their regimes would have to be overthrown before the conflict with Israel could be successfully pursued.[34] Seen in this light, the sabotage and violence against the Hashemite monarchy in Jordan in 1969 and 1970 was logical. The problem was, it ran counter to the non-Marxists' (e.g., Fatah) desire to cooperate with Jordan and retain its support.

Insurgent disunity may also be caused by conflict over which strategies to adopt in the conflict. As we saw previously, many possible strategies are available to insurgents. Take, for example, the contrast between the protracted-popular-war and military-focus strategies. The protracted-popular-war strategy, it will be recalled, emphasizes careful political preparation and the consolidation of a strong political organization (normally a party) before initiating hostilities; the military-focus strategy calls for the commencement of violence and worrying about political consolidation later. Where strategies diverge as greatly as these, their simultaneous adoption by different groups results in quite different, often contradictory, activities. A group committed to clandestine organizational activity during the earliest stage of the protracted-popular-war strategy, for example, may find its efforts undercut by the premature violence of groups following the military-focus strategy because such violence may awaken the government and lead it to crack down on those insurgents who are keeping a low profile and engaging in political undertakings.

Discord over strategy may also center on more specific issues, such as the forms of violence and targets considered advisable at various times. Decisions about whether to carry out acts of terrorism, for instance, have often been a source of disunity. In Palestine during the 1940s, the Jewish resistance underwent considerable internal conflict because the principal group, the Haganah, opposed the terrorist acts by two extremist groups, the Irgun and the Stern Gang. In more recent times, both Basque Homeland and Liberty and the Irish Republican Army (IRA) experienced disruption and defections because of disputes over the use of violence. The latter case led to a split between the so-called provisional and official wings of the movement.[35]

Other strategic questions that can engender disputes among insurgents include whether to expand the arena of conflict to other states, whether to engage in negotiations with the government, and whether to seek support from particular countries. Deciding which, if any, of these is pertinent requires careful inquiry.

When there is agreement on the specific types of issues discussed above, there may be discord over when and where to act. Since these are essentially tactical and operational considerations, they do not generally cause major rifts in an insurgent movement. Nonetheless, they can undercut the effectiveness of political and military efforts.

As the above commentary suggests, there are many possible sources of disunity. While each may be quite damaging, insurgent movements afflicted by several at the same time usually find themselves in an even greater predicament. Although insurgents generally acknowledge the problem and the need to address it, effective remedies are hard to come by.

Quest for Unity

Unity rests on a combination of effective socialization, organizational schemes, and sanctions. Socialization involves inculcating loyalty and a common sense of purpose through propaganda and political education programs. Where social and political cultural factors pose a potential threat to cohesion, insurgents will normally emphasize one or more of the following: the need to close ranks against the common enemy; an ideology or theology that transcends group differences and distrust; and the equitable and mutual benefits to be derived from success.

Organizational schemes are also important in establishing cohesion, and here there are several possibilities. In the first organizational type, the politicians are in charge. This has characterized most Communist movements (as well as some militant Islamic groups like Al Qaida), but there are two variants. In the first, a chain of command descends from the Politburo through the central executive committee, which exercises control over state, district, and branch committees. These, in turn, control the military units within their jurisdiction. The second includes separate chains of command for the military and the civilian organizations. This was the case in the Greek civil war, where the stationary civil administration (parallel hierarchy) ran the liberated base areas, while guerrilla bands, under separate command, moved from sector to sector.

In the second organizational type, the political and military strata exist independently of one another. Such was the situation in the World War II Italian resistance; military resistance was in the hands of the Corps of Volunteers for Liberation, whereas the Central Committee of Liberation handled civil resistance and local administration. During the 1980s, the relationship between the civilian Democratic Revolutionary Front (FDR) and the military Farabundo Martí National Liberation Front (FMLN) in El Salvador followed this format.

In the third organizational type, the military element takes charge. Take, for example, the Irgun, which operated in Palestine during the British mandate.[36] A more recent approximation of the third scheme is the Cuban model, as described by Debray.[37] This also seemed to be the case in the 2004 Iraqi insurgency, where elements of the former regime, local Islamic militants, and foreign groups like Tanzim Qa'idat al-Jihad fi Bilad al-Rafidayn ("al Qaida of Jihad Organization in the Land of the Two Rivers") and Ansar al-Islam ("Partisans of Islam") concentrated on military actions.

Recognizing organizational deficiencies and correcting them are, of course, two quite different things. The FMLN in El Salvador, not without considerable prodding from Cuba, had for several years indicated an awareness of the need to integrate not only its five military groups but also the activities of the civilian FDR. To accomplish this aim, a 1985 strategic assessment indicated, it needed to create a Marxist-Leninist party to provide leadership for a prolonged war that would put more emphasis on popular support and less on military actions.[38] Four years later, the party had yet to appear. Moreover, problems stemming from a lack of cohesion continued, symbolized by the absurdity of the FDR actively competing in the March 1989 election at the same time the FMLN was working vigorously to subvert it.

When socialization and organizational formats fail to curb factionalism, the insurgency's security force may impose obedience, assuming, of course, that it is loyal and effective. The recourse to coercion may succeed if recalcitrant individuals and groups are relatively small and impotent; if, however, dissident groups are sizable and have enough resources to threaten prolonged and costly fighting, larger main-line groups often avoid using coercion to ensure unity. The fact that the majority group in the PLO, led by Fatah, has been unwilling to crack down on smaller groups like the PFLP and PDF, and, more recently, Hamas and Palestinian Islamic Jihad, stems, at least in part, from the reality that Fatah has not had the military ability to deal swift and decisive blows. The sustained use of force against such groups would have resulted in bitter inter-Palestinian strife, which may well have involved outside states intervening on one or both sides.

The reluctance to use force against rival factions and groups can dissipate quickly once a particular group sees that it has gained preponderant strength. In Sri Lanka, the Tamil Tigers emerged as the most important insurgent group by eliminating or silencing their opponents through brutal force and intimidation. Likewise, the Eritrean Popular Liberation Front eventually eliminated the Eritrean Liberation Front as a serious rival in the 1980s—but only after two decades of internal strife that many observers feel was the main factor preventing the Eritreans from fully exploiting severe government weaknesses in the 1970s.

The issue of disunity in an insurgent movement may not be amenable to forceful resolution of the type just mentioned. The fact is that once different groups emerge and gain autonomy and strength, they are difficult to discipline. In order to mitigate the effects of group rivalries and to foster a modicum of cooperation, insurgent leaders may create a unified command for a particular operation, agree on a division of labor among various groups, or establish a unified command. Otto Heilbrunn recalls the following, for example:

> In Greece a unified command was established for one particular operation, while the non-Communist forces in Czechoslovakia decided on a proper division of labour, one movement specializing in sabotage, the second in collecting intelligence and transmitting it to London, and the third engaging in propaganda. In Albania, the Royalists first cooperated with the Communists and then with the Centre, and in Belgium only the extreme Left groups united, while in France, Italy, Holland, and temporarily in Greece, all groups put themselves under a unified command; the Communists, however, always retained their separate identity.[39]

Of the three possibilities, a unified command is generally the most promising, since it is the one most conducive to giving the insurgents a sense of strategic direction and best suited for dealing with the various factors that divide the movement in the first place. For a unified command to be successful, however, the rival organizations must agree to subordinate their parochial interests to the overall interests of the movement, as defined by the unified command. If the unified command's decisions are to be considered authoritative and legitimate, the rival groups must reach a consensus on the mechanics of the decision-making process and on methods for invoking sanctions against deviationists. Consensus on such matters, of course, again raises the question of who will wield dominant power and who will invoke sanctions. Since groups are generally unwilling to make major concessions on these vital matters, the effectiveness of unified commands tends to be marginal, and their durability, limited. This has been the case with various evolutionary Palestinian efforts along these lines (i.e., the Palestine Armed Struggle Command, Central Committee of the Palestinian Resistance, Unified Command of the Palestinian Resistance, and the PLO Executive Committee).[40]

While the fragmentation of the Palestinian, Iraqi, and Islamic insurgents in the early twenty-first century continues this trend, both Palestinian and Iraqi groups have shown some willingness to coordinate specific attacks. In the former case, for instance, operatives from the secular Al-Aqsa Martyrs Brigade (a semi-independent offshoot of Fatah) have carried out joint operations with members of the Issa al din al-Qassam brigades (the military wing of Hamas). To some degree, the same kind of cooperation is true of various Islamic militant groups and cells that make up the increasingly diffuse Al Qaida nebula around the world today. While such diffusion may complicate counterterrorist efforts on the tactical level, it is important to remember its longer-term costs to insurgents in terms of deficient combat support (e.g., intelligence, logistics, training), poor coordination, strategic incoherence, or outright dissention and the danger of sharpening splits and new rivalries. In short, while organizational segmentation may contribute to tactical successes, it is not a formula for strategic victory.

SUMMARY

No analysis of an insurgency will be complete or meaningful if it fails to address the scope, complexity, and cohesion of the insurgent movement. A careful look at the structures and workings of insurgent political and military organizations can reveal a good deal about the progress of an insurrection, as well as the type and magnitude of the threat confronting the government. Three issues are very important in this regard: the organizational requirements associated with the strategy and forms of violence adopted by the insurgents; whether the requirements are being met by extant arrangements; and the status and effects of unity. As one analyzes such issues, relationships between organization and other evaluative criteria should become readily apparent, notably those involving the acquisition of internal and external support. The various aspects of external support are the subject of the next chapter.

NOTES

1. See Ted Robert Gurr, *Why Men Rebel* (Princeton, N.J.: Princeton University Press, 1970), 274–316, for an expanded discussion of the structural and functional aspects of organizations.
2. The *New York Times,* February 7, 1975, reported that defections had reached 1,037 by 1975.
3. William R. Heaton, "People's War in Thailand," in *The Art and Practice of Military Strategy*, ed. George Edward Thibault (Washington, D.C.: National Defense University, 1984), 854, 856–57.
4. Che Guevara, *Guerrilla Warfare* (New York: Vintage Books, 1961), 71–73.
5. A number of specialists on insurgency have noted the importance of parallel hierarchies. See, for example, Bernard B. Fall, *The Two Viet-Nams,* 2nd ed. (New York: Frederick A. Praeger, 1967), 130–38; John J. McCuen, *The Art of Counter-Revolutionary War* (Harrisburg, Pa.: Stackpole Books, n.d.), 31, 33–35; Richard L. Clutterbuck, *The Long, Long War* (New York: Frederick A. Praeger, 1966), 22, 56, 87–88; Julian Paget, *Counter-Insurgency Campaigning* (New York: Walker & Co., 1967), 20–21; Douglas Hyde, *The Roots of Guerrilla Warfare* (Chester Springs, Pa.: Dufour Editions, 1968), 92, 126; and Roger Trinquier, *Modern Warfare* (New York: Frederick A. Praeger, 1966), 30, 70.
6. On cellular development, see Edward R. Wainhouse, "Guerrilla Warfare in Greece, 1946–1948: A Case Study," in *Modern Guerrilla Warfare,* ed. Franklin Mark Osanka (New York: The Free Press of Glencoe, 1962), 223; McCuen, *The Art of Counter-Revolutionary War,* 31–35; Hyde, *The Roots of Guerrilla Warfare,* 67–69; and Paget, *Counter-Insurgency Campaigning,* 24. On the impressive shadow-government structures of the right-wing Colombian paramilitaries, which are described as superior to those of the Marxist insurgent groups, see Juan Forero, "With Chief Missing, Colombian Militias Gain Leverage," *New York Times,* May 19, 2004.
7. See Alf Andrew Heggoy, *Insurgency and Counterinsurgency in Algeria* (Bloomington: Indiana University Press, 1972), 107–29, on the details of the FLN organization.
8. The UNITA organization is composed of a political bureau, central committee, political commissions, and peasant organizations. The political bureau was chaired and chosen by Savimbi. See *Washington Post,* August 13, 1977, and *Christian Science Monitor,* August 28, 1988.
9. The commentary on auxiliary organizations, like that on parallel hierarchies, is extensive. See, for example, Fall, *The Two Viet-Nams,* 134; McCuen, *The Art of Counter-*

Revolutionary War, 34–35; Hyde, *The Roots of Guerrilla Warfare,* 34. An especially good source for the treatment of the role of auxiliary organizations is Douglas Pike, *Viet Cong* (Cambridge, Mass.: MIT Press, 1966), chs. 6, 10.

10. Thomas C. Tirona, "The Philippine Anti-Communist Campaign," in Osanka, *Modern Guerrilla Warfare,* 204; see also Hyde, *The Roots of Guerrilla Warfare,* 90–91.
11. Jerrold Green, "Countermobilization as a Revolutionary Form," *Comparative Politics* (January 1984): 153–68; James A. Bill, "Iran and the Crisis of '78," *Foreign Affairs* (winter 1978–1979): 332–33.
12. Mao Tse-tung, *On Guerrilla Warfare,* trans. Samuel B. Griffith (New York: Frederick A. Praeger, 1962), 113. On the question of military differentiation, see Pike, *Viet Cong,* ch. 13; Virgil Ney, "Guerrilla Warfare and Modern Strategy," in Osanka, *Modern Guerrilla Warfare,* 35–36; Anthony Crockett, "Action in Malaya," in Osanka, *Modern Guerrilla Warfare,* 310; Brooks McClure, "Russia's Hidden Army," in Osanka, *Modern Guerrilla Warfare,* 89; James E. Dougherty, "The Guerrilla War in Malaya," in Osanka, *Modern Guerrilla Warfare,* 302.
13. On Jalalabad, see *Hong Kong AFP,* April 17, 1989, in *FBIS-NESA,* April 18, 1989; *New York Times,* April 13, 1989; *Washington Times,* March 22, 1989.
14. Jessica Stern, *Terror in the Name of God* (New York: Harper Collins Publishers: 2003), 248–80; Rohan Gunaratna, *Inside Al Qaeda* (New York: Columbia University Press, 2002), 54–166; Paul R. Pillar, *Terrorism and U.S. Foreign Policy* (Washington D.C.: Brookings Institution Press, 2001), 54–55; Jean-Pierre Stoobants, "The Western Police Discover the New Forms of Al Qaida," *Le Monde* (Paris), August 21, 2004, in *FBIS-NESA (INE),* August 21, 2004; Didier Francois, "On al-Qa'ida's Trail," in *Paris Liberation* (special supplement), September 9, 2003, in *FBIS-NESA (INE),* September 9, 2003; Federal Bureau of Investigation Assessment, *Al-Qa'ida, Unclassified* (Washington, D.C.: FBI Counterterrorism Division, April 15, 2004), 5. For a contrary view that the hard core does not plan operations, see Arnaud de la Grange, "Al-Qa'ida's Three Circles," *Le Figaro* (Paris), November 21, 2003, in *FBIS-NESA (INE),* November 21, 2003. On Al Qaida's organizational presence and activities in the United States, see Steven Emerson, *American Jihad* (New York: The Free Press: 2002), 151–52.
15. Jerrold M. Post, "Inside the Mind of a Terrorist," *Washington Post,* August 28, 1988, Outlook Section; Konrad Kellen, "Ideology and Rebellion in West Germany" in *Origins of Terrorism,* ed. Walter Reich (Baltimore: Johns Hopkins University Press, 1998), 52–53. Gurr, *Why Men Rebel,* 297–301.
16. Gurr, *Why Men Rebel,* 304.
17. The *Christian Science Monitor* from September 23, 25, 1981, contains articles by Edward Giradet on the Masoud organization. On the Hazara parallel hierarchy, see Christer Lundgren's article in *Gnistan* (Stockholm), April 10, 1981, in *Joint Publications Research Service, Near East-North Asia* (hereafter *JPRS-NENA*) no. 78416, July 9, 1981, 22; *Economist* (May 23, 1981); *L'Unité* (Paris), December 18, 1981, in *JPRS-NENA* no. 79951, January 27, 1982, 27; *Le Monde* (Paris), May 26, 1980; and *New York Times,* March 20, 1979, and March 2, 1980.
18. On the organizational complexity of the PLO, see Bard E. O'Neill, *Armed Struggle in Palestine* (Boulder, Colo.: Westview Press, 1978), 153–56, and Cheryl A. Rubenberg, "The Civilian Infrastructure of the Palestine Liberation Organization," *Journal of Palestine Studies* (spring 1983): 54–78.
19. Ney, "Guerrilla Warfare and Modern Strategy," 36.

20. McCuen, *The Art of Counter-Revolutionary War*, 69.
21. George B. Jordan, "Objectives and Methods of Communist Guerrilla Warfare," in Osanka, *Modern Guerrilla Warfare*, 403, 407, and McClure, "Russia's Hidden Army," 88–89, have stressed the importance of central control to the Russian partisan movement. Hyde, *The Roots of Guerrilla Warfare*, 65, notes that one of the Teo Yong Jin's first acts in Sarawak was to unify disparate groups.
22. Regis Debray, *Revolution in the Revolution?* trans. Bobbe Ortiz (New York: Monthly Review Press, 1967), 73–74.
23. Cited in Jordan, "Objectives and Methods of Communist Guerrilla Warfare," 403.
24. McCuen, *The Art of Counter-Revolutionary War*, 198.
25. For example, the PFLP-GC's seizure of an apartment house in the northern Israeli town of Qiryat Shemona in the spring of 1974 was, according to a PFLP-GC spokesman, aimed at blocking an Arab-Israeli settlement; see *New York Times*, April 13, 1974.
26. The consequences of disunity are reported in *Washington Post*, February 26, 1980; *New York Times*, December 17, 1981, and January 12, 1981; *Christian Science Monitor*, September 28, 1981; *U.S. News and World Report* (January 18, 1980): 38–39; *Le Matin* (Paris), September 28, 1981, in *JPRS-NENA* no. 79364, November 3, 1981, 15; London BBC Service, March 10, 1982, in *FBIS–South Asia*, March 11, 1982; and *Guardian* (London), March 2, 1982. Also see Ilana Kass and Bard O'Neill, *The Deadly Embrace* (Lanham, Md.: National Institute for Public Policy and University Press of America, 1997), 270–73.
27. Internecine violence between Afghan groups has been noted by many sources. See, for example, *Washington Post*, July 12, 1981; *Christian Science Monitor*, August 4 and September 28, 1981; *Baltimore Sun*, September 3, 1981; *Hong Kong AFP*, July 31, 1980, in *FBIS–South Asia*, August 1, 1980; and *Die Zeit* (Hamburg), September 25, 1981, in *JPRS-NENA*, October 30, 1981, 3.
28. On the Islamic Conference Organization's linkage of unity with external assistance, see *Washington Post*, February 26, 1980, and *New York Times*, March 2, 1980, Section IV.
29. The role of Palestinian disunity in the costly civil war in Jordan in 1970 is discussed in O'Neill, *Armed Struggle in Palestine*, 165–66.
30. On Afghanistan, see Alain Chevalerias, "Afghanistan, the Improbable Evacuation," *Le Spectacle Du Monde* (February 1988): 42–44. On several occasions during research trips to the Middle East, I have discussed Israel's penetration of the PLO and its efforts to instigate internal strife among Palestinians. However, given the obvious sensitivity of this matter, the officials requested that they not be formally cited.
31. Besides Saiqa and the PLA units stationed in Syria, the Syrians also had close ties with the PFLP-GC and Abu Nidal's Black June group, both of which carried out acts of violence against rivals from time to time. No doubt the most dramatic instances of Syrian-backed groups fighting against Fatah and others took place in 1976 during the Lebanese civil war, when Syria intervened on behalf of the Christians! From 1983 to 1988, Damascus also backed rebellious Fatah members in several bloody conflicts with Arafat's loyalists.
32. Rohan, *Inside Al Qa'ida*, 23; Bernard B. Fall, *The Two Viet-Nams*, 2nd rev. ed. (New York: Frederick A. Praeger, 1967), 93–94; John McAlister Jr., *Vietnam: The Origins of Revolution* (New York: Alfred A. Knopf, 1969), 83–84.
33. On political style and characteristics in the Arab world, see James A. Bill and Carl Leiden, *The Middle East: Politics and Power* (Boston: Allyn and Bacon, 1974), ch. 3.

34. The role of Marxist ideology and the problems it created for the PLO in Jordan is discussed in O'Neill, *Armed Struggle in Palestine,* 129–30, 134–44, 165.
35. Christopher Sykes, *Crossroads to Israel* (Bloomington: Indiana University Press, 1973), 305, notes the Haganah's critical view of the Irgun and the Stern Gang. On ETA, see Cyrus Ernesto Zirakzadeh, "From Revolutionary Dreams to Organizational Fragmentation: Disputes over Violence within ETA and Sendero Luminoso," *Terrorism and Political Violence* (winter 2002): 71–77. The Official-Provisional IRA discord over the issue of violent tactics is discussed by Don Mansfield, "The Irish Republican Army and Northern Ireland," in *Insurgency in the Modern World*, ed. Bard E. O'Neill, William R. Heaton, and Donald J. Alberts (Boulder, Colo.: Westview Press), 58–64.
36. Otto Heilbrunn, *Partisan Warfare* (New York: Frederick A. Praeger, 1962), 39. On pp. 26–27, Heilbrunn offers three other possibilities, but since they pertain to partisans engaged in direct or de facto support of the army, they are not discussed in this text.
37. Debray, *Revolution in the Revolution?* 95–116. Debray argues that the popular liberation army must command in Latin American insurgencies; further, the army will spawn the party during the struggle.
38. *Washington Post,* November 9, 1985, and *New York Times,* December 22, 1985.
39. Heilbrunn, *Partisan Warfare,* 30.
40. A detailed review of Palestinian disunity and various organizational structures created in an attempt to overcome it may be found in O'Neill, *Armed Struggle in Palestine,* 125–53.

7

EXTERNAL SUPPORT

Up to this point, I have emphasized the part that popular support for insurgents plays in offsetting the strengths of governments and the importance of solid organization in acquiring and utilizing such support. I have also noted that the extent and contributions of popular support vary considerably depending on a number of factors, including the strategies and political skills of insurgent leaders. Yet, as significant as popular support may be in providing assistance to insurgents, it can rarely provide all of the resources necessary for the accomplishment of insurgents' ultimate goals.

Unless governments are utterly incompetent, devoid of political will, and lacking in resources, insurgent organizations must normally obtain outside assistance if they are to succeed. Even when substantial popular support for the insurgents is forthcoming, the ability to combat government military forces effectively usually requires various kinds of outside help, largely because beleaguered governments themselves receive external assistance, which in some cases compensates for their lack of popularity.[1] The viability of governments in Angola, Afghanistan, Kampuchea, and El Salvador in the mid-1980s would have been very dubious if it were not for external assistance from the Cubans, Soviets, Vietnamese, and Americans, respectively; in fact, aid to those governments enabled them to carry out reasonably sustained counterinsurgency military operations. This, in turn, compelled the insurgents to obtain material assets to meet the government challenge and gain the initiative successfully.

If external support is often necessary when insurgents enjoy popular support, it is even more crucial when they do not. Facing a long struggle against government forces with superior arsenals, insurgents must turn to sympathetic nations, other insurgent movements, private institutions in other states, and international organizations in order to increase their political and military capabilities. Fortunately for them, several developments in the international system in the past fifty years or so created favorable opportunities.

Global Context

Among the features of the post–World War II international system that facilitated the acquisition of external support, six were particularly noteworthy: East-West competition, the Sino-Soviet dispute, regional rivalries, the worldwide proliferation of armaments, the activities of private groups, and vast improvements in transportation and communications. For a long time, the greatest impetus to external support for insurgent movements was the continuous rivalry between the major Communist powers and the West starting in the late 1940s.[2] In an era when nuclear weapons made direct military engagements between the two sides extremely hazardous, the Soviets and Chinese served state interests and ideological aims by supporting wars of national liberation against governments friendly to the West. Although the United States and its allies generally found themselves backing governments, in the 1980s they turned the tables somewhat by aiding a number of insurrections against Marxist or partially Marxist regimes in places like Angola, Afghanistan, Nicaragua, and Kampuchea.

The Sino-Soviet dispute also motivated assistance to insurgent groups, especially since the termination of the Cultural Revolution in China and the death of Mao brought to power leaders who were equally, if not more, committed to containing Soviet power. One outcome was Chinese support for insurgents opposed to Soviet-backed regimes (e.g., in Afghanistan and Kampuchea). Both the East-West and Sino-Soviet rivalries thus multiplied the opportunities for insurgent groups to obtain external support of various kinds.

Another development favorable to insurgent groups was, and remains, the tendency of regional states to undermine rival neighbors by providing assistance to dissidents. In Africa, for instance, South Africa backed insurgents in Angola and Mozambique, while the latter two states aided the South-West African People's Organization (SWAPO) and the African National Congress (ANC) in their campaigns against South Africa. In North Africa and the Middle East, similar circumstances marked Sudanese-Ethiopian, Libyan-Sudanese, Egyptian-Libyan, Syrian-Jordanian, Syrian-Iraqi, and especially Iraqi-Iranian rivalries. Once again, the general effect was to increase the overall potential for external support to insurgents.[3]

While states are clearly the most important source of external support, analysts should not discount the inputs of private, nongovernmental groups and organizations, as well as other insurgent movements, for in many instances, they provide not only political and moral support but also money, equipment, training, and other kinds of tangible assistance. The Afghan guerrillas, for example, received help from nongovernmental groups in France, which provided doctors and radio operators and transmitters, and from others in the United States that collected funds, publicized the plight of the resistance, and petitioned the U.S. government to increase its aid.[4] Likewise, the IRA received important aid from the Northern Irish Aid Society in the United States, and the Contras in Nicaragua benefited from assistance provided by private groups, especially following the congressional suspension of aid in 1984 and 1985.[5] And, as chapter 6 suggests, in the 1990s it became apparent that Islamic militant groups were benefiting from the largesse of various social groups, charities, and wealthy private benefactors, especially in Saudi Arabia and the Persian Gulf emirates.

Assistance from other insurgent groups, particularly in the area of training, has also become more prevalent than in the past, as demonstrated by aid from the People's War Group and the Maoist Communist Center (both Indian groups) to the Maoist insurgents in Nepal and by the training assistance that the Palestinian Liberation Organization (PLO) provided to many groups.[6] While aid from both private groups and other insurgent movements may not be decisive strategically, it can be quite important in helping sustain the political activities and low-level terrorism or guerrilla warfare operations of insurgent groups that find themselves in a very weak position.

The unprecedented production of military weaponry and equipment in today's world has also made the acquisition of external support easier. Major and regional powers have a greater capacity to provide assistance, and a flourishing private arms industry can be, and has been, tapped by insurgents.

The final factor facilitating the provision and acquisition of external support is the global transportation and communications revolution. All kinds of material supplies can be moved farther and faster because of quantitative and qualitative improvements in surface, water, and air transportation. Whereas in a previous era potential donors halfway across the world were of little use to insurgents, today distant suppliers can play a major role because effective and expeditious transportation is available.

Also very important, but often underemphasized or discounted, is the impact of phenomenal progress in communications on the provision of moral, political, and material support. Through radio, television, print, and especially the Internet, outside supporters can mount extensive propaganda campaigns on behalf of insurgent groups and reach wider audiences. And, by providing communications equipment, external sources have been able not only to upgrade the command and control of insurgent forces in the field but also to facilitate political and organizational tasks. Reports of National Resistance Front (RENAMO) insurgents using word processors in their jungle base areas inside Mozambique were somewhat of a novelty in the 1980s. But, as the well-known use of laptops by Islamic militants has shown, such reports were merely harbingers of much greater things to come.

All told, insurgent movements seem to have much greater opportunities for gaining external support than at any previous time in history because of a combination of international and technological factors. Whether they take advantage of the opportunities depends on their organizational capability. Nowadays many, if not most, insurgent movements have representatives in foreign countries whose main purpose is to obtain support from private and governmental sources. In some cases, insurgent organizations—like the PLO and, to a lesser extent, the National Union for the Total Independence of Angola (UNITA)—have had a rather extensive de facto diplomatic corps to carry out this mission. How well the mission is performed depends on the quality of the insurgent organization, since many general and specific tasks must be accomplished. In general terms, acquiring external support involves political lobbying and negotiations about what will be provided, how, and under what terms. Specific organizational tasks include provision of policy guidance and coordination and procedures for moving materials (often covert and evasive), as well as funding for representatives' basic needs (e.g., food, shelter, travel, transportation) and for public relations requirements (e.g., computers, fax machines, and videotapes). The point here is simple yet important: external support does not just happen; it must be pursued through serious organizational efforts involving diplomacy and information campaigns. Accordingly, well-organized insurgencies are in a better position to acquire external support than poorly organized ones. The exact nature of that support merits closer attention.

TYPES OF EXTERNAL SUPPORT

To state simply that an insurgent movement enjoys support from particular states or nonstate actors does not tell us much because the kinds of resources made available can differ considerably. Consequently, we must subdivide external support into four basic types: moral support, political support, material support, and sanctuary.

Moral Support

Moral support consists of private and, more important, public statements that indicate sympathy for insurgents in very general terms. The content of such statements may reflect one of several themes. The first and most common emphasizes grievances that justify and explain the insurgents' recourse to violence. Second, attacking governments for denying political rights and allowing repression, as well as for the social and economic deprivations they permit, is a familiar tactic, as is praising the courage and persistence of insurgents in the face of seemingly insurmountable odds. Third, the reputation of the insurgents may be burnished by suggesting similarities between them and heroic groups of the past. Fourth, the righteousness of an insurgent movement may be extolled by linking it to larger global forces seeking to end various exploitations and abuses by governments. The penchant of Marxist governments to associate insurgent groups with such sublime collectivities as "the progressive forces," "the anti-imperialist front," "freedom-loving peoples of the world," and so on typified this theme. Yet, as helpful, comforting, and encouraging as moral support may be to insurgent movements, its contribution is marginal without political support.

Political Support

It is very important to make a precise distinction between moral and political support. Political support for insurgents goes a step further than moral support; it is marked by explicit and active backing for the ultimate goals of insurgents in the diplomatic and public arenas. Although moral support and political support are often given simultaneously, this is not always the case, as two situations involving superpowers make clear. The first was Soviet support for the PLO in the 1970s. On the one hand, the Soviets gave consistent moral backing to the Palestinians by condemning Israel's "repressive measures" and commending the "liberating, just character" of the "patriotic partisans" and their "legitimate nationalist and anti-imperialist struggle." On the other hand, Moscow emphatically dissociated itself from the PLO's goal of eliminating the state of Israel. In a Budapest press conference on November 11, 1968, for instance, Foreign Minister Andrei Gromyko stated that "the Soviet Union, while deploring Israel's views on the Middle East crisis, acknowledges Israel's rights as an independent state," a point that contradicted the ultimate aim of the PLO at that juncture.[7] This distinction between moral and political support was reiterated numerous times, much to the chagrin of Palestinian leaders who came to recognize the limits of what they could expect from the Soviets.

The second situation involved ambiguous American support for the Contras in Nicaragua. Although some Contra leaders were originally led to believe that the United States endorsed their goal of displacing or significantly moderating the Sandinista regime in Managua, American officials, responding to congressional objections, subsequently indicated that the real purpose of U.S. support was to interfere with Sandinista support for the guerrillas in El Salvador. Thus, while American leaders and spokesmen gave moral backing to the Contras by praising them as "freedom fighters" and the like, they disclaimed support for the overthrow of the Nicaraguan government. Not surprisingly, this difference was not lost on the Contras.[8] Since American aid was essential for the survival of the Contras, Washington's influence on the course of events was significant. Unfortunately, incomplete and poorly developed strategic thinking reflected the lack of clarity concerning which goals the United States really backed. For the first several years, the insurgency consisted mainly of cross-border guerrilla attacks from sanctuaries in Honduras and, to a lesser extent, Costa Rica. Later, the insurgents began to make an effort to establish a permanent presence in sections of Nicaragua itself. While the pressure generated by cross-border raids might have been sufficient to motivate Managua to cut off aid to insurgents in El Salvador, it had little hope of compelling the Sandinistas to effect basic reforms or, even less, to change the political system. A prolonged war was necessary to compel such changes, a fact that was recognized only belatedly. The point is that a coherent strategy depended upon a clarification of the main goal, and that vital clarification was largely in the hands of an external-support state that could not decide what it wanted.

While various motives may help explain why external actors withhold political support, one major reason is that it is riskier than moral support. This is because governments whose very existence or territorial integrity is challenged by political support for its adversaries are more apt to adopt diplomatic and economic policies detrimental, if not hostile, to those states giving such support. Governments that fail to punish external supporters run the risk that more states will champion insurgents' goals in the international arena and perhaps even give them tangible assistance. In view of this, it is not hard to see why threatened governments find political support far more damaging and intolerable than the general sympathies and platitudes associated with moral support. Of course, governments deem material support to insurgents even more offensive.

Material Support

Material support consists of tangible resources either used on behalf of insurgents or given to them directly. Obviously, material support is important and often crucial for insurgents. Although the popular image of material support tends to focus on military-related resources, it actually covers a wide spectrum, including, at the nonmilitary end, such things as financing, basic necessities (e.g., food, clothing, medicine, shelter), supply or use of radio stations, and political, ideological, and administrative training. Money serves many purposes, especially funding the acquisition of military supplies, paying the salaries of full- and part-time members of an insurgent movement, and covering expenses associated with sustaining a political apparatus, especially its representatives abroad. Assistance in the form of basic necessities can be quite important because it is directed toward needs that must be met if defection and demoralization are to be avoided. This is particularly true of insurgents who are committed to a prolonged struggle based on popular support. In these situations, Web sites, radio stations (or airtime), and instruction in politics, ideology, and administration can greatly enhance the organizational dexterity and esoteric and exoteric appeals that, as we have seen, are instrumental to insurgents' efforts to gain and retain popular support.

Outside powers can aid insurgent warfare in many ways. To begin with, the supporting state may use its own forces to assist the insurgents, either directly or indirectly. Examples of the direct use of force include Iran's periodic artillery support of Kurds across the border in Iraq in the 1970s and Jordan's occasional artillery support for Palestinian guerrillas in 1968 and 1969; the indirect use of force is illustrated by China's instigation of hostilities along its borders with North Vietnam in response to Vietnam's campaigns against Chinese-supported guerrillas fighting the Vietnamese-backed government in Kampuchea in the 1980s. Since both direct and indirect use of military force from supporting states risk escalating internal conflicts to interstate wars, it is not nearly as prevalent as the provision of advisers, intelligence, training, communications equipment, weapons, ammunition, and other combat-related supplies, which are essential in cases where the insurgents have failed to obtain them from the target government on the battlefield (or elsewhere) or have decided to increase their military operations in scope, intensity, and duration. According to Edward E. Rice, the Mexican Revolution of 1910 to 1920 provides an example of insurgents' inability to obtain outside support for expanded military forces, which led to failure. In contrast, the acquisition of external military supplies played a key role in insurgents' success in Vietnam from 1965 onward, when a North Vietnamese decision to conduct mobile conventional attacks led to the development of an elaborate logistical system (based on massive Russian and Chinese supplies) that stretched from North Vietnam, through Cambodia and Laos, to South Vietnam.[9]

Sanctuary

The Vietnamese conflict also calls attention to the vital role that sanctuaries can play in insurgencies, since all three states adjacent to South

Vietnam contained bases used for training, arms stockpiling, operational planning, and providing safe havens for leaders and facilities for rest and recuperation.[10] The contribution of sanctuaries to the North Vietnamese and Vietcong war efforts was obvious to all who participated in that conflict; thus, the major bombing campaigns and ground operations directed at them came as no surprise.

The Vietnam conflict represented one of two situations in which sanctuaries are particularly important. The first is when insurgents decide to escalate hostilities to widespread guerrilla attacks by large units or to mobile conventional frontal assaults. Both levels of fighting require nearby bases and depots to provide substantial and sustained logistical support. The second situation is when effective government countermeasures deny insurgents permanent bases inside the target country. Under these conditions, the sanctuaries are literally the last fallback position of the insurgents because without them, military activity will cease or be inconsequential (e.g., the PLO after the 1982 Israeli invasion drove its forces from Lebanon).[11]

Students of insurgency have long recognized the importance of sanctuaries to insurgent movements. One astute veteran observer of insurgencies, Bernard B. Fall, argues that "in brutal fact, the success or failure of all rebellions since World War II depended entirely on whether the active sanctuary was willing and able to perform its role."[12] But, while one might agree with the general thrust of this proposition, analysts should bear in mind three qualifications when examining external support: first, there have been exceptions where insurgents accomplished their goal with minuscule or no sanctuaries; second, the presence of sanctuaries may be less important in explaining developments than other factors; and, third, the specific contributions of sanctuaries vary from case to case.[13]

Castro's insurgency illustrates the first point since it succeeded without a contiguous sanctuary. In fact, the importance of all forms of external support was minimal because the Batista government was so weak that it collapsed in the face of low-level guerrilla warfare.[14] The insurrection in Oman during the 1960s and 1970s provides a case in which factors other than sanctuaries were more important in explaining events, especially the demise and containment of the insurgency. Although the Popular Front for the Liberation of Oman (PFLO) had an active sanctuary across the border in the People's Democratic Republic of Yemen that sustained its guerrilla operations for several years, a palace coup in Oman in 1970 brought to power a new sultan who dramatically changed the government response by instituting political, economic, and military reforms that shrewdly exploited the PFLO's shortcomings in the areas of popular support and organization. In a word, an energetic and enlightened government response offset the impact of the sanctuary and other advantages the insurgents' enjoyed.[15]

As far as the third qualification is concerned, a number of situations demonstrate that the contributions of sanctuaries can vary considerably. At one end of the continuum is the most valuable form of sanctuary, namely, a network of extensive fixed bases with headquarters, supplies, training areas, hospitals, and so forth. Current and recent examples include the use of Cambodia, Laos, and North Vietnam by the Vietcong; Pakistan by the Afghan guerrillas and later Al Qaida and the Taliban; the Tindouf area in Algeria by the Front for the Liberation of Rio d'Oro and Saguia el-Hamra (Polisario); Lebanon by the Palestinian fedayeen prior to 1982; and Angola by SWAPO. Somewhere in the middle are smaller facilities and camps used to support terrorism or low-level guerrilla warfare. Iran, for instance, provided facilities for a number of groups, including Al-Dawa ("the Call"), a Shiite terrorist group opposed to the Iraqi Baathist regime; the Bahrain National Liberation Front; dissident Iraqi Kurds; and several smaller groups. Until recently, India permitted the southern state of Tamil Nadu to function as a limited sanctuary for Tamil insurgents fighting in Sri Lanka, and Thailand did the same in its border areas for Kampuchean insurgents. At the lowest end of the sanctuary continuum is an absence of fixed bases but tolerance for the transit of weapons and personnel. Although modest in comparison to more complex sanctuaries, transit privileges and facilities are hardly insignificant for insurgents fighting in landlocked countries like Afghanistan or who are denied easy access to the sea (e.g., the Kurds in Iran and Iraq, the Thai National Liberation Front, the National Union for the Total Independence of Angola [UNITA]). For them, overland shipment of supplies is a veritable lifeline.

A final point with respect to sanctuaries concerns their location. For the most part, sanctuaries in adjacent states are preferable to those a considerable distance away. Although more vulnerable to government counterattacks, sanctuaries in contiguous states facilitate and expedite the marshaling and moving of men and supplies to battle zones far more effectively than distant sanctuaries do, which is very important as insurgents move toward higher levels of military activity. In fact, the absence of contiguous sanctuaries may preclude serious military escalation by insurgents, and their loss will normally result in de-escalation.

The lack of a contiguous sanctuary has severely handicapped groups such as the Tamils in Sri Lanka and the New People's Army, the Moro Liberation Front, and the Moro Islamic Liberation Front in the Philippines when it comes to expanding their small-scale guerrilla attacks into large, sustained, widespread guerrilla campaigns. Accordingly, they must depend on the hope that government ineptitude and demoralization in the army will eventually result in political capitulation. If the government and army do not falter, the lack of an adjacent sanctuary can be a glaring, if not fatal, deficiency.

The sharp regression of Palestinian guerrilla attacks following their expulsion from Jordan in 1971 and the paucity of cross-border guerrilla and terrorist attacks after their exodus from Lebanon in 1982 demonstrate how the loss of contiguous sanctuaries leads to a de-escalation of military activity. Indeed, the hollow nature of the PLO's rhetoric about armed struggle from 1983 to 1990 related directly to its lack of sanctuaries in the confrontation states surrounding Israel.

The importance of contiguous sanctuaries for Al Qaida remains to be seen. Without question, the northwestern tribal area of Pakistan has facilitated guerrilla and terrorist operations in Afghanistan by both Al Qaida and its Taliban and Hezb-i-Islami allies since 2002. That said, a closer look at Al Qaida's strategy thus far reveals the desire for a sanctuary *somewhere* for planning, training, and otherwise supporting its global operations rather than specifying one adjacent to a targeted state. Sudan and later Afghanistan fulfilled this desire. Presumably, Al Qaida's wish to take over a key Middle East state, preferably Saudi Arabia, would as well. The transnational aspect of its strategy and its diffuse organization would both seem to imply that Al Qaida really requires multiple sanctuaries for the various groups in its worldwide constellation, as opposed to one critical, contiguous sanctuary. Reports of an Al Qaida presence in ungoverned spaces in Yemen, Somalia, the southern Philippines, Indonesia, and African states bordering the Sahara lend credence to this assumption.

PRECARIOUSNESS OF EXTERNAL SUPPORT

An accurate description of external-support types, donors, and contributions, while important, is only part of the analytical calculus, since donor-client relationships can entail many costs, risks, and uncertainties. The fact is that few, if any, external states engage in open-ended assistance programs for altruistic reasons; they render support because it serves their interests at specific times. As a result, it is not unusual to find that donors often decrease or terminate assistance or, in some instances, switch sides if it suits their purposes, particularly when the insurgents' ultimate goal and the external supporter's aims are incongruent. For example, during the 1960s and early 1970s, Kurdish insurgents collectively known as the Pesh Merga carried out a persistent, albeit moderate, level of guerrilla warfare against various governments in Iraq. While the Pesh Merga was able to persist largely owing to material and sanctuary support from Iran, this relationship's durability was always in doubt because the shah did not endorse the Kurds' ultimate goals. Essentially, the Kurds tended to vacillate between the goal of outright secession and the reformist aim of autonomy, both of which Iran found unpalatable because their achievement would serve as an example to its own restive Kurdish population. As far as the shah was concerned, the Kurds were a useful instrument for pursuing his own aims of compelling Iraq to agree to border rectifications favorable to Iran, especially with respect to the boundary line in the Shatt-al-Arab waterway. As things turned out, Baghdad agreed to make concessions, and the shah reciprocated by ending his support for the Kurds. Since the Kurds had made the mistake of concentrating their forces, they suddenly found themselves vulnerable to Iraqi military attacks, which they could not withstand in the absence of the external support from Iran. In the end, they were sacrificed on the altar of Iranian state interests.[16]

Situations in which there is equivocation with respect to external political support are also risky for insurgent movements. In the case of assistance to Afghan insurgents fighting the Russians, many key external supporters never clearly endorsed the ultimate political goals of any of the insurgent groups. Moreover, although they appeared to back the intermediate aim of expelling the Soviets from the country, there were questions about whether this meant both Soviet military units and the Soviet-backed government or just the former. The implication for the insurgents was clear. If most or all of their external supporters were willing to settle for a Soviet military withdrawal that left a Marxist government in power, the insurgents could have found themselves locked in a conflict with that government but without the benefit of badly needed outside aid. Similar situations existed in Angola and Mozambique, where the Republic of South Africa aided insurgents not out of commitment to their ultimate aims but because it wanted quid pro quo agreements (i.e., an end to Angolan support for SWAPO attacks in Namibia and Mozambican support for the African National Congress in return for South Africa's termination of assistance to UNITA in Angola and the Mozambique National Resistence).[17]

A current case in point that deserves mention is Syria's moral, material, and limited sanctuary support for Hezbollah and various Palestinian organizations that reject peace with Israel, especially Hamas and Palestinian Islamic Jihad. Never has Damascus agreed to the ultimate political aims of these groups. The idea of a Shiite-based Islamic regime in Lebanon or a Sunni-based one in Palestine is anathema to the secular Baath party, which has long recognized Islamic militants as a mortal enemy. Why then render moral, material, and sanctuary support? The principal answer is to gain leverage over Israel pursuant to the national aim of getting the Golan Heights back. Most analysts and the insurgent groups themselves believe that an agreement fulfilling that aim would include a Syrian commitment to terminate external support to such groups.[18]

A final and somewhat different twist to the ambiguity of external support was illustrated when India allowed its southern state of Tamil Nadu to provide all four types to Tamil secessionists in Sri Lanka while the central government in New Delhi actually opposed the goal of secession (because its achievement could inspire India's Tamils to pursue a similar aim at some point). When it appeared that Tamil success in Sri Lanka might outweigh the short-term political benefits of placating the population of Tamil Nadu, the Indian government accepted an invitation to deploy peacekeeping forces to Sri Lanka, which ended up conducting counterinsurgency operations against the Tamil insurgents.

Even where governments unequivocally support insurgents' political goals, there are no long-term guarantees about the continuation of external support. A classic example is the People's Republic of China's moral, political, and material assistance to the Popular Front for the Liberation of Oman and the Thai National Liberation Front, especially during the heady days of the Cultural Revolution in China. As the Cultural Revolution subsided, a new Chinese leadership reassessed its foreign policy and decided to focus on containing Soviet expansionism. Pursuant to this end, Beijing repaired damaged relations with a number of official governments, including those in Thailand and Oman, by eliminating or severely curtailing assistance to dissidents opposed to these and several other governments. Even Libya's self-proclaimed champion of Third World liberation movements, Muammar al-Qaddafi, has not been above this kind of volte-face; witness the surprise 1984 Oujda agreement with Morocco, which led to his withdrawal of support for Polisario in return for an end to King Hassan's opposition to Libya's role in Chad.[19] In all of these cases, new or reformulated national interests stemming from strategic reassessments took precedence over previous ideological affinities and seemingly shared goals with insurgent groups.

Another negative aspect of external support, one that often occurs in fractious insurgent movements (as noted in chapter 6), is the proclivity of some donor states to contribute to internecine strife within movements by backing one group at the expense of its rivals. This can result from an outright desire to establish hegemony over the insurgents, from a perceived need to check the influence of other donor states, or, as is so often the case, from both. Syria again provides a classic illustration of this particular point. In this context, however, support has to do with assistance to secular elements of the PLO—as opposed to aid to Islamic militants—and is explained by a combination of factors, including a historical conception that the area the insurgents seek to "liberate," Palestine, is really part of southern Syria. In addition, strategic sensitivities stemmed from threats posed to the regime in Syria by potentially unfriendly insurgent groups (both Marxist and Islamic) and their allies in nearby Lebanon, many of which opposed the ideology of Syria's ruling Baath Party. Finally, there were fears that some groups might reach a settlement with Israel that would isolate Syria, thus undercut its effort to get back the Golan Heights (captured by Israel in 1967). A convergence of these factors led Syria not only to sponsor its own group in the PLO, Saiqa, but also to instigate and support hostilities inside the PLO against groups that were following or contemplating policies inimical to Syrian interests. Such hostilities took the form of using various Palestinian groups against each other (e.g., support for the Abu Musa rebels against Yasir Arafat's Fatah from 1983 to 1988) or the use of Saiqa and Palestine Liberation Army units controlled by Syria against PLO groups (e.g., during the Lebanese civil war in 1976). This example suggests that when insurgent movements suffering from disunity and fragmentation receive external support, analysts should pay close attention to who gets what, whether assistance deliberately favors one group over others, what the motives behind the assistance are, and what the consequences are for the insurgency.[20]

The examples above suggest that both authoritarian and democratic governments of states providing external support can be unreliable donors over the long term, although it would seem that the underlying values and institutions of pluralist governments make them more apt to engage in policy reassessments that can lead to a decrease or complete termination of aid. With respect to pluralist values, there is frequently discomfort with, if not outright aversion to (which can be heard in the public debate), interfering in the internal affairs of other states. As with other issues, support for insurgent movements in other countries is not exempt from close and critical scrutiny by the media and various branches of government; witness the impact of the American press and Congress on the policy of supporting UNITA in Angola and the Contras in Nicaragua. While it is premature to reach a firm historical judgment about the relative reliability of authoritarian and democratic external-support states, we need to be particularly alert to domestic political events in democracies that may affect external support for insurgencies.

SUMMARY

The same global factors that have accounted for the increased availability of external support for insurgents (i.e., superpower, Sino-Soviet, and regional rivalries) have had the somewhat paradoxical effect of making such support precarious because in specific situations, political calculations can lead to the conclusion that new circumstances and opportunities render continued support an obstacle to achieving other foreign policy aims. The implication for analysts is obvious: they must pay careful attention to the types of external support rendered and their effect on the insurgency, and they must examine the durability or continuation of support in terms of donor states' motivations and changes in the domestic, regional, and international political contexts that affect them. Although exact predictions may not be possible, the more analysts can set forth underlying factors or developments that could adversely affect external support, the more complete their overall assessment. While the academic merit of such an undertaking is self-evident, it also has very important practical implications for the parties to the conflict. For insurgents, a better understanding of donor nations' motivations may lead to a quest for support from multiple sources, efforts to prevent changes that could result in a decrease of—or end to—support, or adjustments in strategies and plans. For governments trying to cope with insurgents, a better understanding of donor motivations may result in foreign policy initiatives using various instruments of power designed to shape or bring about the events and circumstances that will undercut external support.

NOTES

1. Two examples where the capability to arm insurgents reportedly did not keep pace with an increase in recruits are the Contras in Nicaragua and the Tamils in Sri Lanka. According to Enrique Bermúdez, the operational military commander of the Nicaraguan Democratic Force, only a quarter of his 14,000 troops had adequate ammunition and boots for combat. See *Washington Post,* February 18, 1985. Both Indian intelligence officials and Western diplomats noted in early 1985 that many Tamils could not fight because of a shortage of weapons, according to the *Washington Post,* February 5, 1985.
2. While historians may debate whether the cold war began before or shortly after the Bolshevik seizure of power in Russia or in the aftermath of World War II, no one denies that insurrections in Greece and Iran in the late 1940s and in Malaya, the Philippines, and Vietnam in the 1950s intensified suspicions and fears in the West about perceived Sino-Soviet expansionism. Although support from the Soviets and Chinese varied considerably in these cases, the insurgencies suggested that the Western powers were vulnerable to wars of national liberation in the Third World. Accordingly, by the 1960s both Moscow and Beijing openly endorsed the notion of support for wars of national liberation. On Soviet-bloc support, see Richard Shultz, "The Role of External Forces in Third World Conflicts," *Comparative Strategy* 4, no. 4 (1983): 79–104.
3. In general, support for insurgents in neighboring states appears to be a less risky and costly way to pursue national objectives than interstate conventional warfare.

Moreover, since many Third World states suffer from crises of political legitimacy (i.e., weak political communities, systems, or authorities), they are vulnerable to pressures generated by armed insurgents. The problem with such an approach is that two can play the same game. Hence, governments that have legitimacy crises of their own invite similar actions by their adversaries as time goes by. Where the states initiating external support have greater problems, as Angola and Mozambique compared to the Republic of South Africa, they may end up experiencing greater threats to their own stability than they create for their adversary.

4. Both American and French private groups provided aid to the Afghan resistance. It included, among other things, money, blankets, radio transmitters, and medical care. See, for instance, Claude Malhuret, "Report from Afghanistan," *Foreign Affairs* (winter 1983–1984): 426, and *Christian Science Monitor,* December 28, 1984.
5. In early February 1985, the Nicaraguan Democratic Force had collected some $5 million in the absence of U.S. aid. Part of it was from private sources. See *Washington Post,* December 10, 1984, and February 18, 1985; and *New York Times,* June 15, 1984.
6. "Nepal Maoist Commander Said Admitting Indian Role in Training," *Kathmandu Nepalnews.com,* January 22, 2004, in *FBIS-NESA (INE),* January 22, 2004. Numerous insurgent groups have received training at PLO bases. A succinct account may be found in Claire Sterling, *The Terrorist Network* (New York: Holt, Rinehart and Winston, 1981), 122–26.
7. See Bard E. O'Neill, *Armed Struggle in Palestine* (Boulder, Colo.: Westview Press, 1978), 195–96.
8. The question of whether the primary U.S. aim in supporting the Contras was to destabilize the country and bring about the downfall of the Sandinista regime or to compel the Sandinistas to end their support of the insurgents in El Salvador has never been satisfactorily clarified. The uncertainty and problems surrounding this ambiguity are discussed in the *New York Times,* April 7, 1983.
9. Edward E. Rice, *Wars of the Third Kind* (Berkeley: University of California Press, 1988), 79–80. Numerous other writers have called attention to the importance of external material aid; see, for instance, Virgil Ney, "Guerrilla Warfare and Modern Strategy," in *Modern Guerrilla Warfare,* ed. Frank Mark Osanka (New York: Free Press of Glencoe, 1962), 31–32; Bernard B. Fall, *Street without Joy* (Harrisburg, Pa.: Stackpole Books, 1963), 294; Ted Robert Gurr, *Why Men Rebel* (Princeton, N.J.: Princeton University Press, 1970), 269–70; Julian Paget, *Counter-Insurgency Campaigning* (New York: Walker & Co., 1967), 25; Frank Trager, *Why Vietnam?* (New York: Frederick A. Praeger, 1966), 77.
10. On the importance of sanctuaries, see Ney, "Guerrilla Warfare and Modern Strategy," 10; Peter Braestrup, "Partisan Tactics—Algerian Style," in Osanka, *Modern Guerrilla Warfare,* 376, 380–82; John J. McCuen, *The Art of Counter-Revolutionary War* (Harrisburg, Pa.: Stackpole Books, n.d.), 37; Roger Trinquier, *Modern Warfare* (New York: Frederick A. Praeger, 1964), 97–98; Richard L. Clutterbuck, *The Long, Long War* (New York: Frederick A. Praeger, 1966), 7; and Otto Heilbrunn, *Partisan Warfare* (New York: Frederick A. Praeger, 1962), 51, 60–61.
11. A good example of this situation is the predicament of the insurgents in Sarawak as depicted in Douglas Hyde, *The Roots of Guerrilla Warfare* (Chester Springs, Pa.: Dufour Editions, 1968), 86–88. The Palestinian guerrillas have also relied on sanctuaries in Jordan and Lebanon because they could not establish permanent bases in Israel, the

West Bank, and the Gaza Strip; see O'Neill, *Armed Struggle in Palestine,* 163–64.

12. Fall, *Street without Joy,* 294.
13. J. J. Zasloff, *The Role of Sanctuary in Insurgency: Communist China's Support to the Viet Minh, 1946–1954* (Santa Monica, Calif.: The Rand Corporation, 1967), 80, contends that Fall and others state their case on sanctuaries too strongly. However, in my opinion, Zasloff goes too far in suggesting there is no crucial relationship between external support and success. Whether the Vietcong and North Vietnamese could have succeeded without sanctuaries is very doubtful.
14. Dickey Chapelle, "How Castro Won," in Osanka, *Modern Guerrilla Warfare,* 333–34.
15. See Bard E. O'Neill, "Revolutionary War in Oman," in *Insurgency in the Modern World,* ed. Bard E. O'Neill, William R. Heaton, and Donald J. Alberts (Boulder, Colo.: Westview Press, 1980), 213–33.
16. On the shah's termination of aid to the Kurds, see Paul R. Viotti, "Iraq: The Kurdish Rebellion," *Insurgency in the Modern World,* 202.
17. The mutual commitments to end external support for insurgents between South Africa and Mozambique are summarized and discussed in the *New York Times,* October 10, 1984, and November 30, 1988. The agreement involving Angola is discussed in the *Washington Post,* October 14, 1984.
18. The convoluted relationship between Syria and the Islamic militant groups is discussed in Ilana Kass and Bard O'Neill, *The Deadly Embrace* (Lanham, Md.: National Institute for Public Policy and University Press of America, 1997), 274–77.
19. William R. Heaton, "China and Southeast Asian Communist Movements: The Decline of Dual Track Diplomacy," *Asian Survey* (August 1982): 779–98, and "People's War in Thailand," in *The Art and Practice of Military Strategy,* ed. George Edward Thibault (Washington, D.C.: National Defense University Press, 1984), 850–52; O'Neill, "Revolutionary War in Oman," 223–24.
20. *Christian Science Monitor,* September 7, 1984.

8

GOVERNMENT RESPONSE

That insurgents can pose significant threats to governments does not mean they will achieve their ultimate goals. In fact, it can be argued that most of the time they do not. Yet, even when finally contained, marginalized, or eliminated, insurgents can inflict substantial damage and loss of life. The magnitude of such damage and loss of life depends, as we have seen, on a complex interplay of a number of factors.

Of all the variables that have a bearing on the progress and outcome of insurgencies, none is more important than government response. In words as true today as when written over thirty years ago, Professor Walter Sonderlund puts it succinctly: "As soon as the challenge is in the open the success of the operation depends not primarily on the development of insurgent strength, but more importantly on the degree of vigor, determination and skill with which the incumbent regime acts to defend itself, both politically and militarily."[1] Implicit in Sonderlund's comment is the notion that governments can control their own destinies since they normally have the advantage during the incipient stages of violence due to their higher degree of political institutionalization and control of the instruments of coercion (i.e., the police and military). Whether governments lose, maintain, or enhance their initial advantage depends, in the main, on how they mobilize and use the political and military resources at their disposal, a subject that has spawned a considerable body of counterinsurgency literature. This chapter integrates the most important aspects of that literature with my own ideas and findings.

In most cases, an effective counterinsurgency program depends on an accurate, substantive, and comprehensive profile of the adversary and the environmental context within which he operates. The framework discussed in the preceding chapters is an effective and convenient way to establish such a profile. Understanding insurgents' goals, techniques, and strategies, as well as their efforts and achievements with respect to the physical and human environments, organization, and popular and external support, enables us to focus our analysis on what exactly governments are responding to and how they perceive the situation. When linked to government response, the profile also underscores the dynamic connections among all the factors.

I should note before proceeding that the general use of the term *response* does not indicate that the government is always in a reactive mode with respect to particular threats, issues, and problems. In fact, governments that anticipate difficulties and initiate preventive measures are in a much better position than those that wait for problems to emerge, then react. Both effective reaction and anticipation depend on an informed and comprehensive understanding of the situation regarding both sides of the conflict.

RESPONDING TO INSURGENT GOALS, STRATEGIES, AND MEANS

It goes without saying that no two insurgencies are exactly the same. As we have seen, insurgents pursue various goals, use a variety of techniques or methods, and pose different threats to governments. Consequently, a key point to address when evaluating a counterinsurgency program is how well the government knows its enemy. As self-evident as this may seem, the historical and contemporary record is replete with instances in which governments have misdirected policies because they misunderstood or falsely portrayed the goals, techniques, strategies, and accomplishments of their opponents. Whatever the reasons (e.g., inflexibility, sloppy thinking, ignorance, bias, anger, bureaucratic imperative, or psychological aversion to acknowledging one's own weaknesses), the outcome is flawed, costly, and sometimes fatal policy and behavior.

To begin with, it is important to find out if the authorities have made a conscious effort to ascertain what type of insurgency they are dealing with by carefully examining all information at their disposal—statements, publications, and internal documents of the insurgents, as well as intelligence from human and electronic sources if it is available. Failure to do this can lead them to paint false pictures of their adversary. For instance, reformists can be erroneously identified as egalitarians, secessionists as egalitarians, anarchists as egalitarians, and so forth. In a well-known manifestation of this mistake during the cold war, some beleaguered governments, especially in Latin America, had a penchant for simply portraying all of their adversaries as revolutionary Marxist egalitarians.

A government that misunderstands the type of insurgent movement it is facing can blind itself to policy options that might end the insurgency at lower costs. Conversely, one that does understand is in a better position to craft appropriate and rational responses. For example, a government that correctly views reformists as those who want a more equitable distribution of economic and political power can then see the possibility of a compromise settlement; mislabeling reformists as egalitarians, traditionalists, or anarchists rules out possible accommodations. In turn, ruling out accommodations runs the longer-term risk of transforming increasingly frustrated reformists into one of the other types of insurgents. This happened during the Dhofar insurgency in Oman, where egalitarianism overtook reformism, and some would argue that it happened again more recently in Uzbekistan, where reformism morphed into reactionary-traditionalism.[2]

Careful analysis may also reveal goal disagreements within an insurgency movement, enabling governments to craft policies that may satisfy some rebellious groups, thereby exacerbating divisiveness in the insurgency. The insurgency in Iraq seemed to have just such potential by late 2003. Awareness of different insurgent goals opens up the opportunity to sow discord among insurgents by stressing their incompatible goals through robust and carefully crafted public-information campaigns or by infiltrating the insurgency with agents who try to provoke and intensify distrust among the groups. By contrast, a government approach that treats diversified insurgents as "birds of a feather" is self-defeating because it precludes strategic and tactical responses that can exploit differences between insurgents.

Accurate assessments of insurgent goals, of course, only begin the process of fully understanding an opponent's profile. Early in the struggle, it is also important to identify insurgents' strategy and the prominent forms of violence they employ. In some cases, such as Vietnam, the declarations, writings, and behavior of insurgents clearly reveal their strategy, while in others, such as the Afghan insurrection against the Russians, the strategy has to be inferred because of its amorphous, ad hoc character. Moreover, in some cases there may be no discernible strategic thinking or strategy. Whatever the case, governments that take the time to examine insurgent strategies carefully are better prepared to conceptualize a broad and relevant counterstrategy.

Once analysts understand the insurgents' strategy, they can focus on the most important requirements for success associated with that strategy and look at ways to frustrate insurgents' efforts to fulfill those requirements. To illustrate, if insurgents have chosen a Maoist protracted-popular-war strategy, informed government strategists will be attuned to the need to devise political, social, and economic policies and programs to undercut the propaganda and organizational efforts of their enemies. Since, as we have seen, insurgent activity in the first phase of a protracted-popular-war strategy is largely nonviolent and concentrated on political organizing, it may go undetected or be accorded little significance because the government lacks a basic understanding of the strategy. By contrast, awareness of what tends to transpire early in an insurgency using this strategy can alert the government and motivate it to shed its apathy and complacency, to move quickly to improve and extend its own administrative capability, and to uncover and neutralize the work of insurgent political cadres. If this is done, the insurgency may be contained early on; if not, the insurgency may progress to the point where the stage has been set for guerrilla warfare. Should that occur, the costs of countering the protracted-popular-war strategy will increase sharply. This is precisely what happened in the Philippines during the 1970s when the Marcos government, preoccupied with various political enemies and the Moro Liberation Front's secessionist insurrection in the south, casually dismissed the threat posed by the fledgling New People's Army, which was quietly going about the business of organizing and gaining support for an armed struggle that rapidly became a serious threat once violence commenced.

Where insurgents adopt other strategies, the strategic orientation of the government will differ correspondingly. The military-focus approach calls for a response that emphasizes the military dimension but does not exclude carefully selected and tailored political, social, and economic measures. Conventional warfare threats must be countered with conventional forces. This, of course, was the basic idea underlying the eventual Union strategy to defeat Confederate armies decisively in the American Civil War. The North's difficulties in that conflict stemmed not from an improper strategy but from problems of implementation, not the least of which was mediocre leadership (e.g., General George B. McClellan's indecisiveness in the early years).[3] Where the military-focus strategy of the insurgents emphasizes guerrilla warfare, which has most often been the case in the last sixty years or so, the government emphasis must be on counterguerrilla campaigns (the characteristics of which are discussed below). It bears repeating that emphasizing counterguerrilla operations does not mean that political, social, and economic factors are neglected altogether. Such neglect will, as the first phase of the counterinsurgency campaign in Iraq in 2003 and 2004 demonstrated only too well, exact unnecessary human and material costs. Hence, strategists must anticipate the role these factors play and design appropriate policies to address whatever problems they pose or are likely to pose.

Conspiratorial and urban-warfare strategies necessitate a government response that concentrates on political efforts and on intelligence and police work in the cities rather than on expenditure of resources in the rural areas. Examples here include the responses to the Irish Republican Army (IRA) in Northern Ireland, the Tupamaros in Uruguay, the Red Army Faction in Germany, the Red Brigades in Italy, and Basque Homeland and Liberty (ETA) in Spain.

A transnational strategy like Al Qaida's poses a more complex problem, given its employment of political and military resources across the globe. Organizational threats call for a variety of political and social measures to undercut insurgent appeals and activities, while violent threats call for differential responses to guerrilla warfare and terrorism, depending on which is prevalent in particular places. Since Al Qaida is a polycentric organization operating in many locations, the formulation and implementation of policies must, perforce, vary from place to place. The success of localized policies, however, depends heavily on international intelligence and security cooperation because of the global aspect of the threat. As some countries victimized by Al Qaida have found out, trying to go it alone can have disastrous consequences.

While an accurate assessment of an insurgent movement's strategy is important for the design of an effective general counterstrategy, more specific guidelines and principles for government behavior relate to the political techniques and forms of warfare adopted by the insurgents. All of these have received ample attention in the writings on insurgency, particularly those that set forth lessons learned. There is thus a large collection of propositions, suggested antidotes, and policy prescriptions associated with the different threats.

The political threat posed by insurgents varies in scope and complexity from case to case. It involves organizational activities, information campaigns, demonstrations, fund raising, and the like and can have either internal or external dimensions (or both). Since the political aspects of insurgency movements fall within our categories of popular support, organization, unity, and external support, which this chapter addresses later, we shall defer further comment until then and confine our remarks here to the question of coping with the different forms of warfare (violence) that insurgents may adopt, starting with terrorism.

Experience and experts suggest that internal terrorism and small-scale, *urban* guerrilla attacks against soldiers and policemen are most effectively dealt with by emphasizing police work, good intelligence, and judicial sanctions.[4] Since terrorists operate in very small units or cells and are normally highly secretive, regular military forces are of marginal use because of their conventional training and orientations. Whereas the military is trained to engage and destroy the enemy, police forces stress apprehension, information gathering, and the cultivation of ties with the local community, functions that are crucial for rooting out small, clandestine terrorist cells. The simple fact is that every terrorist killed rather than incarcerated may take invaluable information with him to the grave.

As is well known, regular military forces often resort to indiscriminate violence when frustrated by their inability to cope with elusive terrorists. Two examples include acknowledgments by both the Peruvian and Sri Lankan governments that their armed forces were responsible for large-scale violence against civilians in the mid-1980s when they responded to terrorism.[5] To avoid situations like this, wise governments turn to specially trained police and intelligence agencies for a solution.[6] However, as brutal episodes involving the Peruvian Guardia Civile have also shown, even the police can get out of hand in the absence of discipline and a respect for the law. Accordingly, to be effective, professional police and intelligence work must be disciplined. It is no coincidence that terrorism subsided and became less threatening in Northern Ireland and Italy when governments there emphasized disciplined police forces with more members from the local community. Even when special police forces are part of the military establishment, the latter can be kept out of the day-to-day business of countering terrorists. One way, adopted in Italy for the carabinieri and in Spain for the Guardia Civile, is to transfer units involved in antiterrorist actions to the control of the Interior Ministry.

Reliance on disciplined police and security forces and on intelligence is necessary but not sufficient for effective counterterrorism. Aggressive steps must be taken to insure vigorous coordination within and between the police and security forces. Many governments have learned this the hard way. A case in point was the British effort to deal with IRA terrorism in Northern Ireland. As Keith Jeffery has pointed out, during the 1960s there was no clear policy direction at the highest level and an absence of coordination of the various intelligence and security forces, with the result that the situation had worsened considerably by 1975. This, in turn, led to an urgent review and the adoption of new measures, most importantly, the establishment of a well-coordinated and centralized security structure.[7]

If an emphasis on well-coordinated police and intelligence agencies is important with respect to internal terrorism, the problem of transnational terrorism and the possible use of chemical, biological, and radiological weapons places an urgent premium on international police cooperation and intelligence sharing. In fact, even where terrorism is limited to internal attacks, international cooperation is important because operatives, supplies, weapons, and other forms of aid for terrorists often come from the outside. The obvious question is whether governments facing terrorists with international links are willing to work with the police and intelligence agencies of other countries. Where they are, the situation can improve markedly, as French-Spanish cooperation against Spain's Basque terrorists has shown. In that case, a change in French policy in 1986 led to the arrest and jailing of nearly five hundred ETA suspects in southwestern France, where the terrorists had found a safe haven.[8]

As for officials and citizens who are threatened either at home or abroad, governments may resort to various defensive and offensive measures. Defensively, steps can be taken to enhance the security of embassies, consulates, airline offices, transportation and communications facilities, and the like (e.g., barriers, access control, weapons detection, and the posting of armed guards). Offensively, special operations can be mounted against terrorists located in other countries. As the Israelis have shown, these may involve attacks against the bases and headquarters of terrorists and special operations such as the dispatch of hit teams to eliminate terrorist operatives. Needless to say, such actions risk international opprobrium, retaliation by the country involved, and perhaps expansion of the conflict to involve additional participants; therefore, obtaining the permission of third countries would seem prudent, particularly where a future cooperative relationship with such countries is deemed important. This is not to suggest, however, that under certain circumstances surprise preemptive operations might not merit the aforementioned risks. Where an extant or impending threat is recognized as very serious, as was the case with Osama bin Ladin prior to September 11, unusual boldness may be required, which in this case would have involved the elimination or capture of bin Ladin and his associates. Bold actions in such circumstances, of course, require decisive leadership that can overcome myriad political obstacles, not the least of which are self-serving personal agendas and bureaucratic inertia and turf squabbles that, according to Richard A. Clarke, paralyzed the American national security process prior to September 11.[9]

Guerrilla warfare in the rural areas presents problems different from terrorism. Since guerrilla units are larger and better armed than terrorist units, specialized police units are inadequate and vulnerable. In those rare cases in which guerrilla units are isolated in areas with open terrain, government regular forces can eliminate them with conventional attacks. By contrast, they are difficult to detect and engage when, as is often the case, they operate in favorable terrain and emphasize hit-and-run attacks, dispersal, and reliance on the population. Under these conditions, guerrillas often frustrate regular military forces because, as the United States and Soviet Union found out in Vietnam and Afghanistan, respectively, heavy firepower and large-unit maneuvers are irrelevant, not cost-effective, and sometimes counterproductive.[10]

Numerous cases suggest that the centerpiece of successful counter-guerrilla campaigns is the small-unit operation—that is, sustained and aggressive patrols and ambushes in guerrilla-infested zones. John Nagl has pointed to the U.S. Marine Corps' Combined Action Platoons as a successful example in Vietnam (that unfortunately proved the exception rather than the rule). The main targets are not pieces of territory to be seized and held but rather the insurgents themselves, as well as their supporters, sources of supply, and organization. John J. McCuen argues that the proper response to low-level guerrilla warfare is the positioning of armed units in a large number of small posts where they can protect and mix with the local people. Supported by backup mobile air, naval, and ground forces, they can conduct ambush patrols that engage guerrillas and conduct harassment operations against insurgent units in underpopulated hinterlands. He suggests that French mobile operations in the Atlas Mountains in Algeria might be a model to emulate and that counterorganization using native tribes could prove useful in some underpopulated areas, the French experiences with the Moi and Thai tribes in Indochina being examples. An even more decisive example of using native tribes successfully was the U.S. Army's eventual reliance on rival Apache Indians to quell a tenacious and very sophisticated guerrilla war waged by other Apaches in the latter half of the nineteenth century. Exploiting tribal or clan rivalries presupposes a basic understanding of both social structure and behavioral patterns, something that the American military has come to appreciate—albeit belatedly—in both Iraq and Afghanistan.[11]

When insurgents commence successful large-scale guerrilla operations (e.g., the Vietcong from 1965 to 1966), governments obviously face a more serious threat. McCuen's analysis suggests that smart governments first consolidate the areas they hold (lest they also be subverted) and gradually expand from there with the object of gaining control of the population, food, and other resources.[12] Once this is done, government forces can venture forth from their base areas and seek to defend *vital* lines of communication (the French in Indochina mistakenly tried to defend all lines of communication and, thus, ended up with a large, static defense force), to inflict losses on guerrilla units, and to neutralize the insurgents' political apparatus. Once again, the key components are patrols, attacks, and ambushes by dispersed units operating day and night, supported by mobile forces and airpower. Artillery, air force, and commando harassment of insurgents in remote areas where bases are likely to have been established may also make an important contribution to antiguerrilla efforts. Populated areas cleared of guerrilla bands should be reorganized by military civic action teams that are prepared to play a defensive role in conjunction with forces operating in the region. It is important that any forbidden zones (i.e., areas that can be fired into at will) not be set up in areas where there are innocent civilians; otherwise, such military actions may prove counterproductive by creating more insurgents than they eliminate.[13]

In order to free regular military forces for counterguerrilla operations and to provide security for government officials, civic action teams, and the people, local self-defense forces may be established. Where they are not, insurgent violence can intimidate civilian officials in charge of social and economic programs; witness the plight of unprotected mayors in El Salvador in 1988 who either resigned or were assassinated.[14] The effectiveness of local militias established to prevent this kind of thing will depend heavily on whether they constitute a disciplined force perceived to be a servant of the people (as in the case of the *firqats* in Oman) or are instead ill-disciplined units guilty of excesses against the people (as in the case of the Civilian Home Defense Force in the Philippines).[15]

Governments confronted by conventional warfare are in a more serious situation since the insurgents have calculated that the balance of forces has shifted in their favor to the point where they can deploy larger and more heavily equipped units against government forces in sustained battles (e.g., the terminal phases of the Chinese civil war). One analyst argues that the government's first step should be to stabilize its own base areas, even if this means sacrificing large parts of the country. After securing base areas, it can direct large mobile strike forces, supported by air and artillery, at insurgent bases, as was done with the assaults on guerrilla strongholds during the Greek civil war. If the government is lucky, the insurgents may choose to defend their bases, thus violating a cardinal principle of insurgency warning against engaging a superior force in positional battles. If insurgents decide to revert to guerrilla warfare, the government can then respond likewise, taking the appropriate steps summarized previously.[16]

The last point suggests that *adaptability* is crucial when responding to the various types of threats posed by insurgents. This is easier said than done in many cases because insurgent threats may not only overlap but also vary from region to region. In view of this, an effective response involves a sophisticated military strategy that avoids one form of warfare applied indiscriminately in all sectors and, instead, adopts a flexible policy that coordinates a variety of countermeasures in different areas, depending on the nature of the threats. For example, it would be a mistake for a government facing a substantial conventional threat in one sector and low-level guerrilla activity in another to extend its search-and-destroy operations against conventional formations to the guerrilla area. Such an overreaction could have serious, unintended consequences because guerrillas can easily blend back into the population and, thus, raise the possibility of regular military units striking out against the people, many of whom may be quite innocent. Past experience suggests that under such circumstances, it is more appropriate to conduct conventional operations in one area and patrols in the other. The height of folly would be to rely almost solely on conventional operations while neglecting small-unit operations in key populated areas of the country that face a guerrilla threat (e.g., Westmoreland's overreliance on search-and-destroy operations in Vietnam).

Up to this point, our discussion has concentrated on the different orientations with respect to the use of force against terrorism, guerrilla attacks, and mobile conventional warfare. As we know, however, since the use of force is part of a larger political-military struggle, success depends on its integration with political, judicial, administrative, diplomatic, economic, and social policies. This is particularly true when it comes to dealing with terrorist and, most important, guerrilla threats because nonmilitary factors, all of which the government can influence, largely determine the success or failure of these forms of warfare. To better understand this, we must now focus on the relationship between government response and the other criteria of the framework for analysis.

GOVERNMENT RESPONSE AND EVALUATIVE CRITERIA

Environment

The physical environment, as we saw in chapter 4, can be a tremendous asset for insurgents pursuing protracted-popular-war or military-focus strategies. Large areas with heavy jungles or mountains and poor roads, like the Philippines, Vietnam, Afghanistan, and China, will remain conducive to guerrilla operations for the foreseeable future, despite improvements in defoliation, detection technology, air mobility, and the like. Although the government cannot completely neutralize the advantages conferred on the insurgents by these physical settings, it may be able to reduce those advantages by adopting an appropriate counterinsurgency strategy and skillfully using its own assets. Essentially, government forces need to isolate areas favorable to guerrilla operations by consolidating their own areas of control and then surrounding and gradually moving into the areas with rugged terrain. The British demonstrated that this was possible in Malaya and Kenya in the early 1950s, although doing so required substantial resources and patience. Parenthetically, it should be recalled that the identification of the Malayan Communist Party with the Chinese minority facilitated British efforts.

Many countries, of course, do not have ideal topographical conditions for guerrilla warfare. Although they may have some rugged areas with good cover and few, if any, roads, governments may be able to isolate such zones and decisively reduce their contributions to insurgents' efforts. The insurgency in Oman in the 1960s illustrates this point well. For the most part, insurgents' activities centered on the southern province of Dhofar, a mountainous area with boulder-strewn canyons, abundant foliage, and a poor road and communications system, all of which favored guerrilla operations. But closer inspection revealed that the physical setting of Dhofar had some serious flaws that the government could exploit. Among these was the confinement of the insurgents' transportation and communications lines to the mountains because the latter were bounded on the east by the coast and on the west by the hot, desolate, and inhospitable Rub al-Khali ("the Empty Quarter"). Following the Qabus coup in 1970, the Omani armed forces, aided by Iranian expeditionary forces, took two steps to exploit these vulnerabilities: first, they built roads and extended lines of communications that allowed the army to set up permanent bases in the mountains, and second, they constructed a series of fortified lines that bisected the guerrillas' north-south supply routes and isolated their units. Consequently, they transformed what was initially a favorable area for guerrilla operations into one that rendered the insurgents more vulnerable. Although on a smaller scale, the Omani actions were similar in many ways to those of the Chinese Nationalists during their fifth "extermination campaign" against Mao's base area in south-central China (which led to the famous Long March in the 1930s).[17]

Another illustration of government adaptability and initiative in neutralizing a physical environment that had been supportive of guerrilla operations for several years occurred in the western Sahara. Unlike Dhofar, the terrain there was an expansive desert devoid of foliage. Relatively unhindered by a mediocre government air force and an army made up of recruits from either urban centers or the mountains and unfamiliar with a desert environment, guerrillas from the Front for the Liberation of Rio d'Oro and Saguia el-Hamra (Polisario) took advantage of their knowledge of the desert to conduct numerous attacks, some quite large, and actually reached into Morocco proper. Following a reassessment of the situation, the Royal Armed Forces (FAR) decided to concentrate on defending a so-called useful triangle, an area that contained the majority of the population and phosphate deposits, by building a series of walls (made of sand, dirt, and rocks) that contained intermittent military outposts and detection devices. Although costly, the walls significantly blunted Polisario's guerrilla and mobile conventional operations because insurgent units seeking to circumvent or attack them were relatively easy to detect in the open terrain.[18] Incidentally, it is worth recalling that during the Vietnam War, insurgents rendered a similar effort to construct a barrier along the border between South and North Vietnam (the McNamara line) ineffective by penetrating or going around it via Laos. In that case, the size of the area and the dense foliage would have been too costly to overcome.

Both the Omani and western Saharan situations nonetheless demonstrate that in some situations governments can turn elements of a once unfavorable physical environment to their advantage through calculated policy decisions and effective implementation. The general questions suggested by these two situations are, of course, whether the government has meticulously analyzed the impact of the physical makeup of the country on the insurgency and what it might do to offset the advantages the terrain gives the insurgents.

If understanding the implications of the physical setting is often essential to a sound government response, understanding the human milieu is even more important. A careful and unbiased assessment of demography, social structures and values, economic trends, the political culture, and the structure and performance of the political system is, as we have seen, necessary to uncover the causes of an insurgency and identify obstacles facing both sides in implementing their strategies and policies. From the government's perspective, a comprehensive review—preferably as soon as possible—can reveal critical social, economic, and political problems that it must address, as well as provide insights into the feasibility of various antidotes. Ignoring this step can, as the interim governing authorities learned in Iraq in 2003 and 2004, lead to grave problems and unnecessary losses.

The more complete the assessment, the better it is since partial reviews run the risk of focusing only on part of the problem and ignoring the interrelatedness of demographic, social, economic, and political factors. In response to the insurgency by the New People's Army, for instance, the government of the Philippines conducted a study of the social structure and economic distribution pattern, which suggested a need for land reform. Land reform may not be a panacea, however, as further examination of basic demographic trends reveals an overpopulation problem that would in all likelihood render the effects of land reform inconsequential. This, of course, further suggests that the population dilemma must be dealt with and that other policies may be necessary to cope with the disappointments that will be engendered when hopes associated with land reform are not fulfilled.[19] Of course, the possibility of accomplishing any of this appears dubious in the midterm because the political system allows entrenched wealthy elites to use their leverage to block fundamental changes.

On a more positive note, the insurrection in Oman in the 1960s and 1970s was a case in which an assessment of the human milieu by the government and its British advisers set the stage for adopting more effective policies. In Oman in the 1960s, the human environment was conducive to insurrectionary behavior because the lack of government administration in and commitment of resources to the *jebal* (mountainous areas) exacerbated ethnic and linguistic differences between the *jebalis* ("mountain people") and the coastal population. Under such conditions, insurgent political organizers found it relatively easy to exploit existing social antagonisms. An energetic and enlightened reversal of moribund government policies in the 1970s, emphasizing an administrative and military presence, as well as the provision of health, educational, and agricultural services in the *jebal*, eventually mitigated the *jebalis*' hostility toward the sultan. These developments in Oman showed that governments can affect various dimensions of the socioeconomic milieu in positive ways once they understand the opportunities and challenges it presents.

A comparison of the Omani situation with that in Afghanistan further suggests that an appreciation of social values and structures can help prevent counterinsurgency blunders. Reforms in Oman were effective not only because they met some identifiable material needs but also because they did not involve a substantial government intrusion into local affairs that challenged tribal values and structures. In Afghanistan, by contrast, ambitious land, educational, and marriage reforms in 1978 played a key role in igniting violent resistance. In places such as El Salvador, Guatemala, and the Philippines, such "enlightened" reforms would undoubtedly have been greeted with popular approval; in Afghanistan, they met with scornful and violent disapproval because they threatened widely accepted and deeply entrenched social values and structures legitimized by tradition and religion. The lesson for governments is that officials responsible for counterinsurgency policy making need to understand the social system's tolerance for both the kind and degree of policy initiatives under consideration.

The final aspect of the human environment, the political culture and system, is no less important to governments facing insurgencies. This comes as no surprise since the resolution of social and economic problems often at the root of insurgencies depends on political decisions. Regardless of the type of political system they operate in, political leaders need to be sure that it functions well enough to keep them informed of the extent and intensity of popular demands, which groups espouse them, and how strong the groups are. The basic point here is that blocked channels of communication and expression can be, as the shah of Iran belatedly found out, a major problem because of the misleading and poorly informed images of the popular mood that they may create. In a word, unknown problems are hard to solve.

Aside from the issue of whether social and economic demands are effectively articulated, processed, and communicated, the functioning or effectiveness of a political system itself may be a concern. A major issue here may involve demands for participation in national decision making by various groups. The essential questions are who wishes to participate and what kind of participation they have in mind. Generally speaking, the larger and more educated the groups seeking participation, the greater the problem they present. Smaller groups are easier to manage. The matter of the kind of participation demanded is also important. Not all groups seek Western-style formulas of participation. In the context of the political culture and style of Persian Gulf countries, for instance, participation is more apt to mean playing a role in the consultative process than in "one man, one vote" open elections, political parties, and so on. If this continues to be so and the professional middle class increasingly demands participation, the real solution may not be the adoption of Western institutions but the adaptation and reform of local ones. The idea of co-opting potential or actual dissidents is, after all, hardly a new one.

Much more, of course, could be said about the political system and insurgency. Entire books devoted to the subject of instability have sought to identify specific functions necessary for system maintenance and how the functions are performed in specific cultures in order to assure stability. One point these studies make is the same as ours—namely, that flaws in the political system can be fundamental underlying causes of instability that at times translate into insurgent behavior. The logical prescription here is that governments dealing with insurgencies should take a hard, open-minded look at the political process as part of their assessment of the human environment. They must address in a forthright manner whether and how they can satisfactorily rectify major flaws revealed by an analysis of the political process (e.g., the inordinate leverage of privileged groups like the military, police, or landowners). Reform may well be difficult and, in some cases, improbable, but the absence of an open-minded look at the political process will make it impossible.

While common sense suggests that governments will naturally take the rational step of thoroughly assessing the human environment prior to making policy choices, such an assumption has been proven wrong many times. One thinks again of the political and social blunders of the Afghan government in the 1980s, which, according to Soviet specialists, woefully misunderstood its own society. The government's assessment of the human environment is thus a very significant area of inquiry for all analysts. Superficial, incomplete, distorted, or erroneous assessments are often at the root of political and military policies that are ineffective or have failed altogether, especially when it comes to neutralizing insurgent efforts to acquire and organize popular support.

Popular Support

As noted previously, effective government actions and policies are closely related to insurgent efforts to gain popular support, especially in cases where insurgents are trying to obtain active assistance for terrorists and especially guerrillas. This has commonly been referred to as the battle to win the "hearts and minds of the people." In assessing government efforts to counteract insurgents, it is important to remember our discussion of the various techniques that insurgents use to gain support. Two basic questions need to be asked. First, is the government attuned to the fact that normally the elites and the masses have different interests and respond to different insurgent appeals, thus raising the possibility of the government's adopting policies tailored to each and driving a wedge between the two? Second, how is the government responding to whatever techniques the insurgents are employing?

It is axiomatic that any counterinsurgency effort should aim to destroy much, if not all, of the insurgents' leadership and organization. When the charismatic attraction of the top insurgent leader is thought to play a key role in gaining support, his capture or elimination is especially important; witness Soviet attempts to kill Jonas Savimbi of the National Union for the Total Independence of Angola (UNITA) and the American search for Osama bin Laden.[20] But, since the security surrounding such a personage rarely permits this, other approaches may be tried, including propaganda and disinformation campaigns designed to discredit him. In addition, agents who have penetrated the insurgent apparatus may try to stir up jealousies and rivalries. Where charismatic leaders are operating in a culturally diverse environment, such efforts sometimes emphasize the ethnic, religious, or racial differences between the charismatic leader and the groups he seeks to influence favorably, thereby sowing distrust, if not dislike, between them.

Esoteric appeals based on either religion or secular ideology can be countered by posing alternative ideologies or, short of that, general values.

To help dissuade intellectuals from joining insurgents, persuasive and compelling alternative values, arguments, and ideas need to be presented, and the basic points of the insurgents' theories must be skillfully critiqued and refuted; simple psychological warfare operations directed at the masses will not suffice for dealing with intellectuals. Rather, governments must show that the insurgents' ideas and their implementation are detrimental to the interests of the educated classes. Thus, sophisticated critiques of Marxist class analysis and reminders of the fate of the intelligentsia under Marxist rule can be designed to discourage discontented intellectuals from casting their lot with insurgents. The demonstrable repression and economic failures of regimes that came to power as the result of successful insurrections or political protest movements trumpeting ideologies or theologies intolerant of other views (e.g., Marxist regimes and the Islamic Republic of Iran) can be adduced as further compelling evidence to underscore the point. For the most part, the purpose of this persuasion is to deter members of the educated stratum from backing insurgents; once intellectuals have joined or otherwise actively supported an insurgency for ideological reasons, it is difficult to win them back because of the psychological investment they have made. This is especially so when nationalist or religious ideas are involved.

Nationalism, as we have seen, has a particularly potent appeal in many insurgencies. Whether or not nationalist ideas are part of a larger comprehensive ideological thought system, they continue to play a part in galvanizing popular support for many insurgent movements. Since nationalist appeals are especially powerful because they exploit the natural tendencies of people to distrust and dislike foreigners who rule over them, and because they ascribe psychological (or cultural) traumas, economic deprivation, political disenfranchisement, and repression to foreign rule, it is difficult, if not impossible, for colonial or imperial regimes to counter them effectively with esoteric appeals of their own. Consequently, such regimes generally try to survive by resorting to repression or by meeting the material needs of the people. When their dominions are multicultural, imperial governments have frequently pursued "divide and rule" policies. While such measures may be successful for a time, over the longer term they have generally been ineffective. Indeed, colonial regimes turned out to be exceedingly vulnerable in the post–World War II era (e.g., the French in Vietnam and Algeria, the Portuguese in Guinea, Angola, and Mozambique, the Ian Smith government in Rhodesia, and the Soviets in Afghanistan).

Religious appeals also present a difficult problem for governments because, unlike the appeals of secular ideologies, which are primarily directed at elites, they tend to have much greater influence on the attitudes of the masses; witness the energizing role of Islam in the anti-Soviet struggle in Afghanistan and among radical Muslims today. Where this happens, governments may try to cultivate support from other, more moderate leaders and make the case through propaganda or information campaigns that insurgent religious leaders are disingenuous, selfish individuals who hypocritically violate the most sacred norms of the faith. This, of course, is precisely what the Russian-backed Afghan government tried to do. However, as that case also showed, success will be elusive in the absence of government rectitude since claims regarding moral superiority have little impact when the claimant is engaged in excessive brutality or subscribes to a doctrine (e.g., Marxism) that has well-known antireligious tenets.

Similar dilemmas face those threatened by Al Qaida and its allies today. Repressive policies in many countries, coupled with elite relationships with Western countries, notably the United States, have given militant Islamic ideologues a grand opportunity to exploit fears of externally imposed secularization. Ideologues have effectively and quickly exploited this opportunity by framing the issue as a mortal threat to Islam that must be neutralized by all means, including indiscriminate attacks against noncombatants if necessary. As the Egyptian and Saudi authorities, among others, finally came to understand, coercive measures alone could not eliminate active and passive support for Islamic insurgents; instead, support could be contained and reduced only by a focused, aggressive, and compelling battle of ideas led by respected clerics and intellectuals who could draw on Islamic theology and sacred sources to make a compelling case that militant ideas and behavior, especially terrorist attacks against innocent civilians, are both un-Islamic and anti-Islamic. Whether insurgent ideas are religious or secular, they command attention. Governments striving to maintain and enhance their legitimacy must find effective and culturally relevant ways to communicate and disseminate esoteric appeals of their own, and such appeals must be perceived as relevant and credible. To have enduring value, they must also be truthful.[21]

The manner in which the government responds to exoteric appeals is even more important, for, as we saw earlier, popular support from the elites and especially the masses stems primarily from concrete grievances concerning such things as land reform, injustice, unfair taxation, and corruption. It is over these issues that the battle to win hearts and minds is most directly joined. History suggests that a government can most effectively undercut insurgencies that rely on mass support by splitting the rank and file away from the leadership through calculated reforms that address the material grievances and needs of the people. Governments must distinguish between the motivations of insurgent leaders to change the political community or the political system and authorities, which cannot be accommodated, and the motivations of the masses, which tend to focus on material needs and demands.

Arthur Campbell has noted that in the Spanish guerrilla war against Napoleon, the guerrillas had great difficulty getting aid from the people of Huesca because of the material benefits provided by the French and their restraint with regard to taking things from the people. Likewise, he cites the kindness, administrative reform, and good management of General Suchet in Aragon as factors that undercut support for the guerrillas. In contrast, the repression of General Augereau's forces in Catalonia is said to have played into guerrilla hands and facilitated their quest for popular backing.

Another example of the different effects of contradictory approaches by elements of the same governing authority involved the German administration in the Ukraine during World War II. For the most part, the Germans were their own worst enemy, especially since the Ukrainians had no love for Stalin and seemed ready to help the Germans. As it happened, the German exploitation and repression of the Ukrainians eventually turned them against the Third Reich. Benevolent German administration and effective reforms, such as those carried out by Colonel General Schmidt (which proved effective in harnessing popular support), were few and far between and were undercut by general Nazi policies.[22]

In the postwar era, conscious and determined government socioeconomic reforms reduced active support for insurgents in a number of cases. Besides the previously mentioned Qabus reforms in Oman, one could point to both Israeli policy in the West Bank in the late 1960s and early 1970s and the Huk insurgency in the Philippines in the 1950s. The Israeli case is interesting because the Palestinian Arabs of the West Bank, which had been occupied by Israel in the 1967 war, detest the idea of being controlled by a Jewish military government. Yet, the West Bank populace gave little active support to the Palestinian resistance, even though the latter had experienced a surge in popularity throughout the Arab world in 1968 and 1969. Among the reasons for Israel's success was an improvement in the standard of living in the area, which, the Israelis calculated (correctly as it turned out), would give the people a stake in stability and make them reluctant to support guerrillas and terrorists. Insurgents ruefully conceded Israeli success along these lines, with left-wing ideologues attributing it to the "false consciousness" of the people.[23]

The government of the Philippines faced an increasingly serious threat from the Communist Huk insurgency in the early 1950s, largely because of its poor relations with the people. However, with the election of a new president, Ramon Magsaysay, and good advice from an American, Edward G. Lansdale, the government instituted a number of social, economic, and military reforms to exploit the inherent division between the reformist rank and file and the revolutionary elites in the Huk movement. This generated support for the government and contributed to its eventual victory.[24] It is instructive to contrast this situation with the neglect, corruption, and gross economic favoritism of the Marcos government in the 1980s, all of which played a key part in the striking increase in popular support for the Huks' successor, the New People's Army.[25]

Although less effective than exoteric appeals as a means of gaining popular support, insurgent terrorism can have some impact if it is selective. The major problem for the government is to protect its officials, who must be in place if social and economic reforms are to be implemented. Both rural and urban-based insurgents recognize this, and make officials special targets for assassination, kidnapping, and the like. Many examples come to mind, including the Algerians, the Vietcong, the Tupamaros, the Monteneros, and, more recently, groups such as the IRA, the Red Brigades, the Basque Homeland and Liberty, the Farabundo Martí National Liberation Front (FMNL) in El Salvador, the Sendero Luminoso in Peru, the Palestinians, the Shiites in Lebanon, Al-Dawa in Iraq, the mujahedin in Afghanistan, the African National Congress in South Africa, and various factions in Iraq. To protect their officials from terrorist attacks, governments have found that patient intelligence and police work designed to uncover, detain, or eliminate terrorists is more effective than reliance on the military. Although acts of terrorism may not be eliminated altogether, their incidence and human cost can be dramatically reduced through thc combination of intelligence, disciplined police work, and determined follow-up by judicial officials, as discussed above. It can also lead to informers from insurgent ranks turning against their former colleagues.[26]

Pluralist democracies find it quite difficult and stressful to cope with terrorism because their inherent commitment to due process restricts their actions and, thus, places a premium on patience, determination, and discipline. In contrast, authoritarian states, especially those that exercise extensive control over their citizens' behavior, find it easier to cope with terrorism. The fact that little or no terrorism took place in the Soviet-bloc countries when Communist parties monopolized power is hardly surprising, given the pervasiveness of secret police and intelligence agencies, controlled judicial processes, and a willingness to employ indiscriminate force, if necessary. Authoritarian governments in the Third World, at one time or another, also used harsh and indiscriminate measures to eliminate or reduce terrorism (e.g., Uruguay, Guatemala, Argentina, Syria, Iran, and Iraq). Unlike the Soviet-bloc countries, however, they ran a greater risk of a resurgence of terrorism or popular resistance in the longer term because they lacked the organizational, material, and technological resources of the Soviets and their allies. Indiscriminate brutality (e.g., death-squad activities) risks driving terrorists underground and creating seething hatred among those who are among its more innocent victims.

Recognizing that reliance on coercive measures to eliminate popular support for insurgents is both precarious and costly, even some of the most infamous hard-line authorities have adopted concurrent noncoercive measures. In Iraq, for instance, the government of Saddam Hussein met the challenge of various Shiite insurgent groups, especially Al-Dawa, not only with harsh coercion (including mass executions of insurgents and their families) but also with political and economic measures designed either to win support from the Shiite community at large or to dissuade it from rendering support to the insurgents. These measures included such things as the appointment of Shiites to high-ranking political posts, renovations of urban slums, the building of mosques, and well-publicized visits by President Saddam Hussein to Shiite religious shrines and residential areas.[27]

Whereas the Iraqis had some success with such policies, the Soviets in Afghanistan did not, in part because widespread support for the insurgents grew so rapidly after the 1979 Russian invasion. The Soviet reaction, as noted earlier, was excessively violent, designed to eliminate popular support in the rural areas through the obliteration of towns and villages and the destruction of crops. This situation, as well as a similar one in Eritrea, raises a question that only history will answer: can the physical extermination or expulsion of civilian communities on a widespread scale succeed in coping with the problem of popular support for insurgents? The belated propaganda of the Russian-backed Afghan government in the mid-1980s, stressing support for Islam, accommodation of ethnic nationalism, and economic development, indicated that the Soviets and their Afghan allies had come to doubt the effectiveness of indiscriminate violence. The Soviet withdrawal from Afghanistan in 1989 confirmed the validity of their doubts.

Where governments do not take an overly coercive approach, insurgents sometimes try to provoke repression and an overreaction by government forces against the general population. This age-old ploy to gain popular support can be effective, particularly where governments rely on the military to cope with terrorism, since, as suggested previously, regular military forces, which are not trained for this, often become frustrated and rely on the kind of large-scale violence for which they are trained and equipped. Excessive reactions, as the Peruvian and Sri Lankan governments found out, end up creating more support for the insurgents. Where most of the military and security forces are from a different ethnic or religious group than the insurgents, as in the largely Sinhalese army in Sri Lanka, the danger of overreaction is even greater. Furthermore, even when such behavior does not increase active popular support for the insurgents, it can result in the eventual demise and even punishment of the authorities. Such was the case in Argentina, where the indiscriminate campaign against the Monteneros and other insurgents had the long-term effect of creating pressures on later governments to bring those responsible to trial. To avoid such problems, prudent governments can, as the British in Northern Ireland and the Israelis in the West Bank demonstrated, reassess and alter their policies.

In Northern Ireland during the late 1960s, the British initially reacted to IRA violence by relying on military units and harsh policies such as internment without trial, which was perceived as unjust, indiscriminate, and abusive. When this backfired, contributing instead to increased Catholic support for the IRA, the British rethought their policy, opting for more judicious treatment of suspects, enhanced discipline for military units, and a gradual turnover of the antiterrorist mission to police forces that received support (especially intelligence) from the military. Although imperfect, this turnabout, combined with increasingly indiscriminate IRA terrorist attacks, resulted in decreased Catholic support for the IRA.[28]

Despite their efforts, the British found their policies continuously jeopardized by illegal acts of violence carried out against Catholics by preservationist insurgents from the Protestant community (e.g., the Ulster Volunteer Force). Rather than turning a blind eye to these actions, thereby facilitating IRA recruiting efforts, the British directed police and judicial efforts against the terrorism of Protestant extremists in the same way as they did against the IRA. Despite controversial episodes in 1988 involving the alleged murder of IRA operatives in Gibraltar and a "shoot to kill" policy directed at unarmed IRA suspects, the British performance remained more disciplined than it had been in the late 1960s.

The Israelis faced a somewhat similar problem in their conflict with the fedayeen during the height of the armed struggle in 1968 and 1969. In this case, however, the main source of the problem was spontaneous violence by irate Jewish civilians against innocent Arabs (in reaction to

Palestinian acts of terror) rather than the actions of the military, police, or autonomous pro-state insurgents. Typical of such violence was a response by Jewish citizens after an explosion in a Tel Aviv bus station on September 4, 1968, which killed one and wounded fifty-one. In retaliation, a Jewish mob attacked Arabs in the terminal, beating eight severely, and turned on Arabs arriving in buses, none of whom were among the suspects in the incident. The following day, one of Israel's most respected newspapers, *Ha'aretz*, called attention to the counterproductive nature of such behavior when it said that the perpetrators "must be considered active, unwilling allies of the Arab terrorists." Recognizing the validity of this point and concerned that such violence could lead victims to support Palestinian insurgents, the Israeli government undertook an intensive education drive to prevent recurrences. In addition, government leaders visited Arab representatives in an effort to convince them that such actions did not reflect official policy or attitudes. The crackdown on illegal reprisals extended to the security establishment. In November, two frontier policemen were sentenced to life imprisonment for murdering two local Arabs, and three months later, it was announced that an Israeli captain would be tried for killing an Arab woman and wounding several others.[29]

As a consequence of the attention and effort devoted to the violent reprisals, such behavior decreased and became exceptional rather than normal, until the hard-line Likud came to power in 1977 and ushered in an era of regressive counterinsurgency policies. Among other things, these involved a less discriminate use of force and increased collective punishments, which, in turn, increased Palestinian resentment and led to the first intifada in 1987. Well-publicized and indiscriminate acts of brutality by Israeli Defense Force units that were psychologically and tactically ill prepared for riot duty capped this dramatic regression for the Israelis.[30] Behavior such as this created a groundswell of support for Palestinian dissidents, a fact acknowledged by numerous observers. By 2004, the situation had gone from bad to worse as Islamic militants' popularity soared due to excessive civilian casualties caused by Israeli military forces responding to indiscriminate terrorism by Palestinian insurgents. In a word, the Israelis have provided good—and bad—examples of how governments cope with insurgent attempts to provoke excessive repression.

Finally, insurgents try to gain support by demonstrating their potency through military successes and by providing services. This is obviously a broader method, which ultimately comes down to images and the population's perceptions. Where insurgents can demonstrate relative military and organizational achievements, their chances for gaining support increase, especially if the government is inept, lethargic, and incompetent. While it may sound trite, people tend to gravitate toward the side perceived to be winning. This is particularly true of fence sitters, who have been insufficiently moved by esoteric or exoteric appeals to make a commitment. As for the government response to insurgent terrorism, guerrilla warfare, and mobile conventional warfare, successful counteraction will depend on the various responses discussed earlier, plus traditional military requirements—adequate training, discipline, logistics, transportation, command, control and communications, and, very crucially, astute and flexible leadership at all levels. Since these factors often can affect battlefield outcomes, analysts need to be alert to performance—on both sides—in terms of these traditional military requirements. The failure of the Afghan and the Soviet military to subdue the mujahedin resulted from, among other things, poor leadership, inflexibility, and an overly centralized control system that denied local commanders the initiative required to combat guerrillas.[31] Battlefield reverses for government forces in El Salvador in the early 1980s and in the Philippines in the mid-1980s stemmed partially from shortcomings in many of these areas, especially leadership, while the American debacle in Vietnam resulted primarily from poor leadership marked by self-delusions, prevarication, and a concomitant inability and unwillingness to change a failed strategy, particularly with respect to undermining the political and social activities of the Vietcong.[32]

Through its nonmilitary efforts to demonstrate potency by providing services, the Vietcong intended to take advantage of people's concrete grievances. As we have seen, insurgents try to show that they can meet the needs of the people and provide order and control. This leads us to next consider the government's response to the insurgents' organizational abilities.

Organization and Cohesion

Successful government campaigns to cope with terrorism and guerrilla warfare and to undermine insurgent efforts to obtain, maintain, or increase popular support are closely associated both with a program to address the needs of the people and with administrative competence and capability. Programs without good administrators are hollow. Efficient administrators without programs are powerless, and those with bad programs may exacerbate whatever problems already exist. These qualifiers aside, dispensing basic services, addressing important grievances, and providing security against insurgent violence depends on a good organization that can marshal and wisely use human and material resources. Well-trained and well-motivated political and military officials, especially intelligence personnel, who speak the language and are familiar with the society and culture (as well as subcultures) are essential to accomplishing effectively both the usual tasks of governing and the special undertakings required of coping with terrorism and guerrilla warfare. Those undertakings can involve such things as detention without trial, resettlement of sections of the population, control and distribution of food, curfews, restricting movement of sections of the population, issuing and checking identification cards, and imposing penalties on people possessing unauthorized weapons. Sir Robert Thompson has argued that harsh measures like these can only be applied in areas under government control. To apply them sporadically in regions under insurgent control would leave the people with little choice but to support the insurgents. Beyond this, other experts make the point that to be morally acceptable, governments must impose collective sanctions within the context of providing security against insurgent reprisals. A sound administrative apparatus is vital in assuring that these guidelines are followed and applied in a judicious, fair, and consistent manner.[33]

Resettling portions of the population, for example, may become necessary if the government is to sever links between the insurgents and the populace. While not a desirable course of action, resettlement may be necessary if terror or guerrilla attacks persist and are attributed, at least partially, to the support given insurgents by certain segments of the population. If the government is going to relocate sections of the population effectively, it must give those affected good explanations and assure people that the material benefits of the new locale supersede those of the old one. Civic action and political organization become extremely important during resettlement. The Briggs plan for relocating the Chinese squatters in Malaya, the Kitchener resettlement scheme during the Boer War, and the relocation program during the Mau Mau uprising are examples where moving segments of the population was instrumental in denying the insurgents the support of the population. Conversely, the resettlement carried out by the regime of Ngo Dinh Diem in South Vietnam failed, largely because it was too fast, overextended, and characterized by poor regulatory procedures, ineffective government, inadequate police forces (both quantitatively and qualitatively), and a lack of attention to alternative ways for people to earn a living.[34]

Whenever the government undertakes security measures directed at individuals or groups, it can expect insurgents to make use of legalistic appeals to try to protect their personnel and to portray the regime as a violator of civil and human rights. Essentially, insurgents will seek to have those under detention treated as peacetime offenders.[35] A rebel ploy such as this, designed to further alienate the people from the government, is another reason why the government needs trained officials to implement policies in a judicious and limited fashion.[36]

If the security measures suggested above are to be fairly applied, the government must have accurate information about the insurgent organization, including the identification and location of its members and its intended activities. This requires an effective and educated intelligence apparatus that extends to the rural areas. The government can best obtain the necessary information by establishing a rapport with the people by means of good administration and prudent and diligent police work. That, in turn, calls for well-trained interrogation experts who can minimize violence by knowing the right questions to ask and for competent agents who can penetrate the insurgent apparatus.[37] The best agents are members of the insurgent organization who will betray its secrets and provide "contact" information (what is going to happen in the future).[38] Since the army and police both need intelligence, their cooperation at all levels is, as noted above, imperative. Besides expediting the flow of information, coordination enables military forces to respond as quickly as possible against guerrilla and terrorist units.[39] Governments with diffused power but little coordination among agencies find quick responses hard to achieve.

In light of the fact that insurgents themselves are a potentially valuable source of intelligence, their treatment by government forces is of no small concern. Although it is not likely that members of the hard core (the true believers) will defect, it is possible that less-dedicated insurgents may be induced to surrender, especially if political and military trends portend an uncertain future. Psychological-warfare programs stressing the declining fortunes of the insurgency, contrasting the harsh lifestyle of insurgents with people in government-controlled areas, and promising amnesty, security, and material benefits can play a key part in enticing defections, as the British found out in Malaya and Oman. But if violence is used against defectors, psychological-warfare programs will fail (for obvious reasons).

The successful accomplishment of the political and security tasks noted above depends on the existence of a complex and extensive administrative apparatus. It is no mere coincidence that improvement in the government's political-administrative capacity was a main feature of the successful turnarounds of counterinsurgency programs like those against the Huks in the Philippines, the Popular Front for the Liberation of Oman, and the Malayan Communist Party (MCP). Where the government lacks the ability to establish an efficient administration relatively free of corruption, it runs the grave risk of seeing the insurgents implant their own organizational structures and gain momentum. Both developments become more costly to overcome as time goes by. In the Malayan emergency in the early 1950s, British inattention to the Chinese squatters in areas bordering the jungle enabled the MCP to organize a support base sufficient to sustain a tenacious insurrection. To defeat the MCP, the British eventually had to expend considerable resources to resettle and control the squatters administratively.

The American experience in Vietnam provides a contrasting example. The Vietcong exploited the poor performance, corruption, and neglect that characterized the administration of the South Vietnamese government of Ngo Dinh Diem in the formative years (1958–1964) of the Vietnam War by setting up a political and military infrastructure that ably supported local and increasingly larger regional-force units. By 1965, the victories of the Vietcong led to American and then North Vietnamese involvement on a large scale and to the incredibly costly trial by arms that followed. As a participant on the American side, it was my opinion then that the abysmal political and military performance of the South Vietnamese government in the countryside (due in part to American insistence on conventional military training and operations) was as important an element contributing to the problem as the introduction of North Vietnamese forces. Had the Saigon government done a better job dealing with what was still essentially a southern threat in the early years, the outcome could have been quite different. At a minimum, it might have lifted the mantle of legitimacy and credibility from the Vietcong. If North Vietnam had then proceeded to introduce its own main-force units, the move would have been viewed as an outright invasion rather than an effort to assist freedom fighters against American forces.

More recently, the same organizational failure has been played out in the Philippines and Afghanistan. There is a consensus among observers, including high-ranking Filipino officers, that a poor, inefficient, repressive, and corrupt Marcos government administration paved the way for the increased popularity and growth of the New People's Army, which set up political structures in many parts of the country.[40] Likewise in Afghanistan, Soviet and Afghan government failures in the countryside were due principally to their political and administrative shortcomings, a situation that Afghan leaders Babrak Karmal and later Najibullah candidly admitted a number of times during various conclaves of the People's Democratic Party of Afghanistan. Recognition of the problem, however, was not followed by a solution due to, as is the case in many Third World states, a combination of entrenched political and bureaucratic interests, a dearth of trained administrators (due, in large part, to purges), and insecurity in the rural areas.[41] Whether a belated long-term Soviet plan to compensate for the Afghan government's organizational deficiencies by training officials in the Soviet Union and then returning and dispatching them to the countryside in Afghanistan would have made an impact is doubtful, but we will never know.

Effective organization presumes a significant degree of unity within the government. Like insurgents, governments can suffer debilitating effects from severe political and ideological discord or poor coordination of the various civilian and military organizations under their jurisdiction. The phrase "severe political and ideological discord" refers to a situation in which high-ranking officials and political elites pursue fundamentally different policies for instrumental (i.e., using policies to build political coalitions) or theoretical reasons, or both. Since under such circumstances the primary reason for disunity is often domestic power struggles, the insurgency may receive secondary attention, if that. The familiar results can be paralysis, haphazard behavior, and agencies' failing to share vital intelligence data and working at cross-purposes (e.g., civilian and military officials trying to cultivate popular support through civic action, while various police and security forces commit atrocities). The situation in El Salvador in the early 1980s, which was marked by bitter strife between extreme-right and centrist politicians, is a case in point. This rift not only led to contradictory policies but also resulted in the outright murder of numerous centrist and leftist political leaders (as well as innocent civilians) by right-wing death squads, both developments that benefited the insurgents. Likewise, the chronic and frequently violent disunity between Khalq ("masses") and Parchamite ("banner") factions plagued Afghanistan's ruling People's Democratic Party (PDPA) following its ascension to power in 1978. This disunity, having been widely reported or acknowledged by journalists, diplomats, PDPA leaders, and high-ranking Soviet advisers, is well known to those who follow Afghan affairs to have been a major cause of the failure of the government's policies.[42]

Dealing with disunity is no easier for governments than it is for insurgents when factions or groups have roughly equal (albeit asymmetrical) power, as in Afghanistan. In less severe cases where the central governing authorities have preeminent power but must cope with rivalries among officials and bureaucratic agencies, good leadership qualities appear to be more important than organizational structures. At a minimum, leaders cannot afford to be detached because that simply perpetuates a bad situation. The top leadership must at least clearly articulate a common sense of purpose and common objectives, provide general guidelines, actively coordinate the actions of various agencies, and emphasize initiative, flexibility, and adaptability on the part of local civilian and military officials. While this is quite obviously a challenging agenda, to the extent governments can carry it out, they are better off. Whether regimes are pluralist or authoritarian, they need to steer a middle course between overcentralization and undercentralization. As the Soviet Union found out in Afghanistan, overcentralization undermines the initiative and flexibility at local levels that are vital to coping with guerrilla and terrorist threats. Conversely, as the United States found in Vietnam, decentralization can yield interservice rivalry and poor interagency coordination.

To some degree, the nature of the political system must be considered. Authoritarian systems need to be especially alert to problems of overcentralization as they seek to unify their efforts, while pluralist systems are more vulnerable to excessive decentralization. An extreme case of the latter is Turkey, where poor efforts to cope with both egalitarian and traditionalist insurgents in the 1970s resulted in large part from the fact that the multiparty system produced virtual paralysis in the political, economic, and security spheres. The outcome was stagflation, rising terrorism, and an eventual military takeover that met with popular acquiescence, if not approval.[43]

As a general rule, the chances of having both a broad counterinsurgency strategy and a coordinated and effective organizational structure to implement it seem to be greater under civilian rather than military control, although there are obviously exceptions (e.g., mediocre military rule is better than incompetent and corrupt civilian rule). While military professionals are naturally preoccupied with the management of violence, civilian politicians are apt to have broader outlooks conducive to seeing more dimensions of the problem and to appreciating various nonmilitary responses. Hence, it comes as no surprise that military governments see coercion, sometimes in extremis, as the central feature of a counterinsurgency strategy. The excessive and indiscriminate brutality of military juntas confronted by insurgents in Argentina, Guatemala, Pakistan, and Uganda, to name but a few in the past two decades, is well known. In Pakistan and Uganda, violence contributed to insurgencies' successes; in Argentina and Guatemala, the overwhelming human costs were clearly unnecessary.

While civilian governments have been every bit as myopic about overreliance on force as their military counterparts in ample cases, there are, as we have seen, also many examples of successful counterinsurgency campaigns run by civilians in which force was but one component of strategy. To them, I would add Abraham Lincoln's constant attention to both the larger strategic picture and the importance of political factors in maintaining popular support during the American Civil War, particularly during its most trying moments. It is rare to find military governments that subscribe to and implement multifaceted strategies in which political factors and nonviolent instruments of power are considered as important as force. Hence, other things being equal, civilian governments stand a better chance of success than military governments as far as the organizational response to insurgents is concerned.[44]

External Support

Governments can make a number of possible responses in cases wherein external support for insurgents, particularly in the form of material aid and sanctuaries, plays an important role. Which responses governments choose will depend on calculations of their capabilities relative to external supporters, as well as of potential costs and risks. Since dealing with external support involves interstate relationships, we can analyze government actions in terms of the familiar instruments of statecraft: diplomacy, information, economics, and the military. Before deciding on which instrument (or combination of instruments) to use and how, the governing authorities need to have a clear picture of exactly what types of external support are being provided and the impact that aid is having. This is necessary if the government is to avoid misdirecting its resources because, in some cases, external support either is not a major reason for insurgents' gains, is of little or no consequence, or is nonexistent. The American exaggeration of Soviet and Cuban assistance to the FMLN in El Salvador in the early 1980s, which ignored the real (i.e., indigenous) reasons for the insurgents' successes, illustrates the first situation; the New People's Army's in the Philippines and the Sendero Luminoso in Peru exemplifies the second; and the American invasion of Iraq in 2003, which was justified, in part, by the mistaken assumption that Iraq was assisting Al Qaida, is an example of the third. In all three instances, valuable assets were diverted away from the real problem. Conversely, the accurate assessment that the Taliban regime in Afghanistan was Al Qaida's crucial external supporter (some would even say "center of gravity") led the United States to terminate the rule of the Taliban physically and with it the network of bases it had provided to Al Qaida.

If external support is important and military measures are deemed unwise, one option is to rely on diplomacy. Several actions are possible. On the positive side, quiet negotiations may persuade the external-support state to terminate or alter its support in return for various political concessions if the supporter can be convinced that more important interests can be served by an agreement. This appears to have transpired with respect to China's support for the Thai National Liberation Front in the late 1970s. While we are not privy to the minutes of meetings between Thai and

Chinese officials that led to marked improvements in state-to-state relations, it is probably safe to assume that a Thai desire to see an end to Beijing's support for Thai insurgents was not only discussed but linked to better relations with Thailand, which, in turn, would serve China's far larger aim of containing Vietnamese and Soviet influence in Asia.[45] Successful diplomacy like this, of course, depends on identifying and skillfully exploiting important common interests. Where this is impossible, governments can use coercive diplomacy.

Various courses of action are associated with coercive diplomacy, including the threat or imposition of political, economic, and military sanctions, several of which will be considered when we discuss the other instruments of statecraft. Political sanctions can include breaking diplomatic relations with external-support states and building coalitions with friendly states that will oppose the external-support state on various issues in international forums. Where external supporters are major powers, an important government objective is frequently to gain support from other major powers. However, since major powers pursue a wide range of interests and goals, many of which are more important than those related to a particular insurgency, they are often reluctant to join coalitions or impose sanctions against other major states that are external supporters because to do so might jeopardize the resolution of more important issues with these states. For example, although various European governments shared American concerns about Soviet assistance to various insurgents like the Vietcong in Vietnam or the FMLN in El Salvador, they avoided taking strong stands on behalf of the Vietnamese, Salvadoran, and U.S. governments because to do so might have undercut what they considered to be the far more significant process of rapprochement with the Soviet Union. Since bilateral issues involving major states usually transcend concerns about each other's dealings with third states, governments threatened by insurgents may not succeed in generating international political sanctions against external-supporting states. Accordingly, they frequently place greater reliance on other instruments of statecraft.

The principal aim of the information instrument is to provide ideas, data, and arguments that will convince various audiences that external support to insurgent groups is not in their best interests. There are three targets of information campaigns: insurgents and their external supporters, other nations not directly involved in the conflict, and groups inside the external-support states. As far as the insurgents and their active supporters are concerned, the aim is to create distrust between insurgents and external supporters by stressing their differences or past antagonisms (e.g., ideological, racial, ethnic, religious, and historical animosities). The

Soviet-backed Afghan government's propaganda about putative American anti-Islamic policies, which sought to drive a wedge between the mujahedin and their U.S. supporter, is one illustration; Angola's public castigation of UNITA's external support from the "racist" South African government is another. It should be noted, however, that no matter how accurate and skillful such informational efforts may be, there is little, if any, evidence that alone they have had much impact on insurgents and external supporters.

Information directed at uninvolved nations may be more effective, as the Angolan government has shown. By emphasizing the fact that UNITA's principal external support came from a South African government whose racial policies have been condemned internationally, the Popular Movement for the Liberation of Angola government managed to discredit Jonas Savimbi to the point where other states were reluctant to render any kind of external aid to UNITA. In fact, some states that might not otherwise have done so ended up criticizing Savimbi.

Propaganda directed at groups inside external-support states, particularly in pluralist democracies, may also be somewhat effective; witness the Nicaraguan government's successful 1984–1985 campaign to influence American political leaders and the attentive public by criticizing both the Contras' human rights abuses and their attempt to overthrow the Sandinista government.[46] Other examples of efforts to deny external support to insurgent groups through the use of international publicity efforts are the depiction and excoriation of terrorist acts of the Palestine Liberation Organization (PLO) by Israel and of the IRA by Britain. Although the existence, content, and effectiveness of informational efforts vary considerably from situation to situation, analysts must not overlook them since in specific cases they can be useful.

The use of the economic instrument of statecraft to undercut external support may also have a positive impact in deterring or undermining external support for insurgents in some cases. One of the purposes of Saudi Arabia's largesse vis-à-vis neighboring Arab states, some of which, such as Syria and Iraq, are ideologically opposed to the monarchy, has been to keep them from assisting insurgent groups that could pose a threat to the Saudi regime. A more familiar and negative use of the economic instrument is the threat to curtail or terminate trade and foreign aid, or actually doing so. The problem with this approach is that most governments, particularly in the Third World, simply do not have sufficient capability and leverage to make this work. Hence, they often try to get others who do have leverage to bring it to bear on their behalf. American economic sanctions against Nicaragua and Cuba, because of their support for egalitarian insurgents in El Salvador or elsewhere, would be a case in point. Here again, however, success is not guaranteed because, as Cuba and Nicaragua also illustrate, alternate sources of trade and aid are often available, even though they may not be preferable. All in all, the economic instrument has not been used very successfully as a means of undercutting external support for insurgents. Still, the analyst must be alert to the possibility of doing so and judge such options according to their merits and effectiveness.

The frequent failure of the diplomatic, informational, and economic instruments of statecraft to eliminate external support has, not surprisingly, led governments to threaten or use force against external supporters. Various options are available, and any that are chosen will depend on cost and risk calculations related to the possible escalation of hostilities. The riskiest option is the use of conventional armed forces against external support states or insurgent sanctuaries in such states. Actions here can range from cross-border artillery or air attacks to incursions of various sizes by ground forces. At one time or another, Israel has used all of these against Jordan and Lebanon, with one or two aims in mind: inflicting serious losses on Palestinian insurgents and compelling the external-support state to crack down on the insurgents. Where Jordan was concerned, there was success on both counts because Israel had decisive military superiority, Jordan had no strong ally willing to come to its assistance, and elements among the fedayeen threatened the Jordanian regime itself. While this fortuitous combination of circumstances resulted in the expulsion of the Palestinians from Jordan, similar attacks by Israel in Lebanon during subsequent years were not nearly as successful because, unlike the Jordanian military, Lebanon's was not strong enough to defeat the Palestinians, who had support from the Lebanese leftist and Druze militias.[47] Although the Israelis did crush the PLO militarily with large conventional operations in 1982 and scattered its political apparatus to various corners of the Middle East, they ended up trading their Palestinian adversaries for much tougher Shiite insurgents who proved ultimately successful in driving the Israelis out of southern Lebanon. The Israeli experience suggests that whereas conventional operations can be very effective antidotes to external support under some conditions, under others they may meet with far less success than hoped for or lead to unanticipated costs.

Many, if not most, governments find conventional military reactions too dangerous, either because the external-support state is strong enough to respond in kind or has support from major powers that might intervene on the external-support state's behalf. Not wishing to risk the potential costs of interstate conventional warfare, they opt for lesser uses of force.

Afghan or Soviet troops, for example, would no doubt have crossed the border in the 1980s to clean out mujahedin sanctuaries in Pakistan were it not for fears that the United States might come to the aid of Pakistan. Accordingly, they limited their response to frequent air and artillery attacks, which they usually denied. During the Vietnam War, the South Vietnamese and the Americans did much the same thing, since they were concerned that large ground assaults into North Vietnam might be countered by the introduction of Chinese forces to aid Hanoi.

Where conventional military responses are deemed too perilous, unconventional attacks by commandos and covert operations may be adopted to exert pressure on external-support states. Among the possible targets are insurgent bases, camps, and offices and the military and economic assets of the external-support state. American Special Forces operations in Laos and Cambodia during the Vietnam War, Israeli raids against fedayeen bases and Jordan's irrigation systems (the East Ghor Canal) in the Jordan Valley in the late 1960s, and South African attacks inside Botswana in March 1988 are examples.[48] While such operations may contribute to a crackdown on the insurgents, they are seldom sufficient since they are episodic rather than sustained actions. Because of this, governments have turned increasingly to the support of insurgents inside the external-support state; they consider this "mirror response" a far more effective way of intensifying the pressure on and raising the costs of the external supporter. This stratagem, as noted in chapter 7, is quite common and at one point yielded positive payoffs to the Republic of South Africa, most notably with respect to Mozambique.

Whether other states can replicate the South African–Mozambique situation remains to be seen and will depend on the balance of forces inside the external-support state. Where the external-support state's economic and military capabilities are weak and insurgents opposing it measure up reasonably well in terms of at least some of the criteria discussed so far in this study, insurgents hostile to the external-support state may be able, as they did in Mozambique, to conduct sustained attacks and inflict troublesome costs on the external-support state. Accordingly, if the policy of aiding insurgents in external-support states is adopted, analysts must carefully scrutinize the strengths of the insurgency in the external-support state to ascertain how likely the policy is to succeed.

FLEXIBILITY, INTEGRITY, AND EQUANIMITY

Before summing up, three crucial qualities that are extremely important with respect to government response need to be underscored, namely, flexibility, integrity and equanimity. Their absence can create untold difficulties.

Flexibility

Since insurgencies differ in many ways, no single government response or counterinsurgency program can be applied in all cases. This does not mean that lessons, ideas, and policies from one situation may not be transferred to another. The key question is which lessons, ideas, and policies to borrow and how to adapt them to somewhat different circumstances. Those responsible for counterinsurgency strategy and planning can thus benefit enormously from serious study and analysis of other governments' experiences.

By itself, this is not adequate, however. To avoid mindless borrowing, careful assessment of the overall situation regarding the local insurgency is necessary. That is, the situation, problems, and challenges with respect to the environment, popular support, organization, unity, and external support must be set forth as cogently, comprehensively, and clearly as possible. Once this is done, an overall counterinsurgency strategy *tailored to relevant problems* can be devised. This suggests that the combination of military, social, economic, and political measures will vary according to the problems presented by different insurgencies. By way of example, the kinds of social and economic reforms or civic action programs associated with successful counterinsurgency programs in places like Malaya and the Philippines in the 1950s and Oman in the 1970s would not have been crucial, or even important, in places like Greece in the late 1940s or Belgium and Italy in recent times because in these cases the insurgents lacked significant popular support.[49] Moreover, none of the reforms or programs used in the above cases would be sufficient for coping with the present problems and threats posed by the transnational strategy and operations of Al Qaida since all focused primarily on what transpired within the borders of the nation-state. As the United States found out the hard way, new thinking is required. Only a global orientation that integrates and applies all instruments of statecraft and that is based on aggressive multilateral cooperation among intelligence and security forces around the world will succeed. As we have noted in several contexts, overreliance on the military instrument is fraught with peril in insurgencies confined to particular states. It is even more dangerous and dysfunctional when it comes to global insurgencies based on underground cellular organizations in a multitude of locations. Wherever insurgent units and base areas can be detected, the use of military force is called for. Where they cannot, other means are more appropriate.

This means that counterinsurgency strategic thinking needs to be flexible and adaptable at all times. In most cases, that will mean overcoming psychological and institutional obstacles to rigorous periodic reassessments and change. And that, in turn, places a premium on assertive, nonparochial leadership at all levels that rewards interagency and international cooperation and decisively punishes those who would thwart it.

Integrity

Closely related to the question of flexibility is the matter of integrity, a quality that profoundly affects all aspects of the government response. Webster's definition associates *integrity* with honesty, completeness, and incorruptibility. Needless to say, an absence of these attributes has a corrosive effect on situational estimates, generating either pessimism or, as seems to be more often the case, undue optimism. Ignoring or downplaying problems, for whatever reasons, usually leads to faulty, misguided, incomplete, and sometimes irrelevant policy responses. While many examples could easily be adduced here, noting the Vietnam War is more than sufficient. By now there is clear and persuasive testimony to the fact that self-deception, often deliberate, was a pervasive problem on the South Vietnamese–U.S. side. As H. R. McMaster put it in his compelling work on American decision making in Vietnam,

> The war in Vietnam was not lost in the field, nor was it lost on the front pages of the *New York Times* or on the college campuses. It was lost in Washington, D.C., even before Americans assumed sole responsibility for the fighting in 1965 and before they realized the country was at war; indeed, even before the first American units were deployed. The disaster in Vietnam was not the result of impersonal forces but a uniquely human failure, the responsibility for which was shared by President Johnson and his principal military and civilian advisers. The failings were many and reinforcing: arrogance, weakness, lying in the pursuit of self-interest, and, above all, the abdication of responsibility to the American people.[50]

Inflating the enemy's casualties, portraying defeats as victories, and ignoring the shortcomings of various Saigon regimes fabricated lights at the ends of tunnels and engendered a sense of complacency that undercut needed social, economic, political, and military changes. While the emphasis on integrity may be commonsense and simple, its importance cannot be emphasized enough. Governments that make an honest effort to know themselves and their enemies are in a better position to identify threats and to contemplate effective responses. Those who indulge in killing the bearer of bad tidings court disaster. This being so, the analyst should be especially alert to the absence or presence of integrity when evaluating all dimensions of the government response. In a world where some insurgents, like Islamic militants and members of Aum Shinriyko, have publicly indicated their commitment to apocalyptic forms of violence, nothing less will suffice.

Equanimity

The final attribute that governments should manifest is equanimity when they are successful and approaching the termination of hostilities. Many insurrections that reach this point have been marked by indiscriminate violent retribution, which is a natural result of the passions and anger that accompanied the violence. That victors in a long and especially sanguinary internal war can be cool-headed and magnanimous is clear from the American Civil War where Abraham Lincoln and his principal generals, Ulysses S. Grant and William T. Sherman, unanimously supported a generous peace that would serve the political aim of rebuilding a stable and peaceful union. This does not imply that those who planned, directed, and carried out acts of terrorism should be exonerated; they should be held accountable. Rather, it suggests that long-term political interests might best be served by reintegrating into the political community those who were passively supportive of the insurgency, as well as active combatants not guilty of terrorism. The lesson here is that those who direct and lead counterinsurgency efforts must keep a cool head and never lose sight of the ultimate political outcome they desire. To do otherwise is to risk winning the war but losing the peace.[51]

SUMMARY

The importance of a thorough evaluation of the government's response cannot be overstated. What the government does or neglects to do and how it performs has a direct bearing on the strategies and forms of warfare insurgents choose and the nature and extent of challenges insurgents must cope with as they seek to accomplish their aims. The more government responses are informed, prudent, relevant, determined, and disciplined, the greater the burden on the insurgents.

Responses marked by such qualities do not come easily. As we have seen, they depend on many things, not the least of which is the recognition that an insurgency is a political *and* military phenomenon. It is not an either/or situation. The question is which dimension is most significant and what to do about it. To answer that question, governments should have a comprehensive profile of their adversary fully in mind. A rigorous assessment of the goals, strategy, and forms of warfare of insurgents and the advantages and disadvantages inherent in the physical and human environments is crucial for devising a sensible, relevant, and effective counterinsurgency strategy. Where popular support is important, knowing precisely what techniques the insurgents are using to obtain it is indispensable to devising properly focused policies designed to neutralize their efforts. No matter how hard insurgents try, they will be frustrated if a competent and capable government administration dispenses services, controls the population, and effectively coordinates a multitude of political, economic, and security policies.

Where external support is part of the overall equation, the government's evaluation of the exact nature and role of such support should inform its choices and uses of diplomatic, economic, propaganda, and military means to counter it. In the final analysis, a careful and systematic examination of the government's response in terms of the considerations set forth in this chapter should yield most of the key reasons why an insurgency is progressing or regressing.

NOTES

1. Walter C. Sonderland, "An Analysis of Guerrilla Insurgency and Coup d'État as Techniques of Indirect Aggression," *International Studies Quarterly* (December 1970): 345.
2. Bard E. O'Neill, "Revolutionary War in Oman," in *Insurgency in the Modern World*, ed. Bard E. O'Neill, William R. Heaton, and Donald J. Alberts (Boulder, Colo.: Westview Press, 1980), 216–17.
3. Archer Jones, *Civil War Command and Strategy* (New York: The Free Press, 1992), 173–86. On McClellan, see Stephen W. Sears, *George B. McClellan: The Young Napoleon* (New York: Ticknor and Fields, 1988).
4. John J. McCuen, *The Art of Counter-Revolutionary War* (Harrisburg, Pa.: Stackpole Books, n.d.), 128–42.
5. On indiscriminate violence against civilians by the police and military in Peru, see Mario Vargas Llosa, "Inquest in the Andes," *New York Times Magazine* (July 31, 1983): 23; Cynthia McClintock, "Sendero Luminoso: Peru's Maoist Guerrillas," *Problems of Communism* (September–October 1983): 29–30; *Christian Science Monitor*, February 20, 1985; and *Washington Post*, September 19, 1985. On Sri Lanka, see Jared Mitchell, "A Nation Losing Control," *Macleans* (February 18, 1985): 31; *Far Eastern Economic Review* (September 6, 1984): 18; and *Christian Science Monitor*, February 8, 1985.
6. Past successes by European governments against terrorism (e.g., Belgium, France, and Britain) have been linked to the replacement of untrained local police by police who are full-time specialists on terrorism; see *Christian Science Monitor*, March 8, 1988.

7. On Northern Ireland's and Italy's experiences, see *Northern Ireland: Problems and Perspectives*, Conflict Studies no. 135 (London: Institute for the Study of Conflict, 1982), 20–21, 32–33; Keith Jeffrey, "Security Policy in Northern Ireland: Some Reflections on the Management of Violent Conflict," *Terrorism and Political Violence* (spring 1990): 22–33; David Bonner, "United Kingdom: The United Kingdom Response to Terrorism," *Terrorism and Political Violence* (winter 1992): 197–98; John Newsinger, "From Counter-Insurgency to Internal Security: Northern Ireland 1969–1992," *Small Wars and Insurgencies* (spring 1995): 99–101. In an off-the-record discussion, a major British commander in Northern Ireland pointed out that while the police were emphasized in counterterrorist operations, they lacked some important capabilities, especially in the area of intelligence information. Consequently, the military provided crucial support. This led to a situation he characterized as a police-military partnership. Vittorfranco S. Pisano, "The Italian Terrorist Experience: 1968–1984," *ISUPP Strategic Review* (Pretoria: Institute for Strategic Studies, University of Pretoria [ISUPP], June 1984), 2–15; Franco Villalbal, "The Organizational Structure of the Italian Counter-terrorist Forces," *International Defense Review* (June 1985): 915–17; *New York Times*, October 1, 1981, and September 29, 1983; and *Christian Science Monitor*, March 25, 1985.
8. The impact of French-Spanish cooperation on the Basque ETA is reported and discussed in the *Christian Science Monitor*, February 24, 1988, and January 31, 1989, and in the *New York Times*, January 13, 1989. Discussions I held with Spanish and American officials in May 1988 corroborated the main conclusions of these accounts.
9. On the Israeli countermeasures against transnational terrorists, see Bard E. O'Neill, *Armed Struggle in Palestine* (Boulder, Colo.: Westview Press, 1978), 78, 86–89; Christopher Dobson, *Black September* (New York: Macmillan Publishing Co., 1974), 110–13; David B. Tinnin and Dag Christensen, *The Hit Team* (New York: Dell, 1976). On the American failure to deal with the bin Ladin threat prior to September 11, see Richard A. Clarke, *Against All Enemies* (New York: The Free Press, 2004), 196–204, 227–38.
10. My observation while serving in Vietnam in 1965–1966 was that large search-and-destroy operations against guerrillas (as opposed to regular North Vietnamese divisions and regiments) were futile exercises in which the guerrillas faded into the background during sweeps and then returned when the attacking forces withdrew. Many military and civilian officials have been critical of the clumsy U.S. strategy. See, for example, Charles Maechling Jr., "Counterinsurgency: The First Ordeal by Fire," in *Low-Intensity Warfare*, ed. Michael T. Klare and Peter Kornbluh (New York: Pantheon Books, 1988), 42–43. Amazingly, the Soviets duplicated this error in Afghanistan. See, for example, *New York Times*, June 5, 1988.
11. John A. Nagl, *Counterinsurgency Lessons from Malaya and Vietnam* (Westport, Conn.: Praeger Publishers, 2002), 156–58; McCuen, *The Art of Counter-Revolutionary War*, 119–24, 166–81. One American who clearly understood the nature of the war and how to deal with guerrillas was Edward Lansdale. Unfortunately, like many others, his sage advice did not affect policy. See James McAllister, "The Lost Revolution: Edward Lansdale and the American Defeat in Vietnam 1964–1968," *Small Wars and Insurgencies* (summer 2003): 1–26. On the Apaches, see Robert N. Watt, "Raiders of a Lost Art? Apache War and Society," *Small Wars and Insurgencies* (autumn 2002): 20–21,

and Jacque J. Stewart, *The U.S. Government and the Apache Indians, 1871–1876: A Case Study in Counterinsurgency* (master's thesis, U.S. Army Command and General Staff College, Fort Leavenworth, Kansas, 1993), 109–10. A good summary article on American efforts to take advantage of tribal and clan rivalries in Afghanistan may be found in an article by Scott Baldauf in the *Christian Science Monitor*, June 24, 2004. It should also be noted in this context that the use of airpower against guerrillas has significant limitations, largely because it is hard to locate small guerrilla bands. Needless to say, indiscriminate bombardment creates more problems than it solves. Airpower can be useful for reconnaissance, for movement of troops and supplies, and for very precise strikes against clearly identified insurgents. That said, as Mark Clodfelter notes in his definitive study of the use of airpower in Vietnam, it is indecisive in guerrilla wars; see *The Limits of Airpower* (New York: The Free Press, 1989), 205–10.

12. McCuen, *The Art of Counter-Revolutionary War*, 195–205. The failure of the French to heed General Latour's advice to consolidate their own bases before searching for the Vietminh during the first Indochina war had disastrous consequences.
13. McCuen, *The Art of Counter-Revolutionary War*, 205–45; Douglas Hyde, *The Roots of Guerrilla Warfare* (Chester Springs, Pa.: Dufour Editions, 1968), 205–31; Richard L. Clutterbuck, *The Long, Long War* (New York: Frederick A. Praeger, 1966), 176; Nagl, *Counterinsurgency Lessons*, 95–101. Examples of costly failures to organize the population after an area had been cleared were the French Odine operations in Indochina (cited by McCuen) and Operation Hammer in Sarawak (cited by Hyde). In Oman, by contrast, the role of civic action teams and the extension of the government administration played a key part in the consolidation of the populace; see O'Neill, "Revolutionary War in Oman," 226.
14. The campaign against mayors in El Salvador is reported in the *Christian Science Monitor*, January 13, 1989. Earlier reports indicated army claims to have organized 21,000 civil defense troops of mixed quality; see *Washington Times*, June 27, 1988. However, a *Christian Science Monitor* report indicated that 35 percent of El Salvador's municipalities had no local government.
15. Michael Richardson, "Insurgency in the Philippines: No. 2—The Militia: Help or Hindrance," *Pacific Defence Reporter* (September 1985): 15; O'Neill, "Revolutionary War in Oman," 226.
16. McCuen, *The Art of Counter-Revolutionary War*, 235–45, 258–309.
17. O'Neill, "Revolutionary War in Oman," 219–20; Edward E. Rice, *Wars of the Third Kind* (Berkeley: University of California Press, 1988), 98–99.
18. John E. Bircher III, *Conflict in the Western Sahara: A Dilemma for United States Policy* (Washington, D.C.: National War College, 1985), 14–15, 21–22; *Le Monde* (Paris), June 21, 1984, and March 16, 1985; *Washington Post*, August 15, 1985; *Christian Science Monitor*, April 12, 1989.
19. *New York Times*, July 31, 1988.
20. Max G. Manwaring and John T. Fishel, "Insurgency and Counter-Insurgency: Toward a New Analytical approach," *Small Wars and Insurgencies* (winter 1992): 289. On Savimbi see *INFORMAFRICA* (Lisbon), March 11, 1989, reprinted in *FBIS-Africa*, May 10, 1989.
21. In the 1980s, official government-controlled statements by the Afghan government, speeches by its former president Babrak Karmal, and the media continuously identified

the regime as the defender of Islam and the insurgents as enemies of religion. A typical example is the speech by Karmal to an extraordinary session of the Revolutionary Council on November 9, 1985; see the text in *FBIS-South Asia*, November 12, 1985. On recent Muslim efforts to discredit Al Qaida and its allies, see "Arab Writer: Islamic Terrorism Greatest Enemy of Humanity," *Al Mu'tamar* (Baghdad), September 7, 2004, in *FBIS-NESA (INE)*, September 7, 2004; "Saudi Religious Council Suggests Ways to Combat Terror Groups," *Riyadh SPA*, April 27, 2004, in *FBIS-NESA (INE)*, April 27, 2004; "Friday Sermons Uphold Islamic Ethics, Saudi Imams Forbid Harm to Non-Muslims," *Middle East–FBIS Report*, June 18, 2004, in *FBIS-NESA (INE)*, June 18, 2004. For a more general assessment of the war of ideas against Islamic militants, see Ariel Cohen, "Promoting Freedom and Democracy: Fighting the War of Ideas against Islamic Terrorism," *Comparative Strategy* 22 (2003): 207–21. An example of a culturally relevant transmission of government messages was the reliance on radios in several African insurgencies since radios are a potent form of communication throughout Africa. In particular, radios are credited with encouraging defections from the Lord's Resistance Army in Uganda. See *Christian Science Monitor*, September 21, 2004.

22. Arthur Campbell, *Guerrillas* (New York: The John Day Co., 1968), 10–17, 73–89; Frederick Wilkins, "Guerrilla Warfare," in *Modern Guerrilla Warfare*, ed. Franklin Mark Osanka (New York: The Free Press of Glencoe, 1962), 10–11; Walter D. Jacobs, "Irregular Warfare and the Soviets," in Osanka, *Modern Guerrilla Warfare*, 61; Brooke McClure, "Russia's Hidden Army," in Osanka, *Modern Guerrilla Warfare*, 96–97; Ernst von Dohnanyi, "Combating Soviet Guerrillas," in Osanka, *Modern Guerrilla Warfare*, 102–5.
23. O'Neill, *Armed Struggle in Palestine*, 69–71. Interestingly, the increased terrorism in the West Bank in 1984–1985 came at a time of economic troubles in Israel, which, in turn, had adversely affected the West Bank. One of the major concerns of Israeli political and military leaders about the future was the potential impact of worsening economic problems on stability in the West Bank and Gaza Strip.
24. Rice, *Wars of the Third Kind*, 70; Kenneth M. Hammer, "Huks in the Philippines," in Osanka, *Modern Guerrilla Warfare*, 102; Boyd T. Boshore, "Duel Strategy for Limited War," in Osanka, *Modern Guerrilla Warfare*, 193–96, 199–201; Tomas C. Tirona, "The Philippine Anti-Communist Campaign," in Osanka, *Modern Guerrilla Warfare*, 206–7; Campbell, *Guerrillas*, 129–33; Robert Ross Smith, "The Hukbalahap Insurgency," *Military Review* (June 1965): 35–42.
25. Accounts of contemporary problems in the Philippines may be found in S. Bilveer, "The Philippines: How Much Longer Can the Center Hold," *Asian Defence Journal* (July 1985): 18–33; Denis Warner, "Insurgency in the Philippines: No. 1—Deterioration Marked, Widespread and Demonstrable," *Pacific Defence Reporter* (September 1985), 10–13; Steve Lohr, "Twilight of the Marcos Era," *New York Times Magazine* (January 6, 1985): 30, 32, 34–35, 39, 41, 44, 46, 53.
26. Don Mansfield, "The Irish Republican Army and Northern Ireland," *Insurgency in the Modern World*, 66–67, 74–79, and Pisano, "The Italian Terrorist Experience: 1968–1984," 2–15.
27. Ofra Bengio, "Shi'is and Politics in Ba'thi Iraq," *Middle East Studies* (January 1985): 8–12.

28. Mansfield, "The Irish Republican Army and Northern Ireland," 66–67; Pisano, "The Italian Terrorist Experience: 1968–1984," 2–15.
29. *Arab Report and Record* (November 1–15, 1968): 364, and (February 15–28, 1969), 86–87.
30. The commentary on the Israeli response to the intifada is extensive and consistently paints a harsh picture; see, for instance, *New York Times*, February 8, 19, and March 15, 1989; and *Washington Post*, March 12, 1989.
31. *New York Times*, June 15, 1980, and *Washington Post*, July 8, August 12, September 20, and October 5, 1980.
32. On the problems of military leadership in the Philippines, see Bilveer, "The Philippines: How Much Longer Can the Center Hold," 26; Warner, "Insurgency in the Philippines: No. 1," 13; *New York Times*, November 6, 1984. On El Salvador, see *New York Times*, August 19, 1983. Leadership and other deficiencies in the Salvadoran military led to extensive efforts to better train and equip the armed forces. By 1985, a number of observers reported improved battlefield performance, discipline, and political sensitivity; see *New York Times*, January 29, May 19 (Section IV), and July 28, 1985; and *Christian Science Monitor*, January 24, 1985. By the spring of 1989, numerous observers were reporting that while some attention was being given to winning "hearts and minds," other trends were unfavorable, among them the further deterioration of an already bad economic situation and the resurgence of death-squad activity; see, for example, *Washington Post*, June 12, 27, and August 28, 1988; and *Christian Science Monitor*, August 5, 1988. On Vietnam, see Nagl, *Counterinsurgency Lessons from Malaya and Vietnam*, 151–80.
33. McCuen, *The Art of Counter-Revolutionary War*, 143–58; Ted Robert Gurr, *Why Men Rebel* (Princeton, N.J.: Princeton University Press, 1970), 236–59; Sir Robert Thompson, *Defeating Communist Insurgency* (New York: Frederick A. Praeger, 1966), 53; Charles Wolf Jr., *Insurgency and Counterinsurgency: New Myth, and Old Realities* (Santa Monica, Calif.: Rand Corporation, 1965), 22; Otto Heilbrunn, *Partisan Warfare* (New York: Frederick A. Praeger, 1962), 151–58; Julian Paget, *Counter-Insurgency Campaigning* (New York: Walker & Co., 1967), 169; Roger Trinquier, *Modern Warfare* (New York: Frederick A. Praeger, 1964), 43–50; Campbell, *Guerrillas*, 232–33. A new term, *social intelligence*, has emerged to capture long-standing maxims about the relationship between in-depth knowledge of the society and successful counterinsurgency operations. See *Defense News*, April 26, 2004.
34. On the question of resettlement and its successes and failures, see Ian F. W. Beckett, introduction to *The Roots of Counter-insurgency* by Ian F. W. Beckett (New York: Sterling Publishing Co., 1988), 9–10; Rice, *Wars of the Third Kind*, 96; Clutterbuck, *The Long, Long War*, 56–63, 66–72; Campbell, *Guerrillas*, 36, 148, 218; Paget, *Counter-Insurgency Campaigning*, 36; Heilbrunn, *Partisan Warfare*, 36, 153; and, McCuen, *The Art of Counter-Revolutionary War*, 231–34.
35. Trinquier, *Modern Warfare*, 47. An example is the case brought before the European Court of Human Rights by four Northern Irishmen who were detained without charges under the Prevention of Terrorism Act (which is an important part of the campaign against the IRA). In this case, the court found the law to be a violation of human rights; see *Washington Post*, November 30, 1988.

36. Clutterbuck, *The Long, Long War*, 40.
37. John Pimlott, "The British Experience," in Beckett, *The Roots of Counter-insurgency*, 22–23; Trinquier, *Modern Warfare*, 23–27, 35–38; Campbell, *Guerrillas*, 300, 323; Paget, *Counter-Insurgency Campaigning*, 164.
38. Clutterbuck, *The Long, Long War*, 95–100.
39. Trinquier, *Modern Warfare*, 23–27, 35–38; Campbell, *Guerrillas*, 300–323; Paget, *Counter-Insurgency Campaigning*, 164; McCuen, *The Art of Counter-Revolutionary War*, 113–19; Clutterbuck, *The Long, Long War*, 95–100.
40. Bilveer, "The Philippines: How Much Longer Can the Center Hold," 26–27; *The Situation in the Philippines*, staff report prepared for the Committee on Foreign Relations, United States Senate (Washington, D.C.: U.S. Government Printing Office, 1984), 12–16. That a number of prominent Filipino officials were concerned with the course of events was clear from critical assessments and new strategy proposals that had surfaced by 1989. The need to counterorganize the people and to address their grievances was clearly articulated. See Eric Guyot and James Clad, "Regaining the Initiative," *Far Eastern Economic Review* (September 22, 1988): 40; *Christian Science Monitor*, April 18, 1989; Barry Crane, Joel Leson, Robert Plebanek, Paul Shemella, Ronald Smith, and Richard Williams, *Between Peace and War: Comprehending Low-Intensity Conflict*, National Security Program Discussion Paper Series 88-02 (Cambridge, Mass.: John F. Kennedy School of Government, Harvard University, 1988), 257–58.
41. *New York Times*, January 2, 23, 27, March 5, 6, 30, and August 14, 1980; *Washington Post*, November 7, 1978, January 25, March 5, and November 18, 1980, and February 27, 1981; Kabul Domestic Service, December 17, 1981, in *FBIS–South Asia*, December 21, 1981. Karmal severely criticized several ministries for their poor performance. See Kabul Domestic Service, February 24, 1982, in *FBIS–South Asia*, March 2, 1982.
42. On the fractious politics in El Salvador, see Steffen W. Schmidt, *El Salvador: America's Next Vietnam?* (Salisbury, N.C.: Documentary Publications, 1983), 20, 59–64, 165–78. Acknowledgment of the severe disunity of the Afghan government and its negative impact on government performance was made by Maj. Gen. Kim Tsagolov, Soviet military adviser in Afghanistan from 1981 to 1984 and again in 1987, in the weekly magazine *Ogonyok*. See David Remnick, "Soviet General Predicts Fall of Afghan Communists after Afghan Pullout," *Washington Post*, July 25, 1988; Bill Keller, "Soviet General Declares Kabul Could Collapse," *New York Times*, July 24, 1988; Mohammad Yousaf and Mark Adkin, *The Bear Trap* (London: Leo Cooper, 1992), 142–43.
43. Bruce R. Kuniholm, "Turkey and NATO: Past, Present and Future," *Orbis* (summer 1983): 426–33.
44. A compelling case for civilian control is made by Pimlott, "The British Experience," 17–20.
45. The PRC's diminished support for the insurgency in Thailand had begun by 1973. See William R. Heaton, "People's War in Thailand," in *The Art and Practice of Military Strategy*, ed. George Edward Thibault (Washington, D.C.: National Defense University, 1984), 850–52.
46. An account of the Nicaraguan effort to influence the United States by means of professional public relations efforts may be found in the *Washington Post*, October 9, 1984.
47. O'Neill, *Armed Struggle in Palestine*, 77–86, 168–69, and especially 170–73.

48. O'Neill, *Armed Struggle in Palestine*, 81; *Christian Science Monitor*, March 29, 1988.
49. D. Michael Shafer has made a persuasive case that despite the American assumptions about the positive impact of assistance during the Greek civil war, brute force was the reason for success since the Greek government ignored U.S. prescriptions, did little to improve its relations with the people, did not promote development, and did not control right-wing death squads; see Shafer's *Deadly Paradigms* (Princeton, N.J.: Princeton University Press, 1988), 166–204.
50. H. R. McMaster, *Dereliction of Duty* (New York: HarperCollins Publishers, 1997), 333–34. The problems associated with a breakdown in integrity in Vietnam are easy to document and could fill pages. Neil Sheehan's prize-winning and meticulous *A Bright Shining Lie* (New York: Random House, 1988) brilliantly captures the essence of the problem. Also see David H. Hackworth, *About Face* (New York: Simon and Schuster, 1989). Whether, as some believe, a similar malady has characterized the so-called global war on terrorism and the Iraqi situation is left for historians to judge.
51. Jay Winik, *April 1865* (New York: HarperCollins Publishers, 2002), 173–363.

CONCLUSION

Insurgencies remain a central feature of the international landscape. In fact, the preeminent national security challenges for the United States in the first decade of this century have been the insurgencies in Iraq and Afghanistan and the global insurgency waged by Al Qaida. Insurgencies are present on every continent and will continue to be so for as long into the future as we can project. Moreover, if insurgents acquire nuclear, radiological, chemical, biological, or cyber weapons they will pose an unprecedented qualitative threat. As a consequence, the serious study of insurgency is more compelling than ever.

Analyzing insurgencies is a complicated matter, involving a dynamic interplay of many factors. To facilitate this undertaking, I have presented the factors as part of a structured framework for analysis. Although the framework is neither a formalized model nor a theory, I have set forth a number of important relationships among the factors at various points. This reflects not only the complex nature of the subject, which defies facile generalizations, but also my deliberate aim of providing an analytical approach that emphasizes practicality over theory.

Each of the factors represents an area of inquiry that may be crucial for explaining the course of events in insurgencies. How important the factors are varies from case to case and can only be determined by careful empirical investigation. Since numerous studies give ample evidence that combinations of important factors vary considerably between cases, there is no one model that can be applied to all. In chapter 8, for instance, we saw that the ingredients of a successful counterinsurgency program vary according to the actual or anticipated threats posed by insurgents and the status of the insurgency with respect to the environment, popular support, organization, unity, and external support; there is no pat formula. Far-reaching programs that seek to win popular support through a mix of substantive political, military, economic, and administrative policies may be suitable for some cases in which insurgents follow a protracted-popular-war strategy. In contrast, insurgents who follow conspiratorial or urban-warfare strategies and emphasize terrorism rather than organizing popular support may be countered by a modest but vigorous program centered on intelligence, police, and legal due process.

While acknowledging that the differences between insurgencies do exist, it is important to recognize similarities between them may permit particular lessons to be transferred from one case to another. Whether policies are transferable depends, in large part, on the overall situation. For example, the notion of using small-unit patrols to cope with a guerrilla threat worked well in Malaya and was successfully adopted in Oman. In each case, the insurgents were minorities that could be isolated, and the government side had the resources and will to stay the course. Whether patrols against guerrillas could have been as effective in, say, Afghanistan is another matter. While they would have been preferable to the large-scale search-and-destroy operations conducted by Soviet conventional forces and their Afghan allies, they would probably never have compensated for the inept and misguided political, social, economic, and administrative policies of both the ruling People's Democratic Party and the government. This underscores an important point: analysis of an insurgency must pay special attention to the interrelationships of the factors in the framework. While they help us sort out and make sense of information, the factors are by no means unrelated, discrete categories. What happens with respect to one can have an enormous impact on another (e.g., a loss of external support may undercut cohesion or vice versa). Both the potential criticality of specific factors and their interconnections make it imperative that analyses of insurgencies be as comprehensive as possible.

A comprehensive approach to the study of insurgency demands that analysts ask insightful and penetrating questions about all the major components of the framework. In fact, researchers may wish to add their own questions. Leaving out major factors can be a serious mistake, since major explanations for what has, and is, transpiring may be associated with missing elements. For instance, although a study of developments in the Polisario insurgency that gave no attention to external support might be somewhat enlightening, it would still be woefully distorted, given the crucial role that external support played in that case. In the same context, a study of El Salvador that emphasized external support but ignored the political, social, and economic elements of the human environment could lead to the badly flawed conclusion that simply eliminating external support could have quelled the insurrection. The point is that by addressing all of the factors, one is less apt to overlook a critical facet of the insurgency and will be in a better position to determine what is known and what requires further investigation and analysis.

USING THE FRAMEWORK

Anyone interested in insurgency can use the framework, whether he or she is in an academic setting, involved in the policy process, or a first-hand observer of an internal conflict. In my experience over the past thirty years with graduate students and highly qualified mid-career professionals from the national security policy community, I have found the framework for analysis to be an effective pedagogical tool. As those who have spent time in a classroom know, formal presentations and seminar discussions can easily lapse into "stream of consciousness" exchanges that do little to illuminate the issues at hand. And when it comes to written work, a similar problem surfaces early in the process, as students struggle to organize and present their thoughts. The framework provides a conceptual format for ordering, interpreting, and presenting vast amounts of information related to one or more cases. If we are studying a single case, the concepts or factors that the framework comprises can help identify specific changes in the situation. For instance, the insurrection in country *x* has changed with respect to insurgent goals, strategy, and external support. Or, the insurgency in country *y* has changed with respect to popular support and government response. When we analyze several cases, the concepts can help us see similarities and differences with reference to explicit criteria and what they mean in the broader context of insurgency.

The use of the framework in an academic setting can be quite flexible. Short classroom or written exercises limited by time can use the basic categories, whereas major classroom projects and papers (e.g., theses, dissertations) can use a more detailed version of the framework. Certainly, there is no reason why users cannot add their own modifications, ideas, and concepts to sections of the framework. Finally, the framework is also helpful for critiques and reviews of articles and books because it gives the reviewer a scheme for quickly identifying important subjects that may be neglected and for assessing those things that are covered.

Analysts and supervisors involved in the policy process can also use the framework. For analysts, it provides a clear organizational format for written reports and briefings. One former participant in National Security Council meetings told me after observing classroom use of the framework that clearly organized presentations during policy deliberations are invaluable because they make briefings easier to follow and are more persuasive. For high-level supervisors, the framework, even when reduced to a basic one-page outline, provides a basis for asking explicit, focused questions and for determining what is known, only partly known, and unknown. Ascertaining what is unclear or unknown can be as important as finding out what is known. For instance, a presentation may be quite solid in its portrayal of the type of insurgency, strategy employed, forms of warfare, and environment but have little or no information or insight with respect to one important factor, such as organization. Intelligence analysts and collectors can then be asked to concentrate further attention on organization.

Frequent discussions with firsthand observers of—or participants in—insurgencies (e.g., diplomats, military officers, journalists, insurgents) indicate that they, too, find value in having basic general concepts in mind to aid them in collecting data and structuring their thoughts. While their ultimate purpose may not be to produce the more detailed product of an academic or government analyst, they can still benefit from an overall conceptual format, even if it is abbreviated. On a number of occasions, individuals who spent considerable time observing an insurgency and who had amassed impressive knowledge of social, political, historical, and economic details have told me the one thing they needed to help them interpret and report on their findings was a series of general concepts that generated and framed essential questions. They thought the kind of framework discussed in this book would have met that need.

OBJECTIVITY AND SUBJECTIVITY

Regardless of who they are, users of the framework will always confront the issue of objective versus subjective analysis. While one obviously aspires to achieve dispassionate analysis, it is not uncommon to find ideological and moral predispositions injected into assessments, either consciously or unconsciously, particularly when it comes to insurgencies. No framework is foolproof against this situation. Anyone so inclined can selectively use the data and skew interpretations. The key for dealing with this is the integrity of the researcher. Basically, he or she must inventory his or her own biases on the subject and make a decided effort to see to it that they do not lead to a deliberate manipulation of data to support preconceived notions or to hide unfavorable information.

To give a brief illustration, if one personally deplores the nature of a particular regime, finds some of its countermeasures repugnant, and even sympathizes with the insurgents, there could be a tendency to ignore findings that the insurgents have little support and are disorganized and that government countermeasures are effective. For the serious analyst, as opposed to a polemicist, all of the important findings must be presented, even if they contradict the analyst's prejudgments. It almost goes without saying that the practitioner, regardless of the side he or she is on, also has a great need for objective assessments. Falsifying or ignoring data yields delusions, which can lead to short-term catastrophes and long-term defeats.

In a number of discussions with individuals who have been participants on either the government or insurgent side or who have played supporting roles in various situations, the utility of the framework has been demonstrated. Initially, those with partisan interests tend to exaggerate their own successes and ignore their own shortcomings. When compelled to evaluate the situation point by point in terms of the framework, they find they must confront uncongenial information. By the end of the exercise, they frequently comment that the process of deliberately trying to answer a range of neutral questions objectively is extremely beneficial in a practical sense, especially because the critique of one's own side and acknowledgement of an adversary's strengths is indispensable for improving one's own situation.

SUMMARY

There can be little doubt that insurgencies will continue to pose important domestic and foreign policy challenges for many nations. In situations where nuclear, radiological, chemical, and biological weapons and the malicious use of cyber technology are potentially available to insurgents, those challenges will be grave and the margin for error will be zero. Accordingly, there can be little doubt that insurgencies will be of great interest to a wide range of people—decision makers, government analysts, scholars, students, and journalists. All will find that the analysis of insurgency is a complex and challenging undertaking that they must approach in an organized way and with an open mind. If the framework for analysis set forth in this book facilitates that undertaking, my main purpose has been achieved.

APPENDIX: COURSE SYLLABUS

Note: This syllabus is designed for a graduate course on insurgency with fifteen seminars of two hours each. It could easily be adapted for an undergraduate course with twenty-five or more sessions by spreading out and adding topics and case studies.

INSURGENCY AND REVOLUTION

Introduction

Few nations have escaped insurgent violence, be it terrorism or guerrilla warfare. If such violence were purely internal, it might be of little concern to great powers such as the United States. However, as is well known, most insurgencies have been internationalized in various ways, with outside powers supporting either governments or insurgents in pursuit of their own interests.

Ironically, it was not very long ago that many foreign policy experts concluded the collapse of the Soviet bloc had marginalized the importance of insurgency because it destroyed the Marxist ideological rationale of many insurgent groups. This conclusion proved to be premature, as the tenacity of groups like the Revolutionary Armed Forces of Colombia and the Front for the Liberation of Nepal have shown. Indeed, some organizations, such as the New People's Army in the Philippines, have argued that the deviation from true Marxism-Leninism was the key cause of Soviet problems; others, like the Shining Path in Peru, never put much stock in Soviet thinking to begin with.

We should not be surprised to see several of the leftist insurgencies continue and perhaps new ones appear, given the dysfunctional aspects of the globalization process. Some of these movements will be Marxist, albeit in new guises. Others will be more reformist in orientation (e.g., the Zapatista Liberation Front in Chiapas, Mexico).

The persistence of left-wing insurgencies notwithstanding, insurrections inspired by ethnic and religious groups are and will probably remain more important. While such groups were extant before and during the cold war, the proclivity to equate insurgency with Marxist movements often led to their being ignored or misperceived. That this is no longer so is evident from extensive media coverage of violence perpetrated by various nationalist and religious movements, most notably Islamic militant groups that seek to change the international system fundamentally.

All of this adds to the complexity and disorder in the global arena and makes clear thinking about internal wars more important than ever. Accordingly, the central purpose of this course is to provide a systematic approach for analyzing insurgencies that occur at any time, in any place, and under any circumstances. As you will see, although this approach was used to analyze Marxist insurrections in the cold war years, it has never been restricted to that brief historical epoch. Succinctly put, it can be used to analyze past and present insurgencies and, most importantly, the unforeseen cases that the future will present to us.

Course Objectives

1. To further our knowledge and comprehension of internal wars at a time when internal conflicts are raging in many parts of the world and weapons of mass destruction are but a short imaginative leap away from the arsenals of insurgents;
2. To establish and underscore the crucial role that systematic, objective, and explicit analysis plays in understanding internal wars;
3. To provide a conceptual framework that can be used to systematically analyze insurgencies; in other words, to provide a series of *essential questions* that should be asked about every insurgency;
4. To sharpen and develop analytical skills through the use of case studies in which students apply a framework for analysis to specific insurgent situations;
5. To foster a flexible yet rigorous approach that recognizes the dynamic, varied, and interdependent relationships among the explanatory factors used to analyze insurgencies and emphasizes the importance of using findings from case studies to further refine the analytical framework.

Approach

This course will outline, discuss, and apply a systematic framework for analysis to a number of cases. We shall be concerned with four things: what we mean by insurgency, different types of insurgencies, strategies frequently adopted to accomplish insurgent aims, and factors that are helpful in analyzing the progress of insurgencies.

Besides seminar discussions and readings devoted to case studies, students will analyze several insurrections using the framework and present their conclusions and findings in class.

There are three reasons for adopting and adhering to a common framework for analysis and its inherently comparative methodology. First, it is a convenient means for ordering and interpreting a vast amount of data. Second, it engenders consistency, facilitates communication, and injects coherence into our efforts because it provides us with a series of shared concepts. Third, it not only directs our attention to some of the most important facets of insurgency, but it also suggests crucial linkages among them.

There is no underlying assumption that the framework for analysis is without flaws or omissions. Its propositions and hypotheses should be subjected to careful scrutiny and testing, for only in this manner can we move closer to a reliable body of knowledge that is important to both practitioners and scholars.

Student Requirements

There are three student requirements: completion of class reading assignments, a major class presentation on an insurgency that uses the framework of analysis, and a final exam (note: a paper could be substituted for the exam). The choice of cases has been based on geographic and substantive diversity and availability of adequate information.

The objective in the class presentation is not to create instant area experts. Rather, it is to develop analytical skills and to apply them.

In order to conserve time and facilitate student efforts, files on the various topics will be made available.

As in the past, the ideas and thinking of others remain very important. However, with the much greater availability of information in the twenty-first century, our pedagogical emphasis will shift progressively towards accessing data and analyzing it ourselves. To facilitate the process of discovery and analysis, relevant and timely items drawn from the Internet will be periodically forwarded to you as additional reading.

Course Seminars

As pointed out previously, this is a course about insurgency or internal war. The subject matter is multifaceted and quite complex; hence, analysts, whether in academia or the policy arena, cannot afford to rely on vague impressions, emotional reactions, ideological biases, or sketchy and diffuse data. Nor can they be content with merely gathering facts about specific cases since facts do not speak for themselves. What is necessary is a commitment to systematically analyze insurgencies. Such systematic analysis must, in turn, be based on careful comparisons of historical and contemporary situations.

It is, of course, easier to call for systematic analysis than to do it. Since there is a vast body of literature on insurgency, our first and most important requirement is to structure and integrate much of what we know into a framework for analysis that will assist us in organizing, interpreting, and understanding specific cases.

Seminars 1 to 3 develop the framework for analysis; seminars 4 and 5 demonstrate its use; seminars 6 to 15 are student case studies. The final exam is seminar 16.

As you read the materials for the first three topics, concentrate on developing what you believe to be the generic questions that should be asked about internal wars.

Seminar 1: Analyzing Insurgency

Required Readings

1. Bard E. O'Neill, *Insurgency and Terrorism* (Washington, D.C.: Potomac Books, 2005), chs. 1, 2, and 3.
2. Jack A. Goldstone, "An Analytical Framework," in *Revolutions of the Late Twentieth Century*, ed. Jack A. Goldstone et al. (Boulder, Co.: Westview Press, 1991), 37–51.
3. Gerard Chaliand, ed., *Guerrilla Strategies* (Berkeley: University of California Press, 1982), 1–51.
4. Jennifer Morrison Taw and Bruce Hoffman, *The Urbanization of Insurgency*, (Santa Monica, CA: The Rand Corporation, 1994), 1–29.
5. Shashi Tharoor, "The Future of Civil Conflict," *World Policy Journal* (spring 1999).
6. J. Moreno, "Che Guevara on Guerrilla Warfare: Doctrine, Practice, and Evaluation," *Contemporary Studies in Society and History* (April 1970).

Seminar 2: Analyzing Insurgency

Required Readings

1. O'Neill, *Insurgency and Terrorism*, chs. 4, 5, and 6.
2. Anthony James Joes, "Continuity and Change in Guerrilla War: The Spanish and Afghan Cases," *Journal of Conflict Studies* (fall 1996).
3. Robert N. Watt, "Raiders of a Lost Art? Apache War and Society," *Small Wars and Insurgencies* (autumn 2002).
4. Stathis N. Kalyvas, "New and Old Civil Wars: A Valid Distinction?" *World Politics* (October 2001).
5. Thomas A. Marks, "Urban Insurgency" *Small Wars and Insurgencies* (autumn 2003).

Seminar 3: Analyzing Insurgency

Required Readings

1. O'Neill, *Insurgency and Terrorism*, ch. 7.
2. Max G. Manwaring and John T. Fishel, "Insurgency and Counter-Insurgency: Toward a New Analytical Approach," *Small Wars and Insurgencies* (winter 1992).
3. William H. Miller, "Insurgency Theory and the Conflict in Algeria: A Theoretical Analysis," *Terrorism and Political Violence* (spring 2000).

Seminar 4: How to Apply the Framework–Afghanistan

Note: It is now time to apply the framework to actual cases. We begin with the Russian experience in Afghanistan. The questions below should be kept in mind for this and all remaining seminars. As you will see, they constitute another way of setting forth the issues in the framework.

1. What type of insurgency are we dealing with? What is the insurgents' ultimate goal? Is it egalitarian, reformist, secessionist, traditionalist, preservationist, anarchist, pluralist, apocalyptic-utopian, commercialist, or some mixture of these? Are the goals clear and precise, or are they nebulous and contradictory? Do the insurgents mask their ultimate aim in misleading rhetoric?
2. What strategy (if any) are the insurgents following—conspiratorial, protracted popular war, military focus, urban warfare, or transnational? Is the strategy implicit or explicit? Does its conception and implementation appear to be superficial or carefully thought through? Is the choice of strategy related to the nature of the environment? How?

3. Is the physical environment conducive to terrorism and/or guerrilla warfare? How does the human environment (e.g., demography, ethnicity) affect the insurgency?
4. How much popular support do the insurgents have? What is the role of the educated strata? Which techniques do the insurgents rely on to gain support? How do societal divisions and environmental factors affect popular support?
5. What is the nature of the insurgent organization? Is it a complex one with a parallel hierarchy or is it small-scale (e.g., terrorist cells)? If it is a parallel hierarchy, how extensive is it (i.e., is it limited to a few areas or widespread)? Is the organizational format congruent with the strategy? Are there any connections with noninsurgent groups? If so, what are they like, and how important are they?
6. Are the insurgents unified? If not, what are the reasons and the effects?
7. What kind of external support do the insurgents need? What do they get (e.g., moral, political, and material support or sanctuary) and from whom? How important is it? How durable does it appear to be?
8. Is the government's profile of the insurgents honest, comprehensive, and open-minded? If it is not comprehensive, what has been overlooked and what problems stem from the oversights? Does the government have a coherent and relevant national program for addressing social, economic, and political grievances? Is the government administrative apparatus competent? Does it provide a common sense of direction by integrating and directing both military and nonmilitary undertakings? Is the government's military response carefully tailored to provide appropriate responses to different kinds of threats, or is it indiscriminate? What are the consequences? How does the government deal with external support for insurgents?

Required Readings

1. Mark Sliwinski, "Afghanistan: The Decimation of a People," *Orbis* (winter 1989).
2. Oliver Roy, "Afghanistan: Back to Tribalism or on to Lebanon," *Third World Quarterly* (October 1989).
3. Stephen J. Blank, *Operational and Strategic Lessons of the War in Afghanistan, 1979–90* (Carlisle Barracks, PA: Strategic Institute, U.S. Army War College, 1991).
4. Abdul Rashid, "The Afghan Resistance and the Problem of Unity," *Strategic Review* (summer 1986).

5. M. Afzal Khan, "With the Afghan Rebels," *New York Times Magazine* (January 13, 1980).
6. Keith D. Dickson, "The Basmachi and the Mujahidin: Soviet Responses to Insurgency Movements," *Military Review* (February 1985).
7. Alex R. Alexiev, "Soviet Strategy and the Mujahidin," *Orbis* (spring 1985).
8. Anthony Arnold, "The Stony Path to Afghan Socialism: Problems of Sovietization in an Alpine Muslim Society," *Orbis* (spring 1985).

Seminar 5: How to Apply the Framework—Oman

Required Readings

1. Bard E. O'Neill, "Revolutionary War in Oman," *Insurgency in the Modern World* (Boulder, CO: Westview Press, 1980), 213–234.
2. Special file (library reserve).

Student case studies

Seminar 6: The PKK in Turkey

Note: By this time, you should have a good grasp of how to analyze an insurgency systematically. Accordingly, we shall begin a series of case studies wherein you will be asked to deliver a fifty-minute presentation on a given insurrection that explicitly addresses the questions set forth in seminar 4. Those questions are transposed into the following outline for your presentations:

Historical sketch
Type of insurgency
Insurgent strategy
Insurgent techniques
Status of the insurgency
a. Environment
b. Popular support
c. Organization
d. Unity
e. External support
f. Government response
Brief summation

Keep the historical sketch to *ten minutes* and focus on salient trends or factors from the past that bear on the case at hand. Avoid multipage timelines. *Primary attention* should be placed on analyzing the insurgency in terms of the variables in the framework for analysis. Be sure to consult one or several reputable, up-to-date human rights reports (Human Rights Watch, Amnesty International, the Department of State, or the United Nations) since human rights are often a crucial consideration.

Required Readings

1. Michael Gunter, "The Kurdish Insurgency in Turkey," *Journal of South Asian and Middle East Studies* (summer 1990).
2. Michael Gunter, "Turkey and the Kurds: New Developments in 1991," *Journal of South Asian and Middle East Studies* (winter 1991).
3. Michael Radu, "The Rise and Fall of the PKK," *Orbis* (winter 2001).
4. Stephen C. Pelletiere, *The Kurds and Their Agas* (Carlisle Barracks, PA: Strategic Institute, U.S. Army War College, 1992).
5. Alfred B. Prados, *Kurdish Separatism in Iraq*, Congressional Research Service, May 6, 1991.
6. Nader Entessar, "The Kurdish Mosaic of Discord," *Third World Quarterly* (October 1989).

Seminar 7: Insurgency in Sri Lanka

Required Readings

1. Gamini Samaranayake "Patterns of Political Violence and Responses of the Government in Sri Lanka, 1971–1996," *Terrorism and Political Violence* (spring 1999).
2. Chris Smith, "South Asia's Enduring War," in *Creating Peace in Sri Lanka*, ed. Robert I. Rotberg (Washington, D.C.: Brookings Institution Press, 1999).
3. Daya Wijesekera, "The Liberation Tigers of Tamil Eelam: The Asian Mafia," *Low Intensity Conflict and Law Enforcement* (autumn 1993).
4. Pauletta Otis and Christopher D. Carr, "Sri Lanka and the Ethnic Challenge," *Conflict* 8, nos. 2/3 (1988).
5. Marshall R. Singer, "New Realities in Sri Lankan Politics," *Asian Survey* (April 1990).
6. Nancy Jetly, "India and the Sri Lankan Ethnic Triangle," *Conflict Quarterly* 9 (1989).
7. Robert N. Kearney, "Tension and Conflict in Sri Lanka," *Current History* (March 1986).
8. Robert C. Oberst, "Sri Lanka's Tamil Tigers," *Conflict Quarterly* 8, nos. 2/3 (1988).

Seminar 8: Insurgency in Kashmir

Required Readings

1. Alexander Evans, "The Kashmir Insurgency: As Bad as It Gets," *Small Wars and Insurgencies* (spring 2000).
2. Yoginder Sikand, "The Changing Course of the Kashmiri Struggle: From National Liberation to Islamist Jihad," *The Muslim World* (spring 2001).
3. Stephen Cohen, "India and Pakistan," chapter 7 in *India: Emerging Power* (Washington D.C.: Brookings Institution Press, 2001).
4. K. Shankar Bajpa, "Untangling India and Pakistan," *Foreign Affairs* (May–June 2003).
5. Hamish Telford, "Counter-Insurgency in India: Observations from Punjab and Kashmir," *The Journal of Conflict Studies* (spring 2001).

Seminar 9: Insurgency in Egypt

Required Readings

1. Fawaz A. Gerges, "The End of the Islamist Insurgency in Egypt? Costs and Prospects," *The Middle East Journal* (autumn 2000).
2. Mamoun Fandy, "Egypt's Islamic Group: Regional Revenge," *Middle East Journal* (autumn 1994).
3. Chuck Fahrer, "The Geography of Egypt's Islamist Insurgency," *The Arab World Geographer* 4, no. 3 (2001).
4. Jeffrey A. Nedoroscik, "Extremist Groups in Egypt," *Terrorism and Political Violence* (summer 2002).
5. Alaf Lutfi al-Sayyid-Marsot, "Religion or Opposition? Urban Protest Movements in Egypt," *International Journal of Middle East Studies* 16 (1984).
6. Sana Hasan, "Egypt's Angry Islamic Militants," *New York Times Magazine* (November 20, 1983).
7. Hamied N. Ansari, "The Islamic Militants in Egyptian Politics," *International Journal of Middle East Studies* 16 (1984).

Seminar 10: Insurgency in Sudan

Required Readings

1. Milton Viorst, "Sudan's Islamic Experiment," *Foreign Affairs* (May–June 1995).
2. Randolph Martin, "Sudan's Perfect War," *Foreign Affairs* (March–April 2002).

3. William Langewiesche, "Turabi's Law," *Atlantic Monthly* (August 1994).
4. Ann M. Lesch, "Sudan: The Torn Country," *Current History* (May 1999).
5. Julie Flint, "Under Islamic Siege" *Africa Report* (September–October 1993).
6. Carolyn Fluehr-Lobban, "Islamization in Sudan: A Critical Assessment," *Middle East Journal* (autumn 1990).
7. Gabriel R. Warburg, "The Sharia and the Sudan: Implementations and Repercussions, 1983–89," *Middle East Journal* (autumn 1990).
8. Samuel M. Makinda, "Sudan: Old Wine in New Bottles," *Orbis* (summer 1987).

Seminar 11: Insurgency in the Western Sahara

Required Readings

1. Yahia H. Zoubir, "The Western Sahara Conflict: Regional and International Dimensions," *The Journal of Modern African Studies* (June 1990).
2. Oyvind Osterud, "War Termination in the Western Sahara," *Bulletin of Peace Proposals* 206, no. 3 (1989).
3. John Damis, "The Western Saharan Conflict: Myths and Realities," *Middle East Journal* (spring 1983).
4. David Lynn Price, *The Western Sahara*, Washington Papers, no. 63 (1979).
5. Tony Hodges, *Western Sahara: The Roots of a Desert War* (Westport, CT: Lawrence Hill and Co., 1983), chs. 1, 8, 14, 27, and 30.

Seminar 12: Insurgency in Peru

Required Readings

1. Cynthia McClintock, "Sendero Luminoso: Peru's Maoist Guerrillas," *Problems of Communism* (September–October 1993).
2. Gordon H. McCormick, "The Shining Path and Peruvian Terrorism," *Rand Report* (June 1987), 72–97.
3. G. L. Vasquez, "Peruvian Radicalism and the Sendero Luminoso" *Journal of Political and Military Sociology* (winter 1993).
4. Robert B. Kent, "Geographical Dimensions of the Shining Path Insurgency in Peru," *Geographical Review* (October 1993).
5. James Ron, "Ideology in Context: Explaining Sendero Luminoso's Tactical Escalation," *Journal of Peace Research* 35, no. 1 (2001).

6. Sandra Woy-Hazelton and William H. Hazelton, "Sendero Luminoso and the Future of Peruvian Democracy," *Third World Quarterly* (April 1990).

Seminar 13: Insurgency in Colombia

Required Readings

1. "Colombia: Drugs, War and Democracy," Survey Colombia, *The Economist* (April 21, 2001).
2. Phillip McLean, "Colombia: Failed, Failing, or Just Weak?" *The Washington Quarterly* 25, no. 3 (summer 2002).
3. Julia E. Sweig, "What Kind of War for Colombia?" *Foreign Affairs* 81, no. 5 (September–October 2002).
4. Cynthia A. Watson, "Political Violence in Colombia: Another Argentina," *Third World Quarterly* (July 1990).
5. Gabriel Marcella and Donald Schultz, *Colombia's Three Wars: U.S. Strategy at the Crossroads* (Carlisle Barracks, PA: U.S. Army War College, 1999).
6. Michael Shifter, "Colombia on the Brink," *Foreign Affairs* (July–August 1999).

Seminar 14: Insurgency in Northern Ireland

Required Readings

1. C. J. M. Drake, "The Provisional IRA: A Case Study," *Terrorism and Political Violence* (summer 1991).
2. Steve Bruce, "The Problems of 'Pro-State' Terrorism: Loyalist Paramilitaries in Northern Ireland," *Terrorism and Political Violence* (spring 1992).
3. "UK: Report on Leading Members of IRA," London BBC 2 TV in *FBIS-WEU*, no. 96112 (June 10, 1996), 16–20.
4. John Newsinger, "From Counter-Insurgency to Internal Security: Northern Ireland: 1969–1992," *Small Wars and Insurgencies* (spring 1995).
5. Colin McInnes and Caroline Kennedy-Pipe, "The British Army and the Peace Process in Northern Ireland," *The Journal of Conflict Studies* (spring 2001).
6. Rogelio Alonso, "The Modernization in Irish Republican Thinking toward the Utility of Violence," *Studies in Conflict and Terrorism,"* (2001).

Seminar 15: Transnational Insurgency–Al Qaida

Required Readings

1. "Al-Qa'ida Political Bureau Releases Statement Promising to Stay the Course," *Alneda* WWW-Text in Arabic, in *Foreign Broadcast Information Service—Near East–South Asia* (hereafter *FBIS/NESA*) (September 11, 2002).
2. "French Daily Analyzes Evidence of Changes in al-Qa'ida's Organization," *Liberation* (Paris), in *FBIS/NESA* (September 9, 2003).
3. "Writer Attributes Origins of Violence in Saudi Arabia to Wahhabist Doctrine," *Shu'un Sa'udiyyah* (London), in *FBIS/NESA* (May 4, 2004), 4.
4. "Global Analysis: Is There an Islamist Internationale?" *Herzliyya International Policy Institute for Counterterrorism*, in *FBIS/NESA* (July 12, 2000), 9.
5. "Afghan Weekly Details New Generation of Al Qa'ida Network," *Kabul Weekly*, in *FBIS/NESA* (February 18, 2004).
6. "French Report Examines Different Circles of Al Qa'ida Activity," *Le Figaro* (Paris), in *FBIS/NESA* (November 21, 2003).
7. "New Jihad Handbook Shows More Strategic Analysis Than Previous Al Qa'ida Publications," *Hamburg Spiegel Online*, in *FBIS/NESA* (March 18, 2004).
8. Federal Bureau of Investigation, Intelligence Assessment, *Al Qa'ida*, April 15, 2004, 1–5.
9. Parts 1 through 5 of book review: "Egyptian Islamist Leaders Fault Al Qa'ida's Strategy," *Al Sharq al Awsat* (London), in *FBIS/NESA* (January 11, 12, 14, 16, and 18, 2004).
10. Rohan Gunaratna, *Inside Al Qaida* (New York: Columbia University Press, 2002), chs. 2 and 3.

Seminar 16: Final Examination

Index

J

K

Q

R